From B. M. R & C

Christmas 2009.

Stitching

for

Victory

Stitching for Victory

SUZANNE GRIFFITH

With deepest gratitude to Julia Caprara, Alex Caprara and Constance Howard, and all those who stitched or used stitched items 1939–1951.

The Author and Publishers have made every possible effort to trace copyright holders; we apologise for any erroneous use of copyrighted material and would welcome contact from the original copyright holder.

First published 2009

The History Press
The Mill, Brimscombe Port
Stroud, Gloucestershire, GL5 2QG
www.thehistorypress.co.uk

© Suzanne Griffith, 2009

The right of Suzanne Griffith to be identified as the Author of this work has been asserted in accordance with the Copyrights, Designs and Patents Act 1988.

All rights reserved. No part of this book may be reprinted or reproduced or utilised in any form or by any electronic, mechanical or other means, now known or hereafter invented, including photocopying and recording, or in any information storage or retrieval system, without the permission in writing from the Publishers.

British Library Cataloguing in Publication Data.
A catalogue record for this book is available from the British Library.

ISBN 978 0 7524 4533 5

Typesetting and origination by The History Press
Printed in Great Britain

Contents

War

War torn...

War tears...

War tears mind from body
        soul from body
        heart from soul.
It breaks open the sweet shell of humanity
        for the guts to fall quivering
        in an agony of air.

The adversary is defined.
And suddenly becomes uniforms
Just happened to be filled with flesh and blood.
Objects in the way of tanks.

Faceless face faceless
Over a chasm
Formed from a well of destruction.

War tears and rips humanity to shreds.

'*Why?*' echoes and re-echoes.

'*WHY?*' ...

SG

Acknowledgements

My thanks to Amy Rigg, Emily Locke and The History Press.

Deepest thanks also to:
Bertha Leverton for permission to quote so substantially from *I came alone*; British Red Cross and St John Ambulance for permission to quote from the personal memories in *Caring on the Home Front*; Charlie Workman for allowing me to quote from his *From Hardships to Steamships*; Delcia Miles whose committed support produced such a rich and invaluable fund of photographs, drawings, embroidery and personal memories; Dorothea Abbott for giving her permission to quote from *Librarian in the Land Army*; Ester Friedman for allowing me to quote from her autobiography; Len Chester for permission to quote from his book, *Bugle Boy*; Lynn Szygenda of the Embroiderers' Guild for permission to quote so extensively from *Embroidery*; Matthew Dring for access to images of the work of his mother, Lilian. And deepest thanks to Joan and Edie Rundle for their unfailing, generous hospitality.

This book could not have been researched without the kindly help and forbearance of the staff of St Ives Library – Christina, Florence, Jane, John, Pam – and Simon at Penzance Library. Grateful thanks also to John Allen of St Ives Archive Trust for his hours of scanning.

My grateful thanks for the expertise and kind support of the following:

Alan Jeffries, Imperial War Museum; Andre Gaillano of *Punch* archive; Andrew Whitmarsh, Portsmouth Museum; Chrysanthe Constantouris of the V&A for her patience; David Bell of the Imperial War Museum Photographic Archive; David Pearce for his kindness and professional expertise; Dorothy Tucker, Embroiderers' Guild; Dr Nick Hiley at The Centre for the Study of Cartoons and Caricature; Elizabeth Griffith for reading and commenting on first drafts; Fiona Watson of the National Trust Chartwell; France Beauregard, National Gallery of Canada; Gabrielle White of Random House; Jen Young of the British Red Cross Museum and Archives for her help and advice; Loreen Brown of Hodder & Stoughton; John Delaney of the Imperial War Museum, Duxford; John Martin, Flambards Experience, Helston, Cornwall; Kate Farrer of the Kent Institute of Art and Design; Kate Williams, Getty Images; Liesl Munden for her advice, support and memories; Louise Oliver and Miss Clark, Royal Collection Buckingham Palace; Lynn Openshaw for her research into Occupational Therapy; Lynne Beckley, computer wizard; Mandy Fay, Darlington Libraries & Community Learning Service; Margaret Coleman for kindly reading first drafts; Marzanna Misztela of Solo Syndication, London; Meriel Pardoe; Michael Griffith for the computer; Peter Garwood of the Barrage Balloon Re-union Club; Peter Merton of the Imperial War Museum, Duxford; Rosemary Griffith for her comments on first drafts; Rowland Lowe-Mackenzie, Turnbull & Asser; *The News*, Portsmouth; Tom Eaton of the Imperial War Museum Photographic Archive; Vicky Stubbs of the National Trust Chartwell.

Grateful thanks to members of the Embroiderers' Guild and National Federation of Women's Institutes who so generously contributed their memories, photographs, sketches and pieces of embroidery: Alice Livie; Angela Cole; Angela Davies; Anita Seamons; Ann Walker; Ann Williams; Anne Blakeney; Anne Honeybone; Anthea Geddes; Audrey Hussey; Audrey Pevy;

Barbara Adams; Barbara Parsons; Barbara Saunders; Bettina Cohen; Betty Clease; Betty Deacon; B.M. Hall; Carol Ewen-Hennessey; Chris Watkins; Christine Goldie; Clare Williams; Cynthia Savory; Denise Cochrane; Derry Timmer; Diana Trotter; Doreen Buchanan; Doreen Green; Doreen Newson; Elizabeth Wade; Enid Mason; Evelyn Taylor; Florence Bomber; Frances Wilson; Gillian Garratt; Gloria Adams; Gloria Barker; Glory Chenery; Gwen Jones; Hazel Brannon-Sim; Heather Fogg; Heather Shearing; Jane Rodgers; Janet White; Jean Brown; Jean Hooper; Jean Panter; Jessica Rix; Jill Rickard; Joan Angus; Joan Head; Joan Trethewy; Joan Walters; J. Sixmith; June Simper; Kathleen Lever; Madge Warne; Margaret Gibson; Margaret Naude; Margaret Woods; Maureen Spenceley; Mary Cole; Mary D'Escofet; Mary Harman; Mary Howse; Mary Thomas; M.E. Harris; Muriel Pushman; Olive Ball; Olive Caselton; Pat Burton; Pat Crocker; Pat Salmon; Peggy Brown; Penny Hodgson; Rita Williams; Roberta Page; Rosalind Abbott; Rosemary Culshaw; Rosemary Dishington; Rosetta Price; Sheila Brooks; Sheila Fowles; Sheila Westall; Stella Fox; Stroma Hammond; Susan Lindley; Susan Monk; Susan Reynolds; Sybil Cross; Sylvia Foster; Thelma Castlemaine; Valerie Bush; Valerie Crooks; Valerie Green; Valerie Watson; Vera Goode; Virginia Leonard-Williams; Wendy Connor; Wilma Raumati; Ann Wright; Jean Wright; Wyn Trevitt; Yvonne Blackith; Zoe Rains.

Also: Nicolete Anderson, Jim Broyad, Jim Peakman, Jo Humphries, John Williams, Mike Osborne and Robin Tabusor.

This book could not have been written without reference to the sources listed in the bibliography. My grateful thanks, therefore, to the writers, researchers, archivists and those who have published their memories of the Second World War.

Foreword

When I was a child, just after the Second World War, my mother stitched complicated tapestries, smocked my dresses, and made my green gingham school dresses; I stitched dolls' clothes, looked at the illustrations in *Needlewoman and Needlecraft* and *Vogue*, learnt to speak with awe of The Needlewoman on Regent Street, London, and treasured every little scrap of material. At school I embroidered, hemmed, and was taught more about dressmaking, which enabled me to make my own clothes, including my wedding dress, through into the 1960s.

But it wasn't until I researched the stitching of the Second World War and the 1950s for a degree in Textile Art and Design that I began to understand how the centuries-old tradition of home stitching in Britain was fading to a close in these years. It also became clear that the British war effort had relied heavily upon its stitchers and that their endurance and skill had been overlooked against the compelling drama of world events.

This book can only convey just a brief idea of the enormous quantity of stitching which was generated by the Second World War – and the effects which the items produced, as Britain stitched for victory and then faced the challenges of recovery, 1939–1951.

S.G.

Weights, measures and currency, 1939–1951:

£1 = 20s (shillings) 1s = 12d (pence) (The average weekly wage was around £4)

1in (inch) = app. 2.5cm 12in = 1ft (foot) 3ft = 1yd (yard) (app. 91.5cm)

1 mile = app. 1.6 km

1lb (pound) = app. 0.5 kilos

Introduction

From the moment of birth our closest bodily relationship is with stitch. Stitch constructs some of the most intimate essentials of our personal existence. Our stitched belongings move and change with us through our every waking and sleeping hour, fulfilling our needs, sending messages to the world on what we are, what we would like to be, or what we *have* to be. Stitch even accompanies us in death.

In the 1930s, the production of stitched goods was a fundamental part of industry and home life in Britain. Clothes had to last for years and they were made in Britain's many textile factories, by the thousands of independent dressmakers and tailors – or were created at home. Stitch was a form of relaxation, maybe when the family gathered together in the evening around the sitting-room fire to 'listen in' to the radio.

It was usually cheaper and more satisfying to make garments, furnishings, toys, dolls' clothes, party clothes and fancy dress costumes at home and stitch was one of the essential feminine skills. Girls were taught to sew and embroider, maybe before they could read and write, and to appreciate, even feel affection for, the qualities of fabrics and embroidery stitches. It was not expected that the items would be made quickly, but rather, stitchers looked forward to spending satisfying hours in the creation of something to be treasured, worn, played with, or used in the home.

Upon the outbreak of war and until Britain was fully recovered, stitch became an important part of the nation's resources. It became an essential process in the production of military uniforms and equipment and hospital clothing; a means of keeping up morale and a healing activity for minds traumatised by pain and horror.

The stitching of 1939 to 1951 could be viewed as unworthy of recognition, but without stitch the fight for the nation's freedom, peace and ultimate recovery could not have been organised or carried out, and the skillful use of stitch added considerably to Britain's chances of success.

This book offers a brief glimpse into the experiences of the stitchers of the Second World War and the millions who depended upon stitch to bring them through. It is intended as a memorial to their endurance, ingenuity, courage and the essential part which they played in the achievement of peace.

one

Ten Thousand Children

The Beginnings of War

It is an act of selfless love and complete desperation for parents to send away a child, or children, alone, on a train bound for a foreign country, trusting them into the care of relatives or strangers, knowing that they may never see them again. Yet such was the terror under which the Jews of Germany and Nazi-occupied countries were living, that thousands of frightened parents struggled for places for their children on the *Kindertransport* trains which had been organised to carry Jewish children to safety in Britain.

After Adolf Hitler's rise to power in 1933, life had become increasingly isolated, restricted and dangerous for Germany's Jewish population. Nazi cruelty was such that many adults committed suicide, suffered a nervous breakdown or fled their homeland, but many more believed that the majority of Germans would not accept such behaviour and that it would soon 'blow over'. However, on 9 November 1938 – the 'Night of Broken Glass' or *Kristallnacht* – the signs became absolutely clear: anyone of Jewish descent in Germany was in mortal danger, for during that night, Nazi Stormtroopers entered every Jewish home, business, school and orphanage, which they systematically smashed and ruined. Every Jewish synagogue was irreparably burnt down. Thirty thousand Jewish men were marched away to concentration camps,[1] beaten violently and held in captivity for weeks or months before being allowed home, with heads shaven, bodies broken and bruised.

The world was horrified. Organisations such as the Refugee Children's Movement and Quaker Society of Friends rapidly lobbied the British Parliament for humanitarian aid, and on 21 November the House of Commons stated that Britain would accept 10,000 children up to the age of sixteen years from Germany and German-occupied countries on condition that each was sponsored by £50 to ensure that they would not be a financial burden to the nation. A very strict quota was laid down by the German authorities regarding the number of children who could leave for Britain and it was left for Jewish families to find out about the *Kindertransport* quite by chance.[2]

It was found that the best route for the trains, which travelled from Berlin, Hamburg, Munich, Frankfurt, Vienna or Prague, was to pass through Holland or Belgium then the children would be transported by ferry across the Channel to Harwich. It was on 1 December 1938 that the first 200 children left, including some from a Jewish orphanage in Berlin which had been ransacked by the Nazis, and they were followed by just 9,154 more, for the border with Holland was closed on 14 May 1940 under Nazi occupation and by September 1940 only 9,354 children had been taken to safety. In some of the towns which they had left not one child would survive.[3]

For their journey to a new life in Britain the *Kindertransport* children were allowed to carry just one small suitcase, maybe also a rucksack, and parents had been warned that if they

This photograph of Liesl Heilbronner aged fifteen years with her parents Ludwig and Emma was taken a fortnight before she left by *Kindertransport* train from Dusseldorf, Germany, in 1938. (By kind courtesy of Liesl Munden)

attempted to include more than 10 Reichsmarks, or any valuables, the whole train would be sent back, indeed it was stitched items which were to compose the majority of the contents. These few possessions, packed with love by the grieving and desperate parents, were mainly clothing and toys, sometimes a shoe-bag, sewing kit, tefillin bag or prayer book cover, or a mother's apron or scarf – even a wedding veil. Later, some children were fortunate to receive additonal boxes or parcels of treasured household items including their mother's housecoat and family linen. Within the two wooden chests which Liesl Heilbronner (above) received was her mother's grey silk apron edged with lilac crochet and incorporating a drawstring pocket to hold knitting and embroidery. She also received a crochet-edged cross-stitched tablecloth which had been made by her mother. (See colour illustration 1.) After she left Dusseldorf, Liesl's mother and father were deported to a concentration camp in Minsk and there they were separated and shot. No other members of Liesl's family survived.

Many parents made sure to describe England as a place of freedom and safety and the journey as an exciting adventure, looking forward to a time when they would be re-united, hoping that they also could travel to Britain. However they had no clear idea of British clothing.

> We thought of England as a land of lords and ladies because of the king and queen, and the two little princesses appealed to us very much. A year or two before we saw pictures in newspapers of the coronation with their ermine clothes and their crowns on their heads. And we really thought in England that's how people got dressed – perhaps not every day, but sometimes on Sundays. So that was our expectation of England. (Bertha Leverton)[4]

> We all had curious, if somewhat stereotyped pictures of England in our minds. We imagined that all English people walked about dressed like Sherlock Holmes or like the prim English girls seen in old copies of *The Tatler*.[5] (Gerta Ambrozek)

Preparations were hasty. Liesl Heilbronner's parents were notified just one week before the train was due to depart. Sometimes, as a last chance to express their love, mothers embroidered their child's name onto the clothing, perhaps on every single item, as if the stitches would keep this dearest relationship alive far away in another land. It was true, love was strong, and these stitches would indeed create a link with home which would last for the rest of their children's lives.

> Everything was happening much too fast for a seven year old. Suddenly I was taken to shop for every conceivable item under the sun, from underwear to coats, dresses and even two suitcases. (Edith Forrester)[6]
>
> Since my mother was not well I bought all the clothes for England myself and sewed name tags on everything. (Gabrielle Gatzert)[7]

The contents of the children's suitcases had to be inspected by Nazi officers to make sure that no valuables had been included and then they were officially sealed.

Many grief-stricken parents pretended that they would also be travelling and the children did not understand that they were going on alone until just before the train was due to depart.

> We were going on a journey, perhaps we were about to embark on a wonderful holiday. … I assumed, of course, that I would be going on this journey with my parents. … We waved goodbye to my father in such a way that I felt sure he would be joining us shortly. … My mother tried to explain, but with the trusting nature of a much-loved only child, I felt secure and did not grasp the awfulness of the situation until I found myself alone on a train which was bursting at the seams with what seemed to me to be hundreds of children. Suddenly I heard my cry of 'Mutti! Mutti!' and somebody lifted me up and I was able to catch a last glimpse of her face, her lovely, sad eyes frantically searching for me. … I was no longer a bewildered child, but a very frightened one. Where was I going and what was going to happen to me? (Edith Forrester)[8]

Sometimes, Nazi guards enforced silence as parents and children were parted.

> My father had sewn me a cloth pocket to wear next to my body, with all papers, passport etc. … My mother, my suitcase and I went to the Vienna train station. There was an ocean of humans everywhere – panic, fear, confusion in the air. All of a sudden, as a Nazi shouted into a bullhorn 'No talking or waving goodbye – or you'll be arrested', there was a deadly silence. I remember looking out of the open train window, my arms by my side, looking at Mutti. She was so thin, so white, so shabby. I loved her so … Someone handed me a baby through the window. The baby didn't cry … The train pulled out. No waving – not a sound, just like that. (Lisl Saretzky)[9]

Nazi guards continued to harass and intimidate the children as the great steam trains passed through Germany, patrolling the corridors and entering compartments to check papers and ransack suitcases, leaving the children with just one change of clothes.[10]

As the train crossed the border into Holland, the children immediately felt an enormous sense of relief, as if a nightmare had ended. The Dutch Red Cross were waiting to greet them with trolleys of refreshments, smiles, hugs and comfort; it was another world of kindness without fear, which the children had not known for a long time; it even made them smile again.[11]

Upon their arrival at the port of Harwich, most children were taken either to Liverpool Street Station in London, where they were met by friends, relatives or guardians, or to Dovercourt Bay and Pakefield converted holiday camps. More than half were finally housed in hostels, converted barracks, houses and convalescent homes – in fact, anywhere that the many regional Refugee Committees or committed individuals could obtain, including Gwrych Castle in Wales. At Lyon House in London, each child was greeted by the gift of a soft toy on their bed. The children who were taken to Dovercourt Bay, which had been built by Billy Butlin as a summer holiday camp, needed all the warm clothes they could get in the unheated rooms during the exceptionally cold winter of 1938, when snow drifted into the dining hall to land on their unfamiliar breakfasts of kippers and they had to sleep in sweaters and coats.[12]

It was most important for every child to be clean, neatly dressed and appealing on Saturdays and Sundays when prospective foster parents and organisers of hostels visited to 'choose' their children. Perhaps wearing unfamiliar borrowed clothes or things newly received from the Refugee Children's Movement, surrounded by adults discussing them in a language which they could not understand, the children often felt more like animals on show in a zoo.[13]

With more children constantly arriving, by Christmas 1938, the Refugee Children's Movement funds were in crisis, but a programme entitled *Children In Flight* was broadcast on the radio in January 1939 which spoke so vividly about the children's plight that across the country groups such as Women's Institutes and Rotary Clubs organised fundraising events and parcels of clothes and food began arriving from a compassionate public, including shoes and coats from Marks and Spencer, a trunk full of warm knitted clothing from a ladies' group in Johannesburg and a pair of boxing gloves from the National Boxing Club.

But even when settled, clothes could again become an issue for the *Kindertransport* children. As soon as war was declared on 3 September 1939 it was not wise to be seen wearing their foreign-style clothes from home, so those few, intimate, dearly cherished possessions had be taken away. Such was the shortage of clothing in Britain that they were later given to British children who had been bombed-out or made orphans in the Blitz![14]

Yet sometimes a child was allowed to keep an item from their suitcase such as the little toy dog given to Evelyn Kaye by her father to comfort her on her journey from Austria and which he called an *Ausieschaner*, 'a present peeking out of a pocket'.[15] (See colour illustration 2.)

Older children quickly did what they could to help their parents and relatives also to escape and tried every means of finding work for them so that they could be accepted into Great Britian. A few were successful,[16] but the majority remained alone, far from parents and homeland. The fortunate ones found love, support, lifelong friends and a 'second family' in their foster homes, but some were to be cruelly treated, abused or used as servants and they would not know again the comfort and security of home until they were old enough to make one for themselves.

Their lives were soon to be interrupted once more in June 1940 when German invasion forces began to mass along the coast of France and the British Government took measures to ensure that there should be no enemy spies or collaborators on British shores. German and Italian adults and children were either moved thirty miles away from the south coast of England, interned, or shipped to Canada or Australia in shamefully appalling conditions, and tragically, many of the children lost their lives when the *Arandora Star* was torpedoed off the coast of Ireland.[17]

At the age of fourteen, when young people in Britain were expected to start work, many of the *Kindertransport* children were advised to take jobs in the catering or clothing industries where, sadly, suspicion and anti-Semitism sometimes increased their loneliness. Girls gave valuable service as nurses, members of the Auxiliary Territorial Service, the Women's Auxiliary Air Force, the Women's Land Army, or the National Fire Service and the Refugee Childrens' Movement supplied them with clothing when necessary, including the rather expensive 'Nippie' outfit of black dress, white frilled hat and apron, for waitresses at the popular Lyons Corner Houses. Boys could sign up with the Jewish Pioneer Corps and were later allowed to serve Britain in the regular services, finding their native language much in demand when interpreters and interrogators were needed to accompany Allied troops as they finally entered Europe.

> Being beyond school age, I was given an errand boy's job at a gentleman's outfitters in Kentish Town. On the first morning, when I reported for work, dressed in continental fashion in plus fours, I dutifully clicked my heels and bowed my head and offered my hand to be shaken. The boss looked quizzically at me, examined me from head to toe and then burst out 'You haven't come to play golf.' A second-hand suit was quickly organised. (Walter Fulop)[18]

The enduring dream of the children was, of course, to be reunited with their parents and relatives as soon as the war ended and it was devastating after years of longing to discover, with the rest of the world, the extent and unimaginable inhmanity of the Nazi Holocaust and that their loved ones had not survived the years of brutality. Only a few were to find their parents again, but then the relationship had changed: now *they* had to be the ones of strength and understanding to slowly overcome the appalling traumas which their parents had suffered in the Nazi camps. Some of the children, now young adults, went back to their homeland to do what they could to aid its recovery, but many never returned to the places which they had left six years before, deciding instead to settle in Britain and start families of their own or travel on again to find new lives in America or Canada.

For the majority of the *Kindertransport* children, their pieces of stitched clothing, linen or toys had become all that was left of home. However, Ester Friedman found her most treasured stitched possession after the war had ended. She recounts in *I came alone*:

> … the story of the tapestry started seventy years ago, when my mother started embroidering it before her marriage to my father. My mother loved sewing, so she became a dressmaker. Here in England you would call her a Court Dressmaker … She had little time to relax, but sometimes, and that very seldom, she would take out the tapestry and sit and embroider it. And I would sit on a little wooden stool at her feet, so happy oh, so happy, to have my mother to myself and to know that she was relaxed and content. I would sort out the colours and tidily roll up the silks. What precious moments – what happy memories! … The transport left Vienna on 12 December 1938 and I was fourteen years old … Time passed, the war continued. I had a few letters from my parents through the Red Cross until 1941 and then SILENCE. We children, like so many others, had no idea what was going on in Germany, Poland and Czechoslovakia and we did not know about the concentration camps.
>
> … [after] contacting the authorities and governments involved … I contacted a firm of private investigators, sent them photos and particulars and they put up posters in public places with pictures of my parents and sister, their old address, and, as by then I was training to be a nurse, my hospital address.
>
> One day I was studying in my room in the nurses' home when there was a knock at the door. A stranger stood in the doorway and he told me the following: He saw one of my notices and as his intention was to come to England, he went to my old address. Someone who knew nothing of my parents opened the door. Unable to get information from her, he

tried the neighbour below our flat. … This Mrs Silber, not being Jewish, was still alive and she told my visitor the following: My mother lost most of her clients as they were not allowed to give Jews work. In 1940 my family was forced to give up three rooms of our flat to another family and had to move – the three of them – into the fitting room. A tiny room with the window facing the wall opposite. How long were they there? How did they live? My mother's permit to work was withdrawn. It was then that my mother found time to work on the tapestry. This tapestry, when finished, my mother gave to Mrs Silber for safekeeping.[19]

I remember her words as if it had been yesterday. 'This is all I have to give my child. We had many happy moments together while I embroidered it and Elsie sat at my feet on a little stool. Be sure to give it to her and to no one else. All my love is in this tapestry and all the love we felt for each other we expressed while working on it. She will know what I mean, if you tell her that. Tell her to feel my love for her when looking at the tapestry.'[20]

One day the SS came – heavy boots on the stairs, truncheons splintering the door, truncheons wrecking and breaking the furniture, breaking all that was breakable. Strong, rough hands grabbing my beloved mother, father, sister – dragging them downstairs into the lorries already full with other helpless men, women and children. That ended Frau Silber's story – she did not know any more.

She kept the tapestry throughout the war.

And so, he, a stranger, came to me.

What is there of greater value to me than this heirloom worked in times of happiness with love and in utter despair.

The only thing that escaped destruction – the only thing left of them except their ashes in a mass grave in Auschwitz. Please God, let them rest in peace.

(Ester Friedman *née* Muller) (See colour illustration 3.)[21]

two

The Royal Family

In 1939 the British royal family were at the apex of an Empire, Dominions and Colonies encompassing a quarter of the globe. However, King George VI and Queen Elizabeth had inherited a difficult situation, for war threatened in Europe and loyalty to the Crown was low both at home and overseas. Stitch had played a part in this situation and would also be a remedy.

Clothing in the 1930s rested firmly upon an appearance of respectability and everyone looked to the British monarchy for their example. As Prince of Wales, the handsome and charismatic Edward VIII had charmed the world with his fashion-leading, innovative style of *chic fatigue* which mixed bright colour and pattern in a relaxed, modern look, completely against the wishes of his father George V whose strict dress-code was firmly rooted in the Victorian era. Yet, in an age when divorce was morally unacceptable, Edward VIII had chosen to abdicate the throne in favour of marrying his twice-divorced American mistress. The world was shocked; loyalty to the monarchy plummeted in Britain and throughout the Empire and Dominions.

Unfortunately his younger brother, who reluctantly took his place, seemed dull and inhibited in comparison, with a stammer, weak health and the sense of conformity and correctness in dress which he had inherited from his father. However, he had married the sparkling and much sought-after Lady Elizabeth Bowes-Lyon whose warmth, optimism and constancy came to be adored by the British public, and with their two young daughters, the Princesses Elizabeth and Margaret Rose, they had become the 'ideal family' of Britain. Their Coronation had done much to restore trust in the British monarchy at home and overseas.

Glimpses of royalty were a rare treat in the 1930s, an avid public studied their images in newspapers, magazines, books and cinema newsreels across the world and the nation's mothers sat at their sewing machines or hand-stitched copies of the two little Princesses' identical wardrobes.[1]

This public interest, almost obsession, was shrewdly exploited by the Queen as a means of enhancing the monarchy's popularity finding her perfect couturier in the young Norman Hartnell, whose sense of theatre ideally suited the splendour and pageantry of royal ceremonial occasions, and whose designs were also appropriate for the more restrained clothing required for less formal public engagements. Hartnell, in turn, regarded the Queen as his 'first star' of fashion and his clothing beautifully enhanced her image of gentle, approachable, maternal, royal femininity. Their successful relationship lasted a lifetime. The Queen's favourite soft pastel shades of light blue, subtle green, pale pink and violet were translated into romantic, floating, delicate, sequinned and embroidered gowns,[1] to which she added ropes of pearls, a corsage, peep-toe shoes and graceful Aarge Thaarup hats. She was also able to use the lavishly applied sparkling jewels and beading as a subject to open conversations with shy guests at banquets or State dinners.[2]

Hartnell's most famous designs for the Queen were his off-the-shoulder, tight-waisted, crinoline-skirted evening gowns, which was actually suggested by the King, from the paintings by Winterhalter at Buckingham Palace of the Empresses Eugénie of France and Elisabeth

WE thought you would admire —as we do—these charming studies of the Royal family "off-duty" . . . enjoying to the full a holiday from State occasions.

Photos: Studio "Lisa."

Home CHAT

September 21st, 1946   441

(© IPC+Syndication)

of Austria.[3] In this preference, he was echoing a beloved British image of the time, that of the 'crinoline lady', who tended her luxuriantly blossoming garden in embroideries across the land on pictures, fire screens, table linen, dressing-table sets, anti-maccassars and chair arm-protectors, cushions and curtains (see colour illustration 4) for stitching the comforting images had supported the women of Britain through the hungry years of the Depression, perhaps after the loss of a fiancée, husband or brother in the First World War, and their love of the design had been passed on to their daughters. Although, the Queen found that there could be problems of practicality when actually wearing the crinolines' voluminous skirts – she was heard to remark 'I have a hard time fitting into these chairs with these new dresses…'[4]

It was Hartnell's task to ensure that she appeared immaculate at all times – when kneeling, standing, walking, and sitting – and whilst being a centre of attention, she must at the same time appear both dignified and discreet. His clothes also had to complement the priceless royal jewels with which they might be worn, or match the colour of ceremonial ribbons, and – most important – the Queen must dress with style, yet not appear dated when photographs and films were seen in future years.

In March 1938, Austria joyously welcomed its annexation by Germany and a strong pro-German feeling began to emerge in France, Britain's only ally, upon whose powerful Army Britain depended. War seemed ever more certain, and to strengthen the vitally important Anglo-French *entente cordiale*, a State Visit of the King and Queen to Paris was planned for June 1938. Hartnell was commissioned to create a wardrobe of day dresses and a dozen gowns,[5] but as it transpired, this was to be his greatest challenge – for just five days before the visit, the Queen's dearly loved mother, the Countess of Strathmore passed away, yet the Queen was determined to accompany and support the King who was just recovering from a bout of influenza. The Queen would be in deep mourning and Hartnell's prepared collection was rendered obsolete: he had only three weeks to produce an entirely new wardrobe before the postponed visit was due to take place.

As black crêpe or deep mauve would be inappropriate for summer, especially in Paris, the world's capital of couture, it was decided to dress the Queen in white, a colour used by the French for mourning, and Hartnell's workrooms plunged into an emergency round-the-clock race to stitch a wardrobe of gowns in white, including satin, tulle, organdie, lace, crêpe and fur. For the State Banquet, a silk tulle crinoline was made, covered with hundreds of yards of Valenciennes lace glimmering with silver. The State Visit was an enormous success and the Queen's 'White Wardrobe', including a parasol which had once belonged to Catherine the

Great, newly trimmed with transparent lace over silk tulle,[6] was a sensation both in Paris and New York. Tongue-in-cheek, Parisian newspapers dubbed the Queen as *soutien*-George, or George's support (*soutien-gorge* meaning 'bra' in French)[7] and Norman Hartnell was awarded the highest accolade in Parisian couture – Officer of the Académie Française.[8]

In February 1939, the danger of war deepened as Germany signed a 'Pact of Steel' with Italy, a Tripartite Pact with Italy and Japan, and a non-aggression pact with the Soviet Union. Britain and France decided to negotiate the Munich Agreement which allowed Hitler to take the historically German Sudetenland of Czechoslovakia, whilst at the same time giving warning that should Germany invade Poland, they would lend military aid. There followed an uneasy peace.

In Britain, Anderson air-raid shelters were distributed, conscription began for men over twenty years of age and the Government sought sorely needed support from isolationist Canada, and also a similarly isolationist America, which feared that Britain must inevitably succumb to the enormous power of the Nazi war machine.

The King and Queen were now given the essential task of revitalising Canada's loyalty and in May 1939 they set sail to cross the Atlantic on a State Visit, having also received an invitation from President Roosevelt to visit the United States. Hartnell's brief on this occasion was to provide separate wardrobes to be worn in Ottawa and Montreal; clothing for the varying climatic temperatures which would be encountered on the journey, and informal clothing to be worn on short train stops, maybe in the middle of the night.[9] Once more, the royal couple were a resounding success in planting the seeds of a vitally needed support for Britain – and once more, the Queen's parasols caused a sensation, resulting in a huge demand for copies.

On 1 September 1939, Nazi troops invaded Poland, and on 3 September Britain declared itself at war with Germany.

Immediately, Nazi U-boats began their strategy of decimating British shipping to cause massive losses in supplies of food and raw materials and when the Government introduced stringent rationing, the King and Queen joined the nation in saving resources through stitch. The King replaced the rich livery of Palace staff with a more suitable khaki, had his shirts' collars and cuffs repaired from the shirt-tails and he also applied himself to making ammunition on two evenings each week.[10] Again stitch played an important role in the welfare of the nation when Hartnell was commissioned to produce a wartime wardrobe for the Queen – this time to comply with

Cecil Beaton's photograph of Her Majesty Queen Elizabeth wearing a gown from the 'White Wardrobe'. (Courtesy of the Victoria & Albert Museum)

Visiting an ARP post at 'Hell's Corner, Dover, October 1944. (Courtesy of the Kent Messenger Group Li9451)

the Government's regulations in economy of fabric and design. Colours were carefully chosen
to blend with the wartime uniforms now filling the streets, at the same time ensuring that the
Queen could easily be seen in the rubble of bombed areas, the dim light of factories, air-raid
shelters and on military inspections. Using dusky pinks, blues and lilacs, painted fabrics and
drawn thread work to replace the now-forbidden embroidery, his designs were exactly what
was needed and perfectly enhanced the Queen's morale-boosting position of figurehead and
inspiration for the women of Britain, her motherly image, inner warmth, empathy and charm.

To celebrate her fortieth birthday in 1939, the Queen asked the revolutionary photographer
Cecil Beaton to photograph her in the celebrated 'White Wardrobe', and he was to remark that
his subject was one of 'overwhelming' charm, goodness and sympathy,[11] which was beautifully
captured in his photographs. Stitch had provided magnificent propaganda – the gentle and
serene Queen, dressed in white, who contrasted markedly with the brutal aggression of the
Nazis' war machine, their forbidding uniforms, metal helmets and leather jackboots.

In the 1940s, it was the experience of a lifetime to catch a glimpse of the King or Queen in
'real life' and the royal couple embarked upon what would be 4,766 public engagements to
boost the nation's morale. They inspected troops, visited factories and bomb-damaged areas,
shook hands and offered kind words of support and encouragement. The King personally decorated some 32,000 servicemen[12] and stitch became an aid to ensure that his own version of active
service was perfectly clear – that of total commitment to the nation – when he always appeared
in the uniforms of Admiral of the Fleet, Field Marshal, or Marshal of the RAF.[13] However,
the Queen visited to remind Britain of the peace for which everyone was fighting by always
appearing in civilain dress. Asked if she was quite sure that she wanted to wear her best clothes in
the smoking, dust-filled, rubble-strewn streets, she explained that the people would put on *their*
best clothes to visit *her* home.[14] Her sympathetic concern was deeply appreciated.

> The Queen came down yesterday morning – God bless her. She was so kind and she said to
> me: 'I am so sorry for you. I know what you are feeling.' The way she spoke was like the voice
> of an angel. Though I hadn't shed a tear over my home in ruins, and my little dog dead, I cried
> like a baby. There's never been a lady like her – and that's the truth.[15]

> People couldn't believe it. She just came and chatted as if she had known them all her life. She
> was in the same predicament and it was a real morale booster to the whole of the East End.
> My mother and her friends were in tears, something I had never seen before and was never to
> see again. She was fabulous. We never forgot her and she never forgot us.[16]

In their unstinting wartime service, aided by stitch the royal couple expressed all that Britain
held most dear. King George VI proved to be a bedrock of British wartime fortitude and self-
lessness; quietly correct in appearance, sincerely religious and completely committed to the
achievement of victory. The Queen, as always, was tirelessly optimistic, charming and sympathetic, her wartime service to the nation being celebrated in this poem by Mary A. Winter of
Chicago:

> London Bridge is falling down
> My fair Lady!
> Be it said to your renown
> That you wore your gayest gown
> Your bravest smile, and stayed in town
> When London Bridge was falling down
> My fair Lady.

(First published in the *Daily Colonist*, Chicago. Sent to the British *Times*, then sold on hugely
popular postcards.[17])

three

Mr Churchill

'If he isn't fast asleep, he's a volcano.'
General Ismay[1]

'To choose clothes … is to define and describe ourselves',[2] yet occasionally a great and independent spirit will disprove this statement. Maybe Winston Churchill was one of these, for whatever he wore during his years as Britain's wartime Prime Minister, the power of his 'sheer personality'[3] was the first impression which one gained – often *despite* his clothing.

Winston Churchill had the deepest belief that he had 'a mission to perform and That Person will see that it is performed'.[4] It seems that with this inner assurance came a total disregard for personal safety and a lack of the need for pretension in appearance, allowing him to indulge an often colourful and at times distinctly uninhibited use of dress – or undress.

In public, he would appear, according to the occasion, in his own individualistic, impeccable, formal dress, military, or quasi-military uniform and always, in public or in private, his clothing was always of of the very highest quality in fabric, design and craftsmanship from the workrooms of Britian's world-renown tailors. His shirt pattern at Turnbull & Asser, London, was carefully re-cut every two years to maintain a perfect fit and allow for any changes in measurement.[5] In private, however, stitch provided the comfortable clothing which was to play an intimate and supporting role in his almost superhuman capacity for work.

When the bombing of London started in earnest, the press and public were to see Churchill in perhaps his most famous garments of the war – his 'siren suits' – or as he called them, his 'rompers', as they were similar in design to a child's all-in-one zip-fronted playsuit. In fact, they were an immaculately tailored development of the protective overalls which he had worn during his more leisured years out of political office when building brick walls in the gardens of his home at Chartwell, Kent.[6] Clementine Churchill also possessed her own collection of siren suits, as did the Princesses Elizabeth and Margaret Rose,[7] and tartan Viyella siren suits with hoods were made by British couturier Digby Morton.[8] Thousands of women bought, or stitched, siren suits for themselves and their children and it was said that Churchill was 'quietly pleased' to have started a fashion[9], although it is amusing to note that while the general public quickly slipped *their* siren suits on over night-clothes as the air-raid warning siren sounded, ready to run to the Anderson shelter in the garden, Churchill wore *his* siren suit to watch enemy bombing, standing out in the open, high up on the roof of the Annexe (the present-day Treasury), even refusing to wear his protective tin helmet. (See colour illustration 3.) The British public soon came to feel an affectionate familiarity for his air force-blue version and his Air Force greatcoat.

It was on the first day of the Blitz, 10 May 1940, that Winston Churchill took over as Britain's wartime Prime Minister[10] after Lord Halifax had refused the position, saying that the only option left for Britain was to sue for peace with Germany. This was not Churchill's plan –

Winston Churchill:
First Lord of the Admiralty, September 1939 to
May 1940.
Prime Minister and Minister of Defence, May
1940 to July 1945.
Prime Minister, 1951 to 1955.

German military leaders always appeared in full
Nazi uniform and this image of Churchill in
civilian clothes holding a 'Tommy' gun was a gift
to Nazi propagandists having to deal with the
latest British attacking force, the Commandos.
Stitched clothing was subverted to 'prove' that
the British War Cabinet were 'lawbreakers' with
the Commandos as their 'terror merchants',[2] for
Churchill did indeed greatly resemble a 1930s
American gangster. In fact, in the original photo
he was inspecting the gun whilst surrounded by
Army personnel. (Courtesy of the Imperial War
Museum, London H 2646a)

'He did not care what anyone else wore …'' On this occasion Churchill wears a dressing gown in the company of the American President Dwight D. Eisenhower and General Alexander. (Courtesy of the Imperial War Museum, London NA 10074)

Inspecting bomb damage, accompanied by the Mayor of Portsmouth. (By kind courtesy of *The News*, Portsmouth)

immediately he formed a coalition government which had the effect of a depth charge on the 'leisurely and gentlemanly' British response to Germany's massive war machine.[11]

Nazi U-boats were decimating Britain's greatest strength, the Royal Navy and Merchant Navy; the British Expeditionary Force (BEF) in Europe was in retreat, and there was no offer of support forthcoming from a determinedly isolationist America. Only days after his arrival at Downing Street, the situation grew yet more serious when the BEF with French and Belgian troops were forced back into the sea at Dunkirk and only by a seeming miracle were 338,226 men and women brought to safety across the English Channel. Virtually all of the BEF's equipment and ammunition had to be abandoned in the sand.

Churchill's most pressing task was to convince the free world that Britain would fight on – and fight on to victory – but within Britain, he lacked both the trust of fellow politicians and also that of the British public, which assumed from his aristocratic upbringing and appearance that his policies would be certain to continue the usual governmental disregard of the working classes. It quickly became evident, however, that he possessed just what the country needed, the power of an indomitable vision of victory, which, when communicated through his soul-stirring speeches, generated immense respect from all those who had doubted. Politicians and public alike caught his spirit of energy and courage and 'an elating rush of confidence'[11] swept the nation which made it seem a privilege to be part of his unquenchable determination to see it through at all costs.

In this most tremendous task, Churchill was to use his somewhat eccentric wardrobe of stitched garments as an essential aid in keeping up a breathtaking pace of work for eighteen to twenty hours a day. Day and night, stitch – and the lack of it – provided relaxation and comfort. After breakfast in bed around 8.30 a.m., he worked in one of his brightly coloured quilted dressing gowns until his bath at 1 p.m., keeping three secretaries busily working in shifts on a silent typewriter in his room, and sometimes attending to important visitors whilst dictating. Dictation often continued during his bath. Work resumed after lunch including champagne, only to be interrupted by an hour's sleep before dinner when, once inside his bedroom, he would disrobe during the few steps to the bed where he often have put on his silk vest and black satin eye-shade and be asleep before his bodyguard, Walter Thompson, had picked the clothes up from the floor.[12] The evening's work began after a walk, clad in a siren suit, from Downing Street to the bomb-proof Annexe even during enemy raids, and dictation continued there until around three or four o'clock in the morning, maybe with a break to watch enemy bombing from the roof.[13]

At weekends, the work of Downing Street was transferred to the Prime Minister's mansion at Chequers or, if the moon was full and the sky clear, with a risk of enemy bombing, to Ditchley Park near the Churchill family seat at Blenheim. There, the routine continued, to which any invited Cabinet Ministers, overseas visitors, chiefs of staff, politicians, or generals were expected to conform. Again, Churchill dressed himself comfortably in siren suits or dressing gowns, and again he would rush out of doors to see enemy aircraft – a brightly coloured target in a dressing gown.[14]

After his evening bath, Churchill would wear a siren suit for dinner, then, changing into a dressing gown, he would watch a film with his guests and if he happened to be occupied by a particular problem there would be a game of bagatelle, to be immediately followed by work until three or four in the morning – which, of course, demanded the attendance of his guests.[15] Then sometimes before bed he would march up and down the Great Hall of Chequers, humming to the tunes of brass bands played on the radiogram.[16]

Immensely busy though he was, Churchill always had time to visit troops, or areas of Britain which had suffered severe enemy bombing. Stomping through the rubble, chewing his cigar and giving his V sign for victory, he was warmly greeted by a public willing to support him to their utmost and grateful for his obvious care for their wartime struggles. The deep respect in which Churchill held the British public, particularly the poorest who were suffering and losing the most, yet giving their all – the sight of which could reduce him to tears – was returned by great affection for his figure in the familiar blue-grey siren suit and greatcoat, formal pin-striped suit or black jacket and striped trousers worn with a spotted bow-tie, walking stick and black hat.[17]

Secretly, during his years as Prime Minister and Minister of War, Churchill travelled some 200,000 miles across the world to attend high-level meetings, witness the progress of the war at first hand, and boost the morale of the services. At these times, when Churchill was overseas, the actor Norman Shelley took over his wireless broadcasts to the nation,[18] adding just one more impersonation of Churchill to the many with which the British public entertained themselves.

Churchill's conscious use of stitch to provide relaxation and comfort contributed enormously to his ability to sustain a position of immense responsibility, but ultimately the intensity of pressure over such a lengthy period of time took a toll on his health, and at one point it was expected that he would die from pneumonia following a second minor heart attack. But neither this, nor the determination of the Nazis to assassinate him, nor the dangers to which he constantly exposed himself, could prevail against such a fighting spirit, and at 3 p.m. on Sunday 13 May 1945 it was Churchill's deeply deserved honour to finally make the wireless broadcast which announced to the nation the cessation of hostilities in Europe. In an unobtrusive suit, beaming with obvious satisfaction, he took his place before wildly celebrating crowds on the balcony of Buckingham Palace – with the King and Queen as the focus of a relieved and jubilant free world.

'They had the lion's heart. I had the luck to be called upon to give the roar.'[19]

Appearing to celebrating crowds on the balcony of Buckingham Palace, VE Day. (Courtesy of Getty Images 2638153)

four

Home

Everything conspired to disrupt or destroy the homes of Britain in the years 1939 to 1945. Upon the outbreak of war, many families were broken up, for adults could be sent away on war service and children evacuated. Wealthier people in areas most vulnerable to bombing shut up their homes and went overseas or rented a house in the countryside.

Then, when the bombing started in earnest, the blast from explosions destroyed possessions, covered everything in dust or soot which had been shaken down from chimneys and filled the air with the stench of explosives. Cut off water supplies made cleaning up more difficult and home owners might have to replace shattered windows or have damaged roofs temporarily covered in tarpaulin. Those who remained at home became tired and worn down by uncomfortable, sleepless nights in air-raid shelters and little time was left for home-making after the demands of war work, queuing for necessities and the challenges of making the most of rations.

When a home – with all its family memories, privacy, security, and position in the neighbourhood – was obliterated by a direct hit, it was the sad task of the Civil Defence Services to search through the rubble for occupants, pets and any undamaged belongings. Lives had to be rebuilt, maybe somewhere else to live had to be found and the process started of replacing essential possessions. The homes of around 2¼ million people were destroyed in the nine months between September 1940 and May 1941, and nearly two-thirds of these were in London.[1] By the end of the war, one in five homes had been either damaged or destroyed, and some streets no longer existed. Victims felt completely disorientated by such sudden and devastating changes. Shocked survivors, or 'bombees', were directed to Rest Centres, and when these overflowed, local authorities requisitioned unoccupied furnished houses.[2]

However, people were absolutely determined to go back to their own neighbourhood if at all possible; no matter how devastated and ruined, it was still home[3] – and this love of home was skilfully transformed into a national strength by the British Government: Britain itself became the nation's 'home' in which everyone would be called upon to share their own private homes.

Local Defence Volunteers were re-named the Home Guard, the BBC Radio Home Service united all those who were 'listening in' and windows were left open to share important news broadcasts. Countless householders welcomed passing strangers into their Anderson air-raid shelters when the warning sirens sounded, and it was – if reluctantly – accepted that one should take into one's home an evacuated child or children, a billeted serviceman or woman; or, in the case of much larger houses, volunteer one's home for the use of a school, hospital or convalescent home.

The *Housewife* magazine of December 1939 gave advice on how to cope with these extra people by turning the dining room into a bedroom and replacing this with a lounge-dining room for which could be made 'quite adequate' seats out of wooden packing-cases '…painted or covered with fabric … The tops should be padded or have gay loose cushions'. This clever new seating also acted as storage for household items which had to be packed away in order to

This mother and son are looking at what remains of their home. (Courtesy of Kent Messenger Group PD 800610)

make more space. It was also recommended that bedrooms should be turned into bed-sitting-rooms to afford a place of 'peace and privacy'.[4]

Determined home-makers treasured the times – even in an air-raid shelter – when they could sit down as they were used to do, and stitch some decorative or utilitarian item for their home. There were many options:

Things that were home-made in our house, or at the least home decorated, were cushions, chair backs, arm rests, table runners and table cloths, decorative mats – the sideboards in the living rooms, and of course curtains. Dressing table sets were always prettily embroidered in our bedrooms. … In the kitchen we had tray-cloths for tea trays when we had visitors, also tea cosies – embroidered material for 'posh' … It was the decorative things that were embroidered – utilitarian things like sheets or towels were mostly left plain – but the embroidery cheered things up as well as protecting things from wear and damage – hence the chair backs and arm rests for the upholstered furniture and mats under anything that could scratch the polish on sideboards and dressing tables – as I said, my mother liked to keep things nice. [She] had been in service, and also a lady's maid with whom she travelled on the Continent, and so she was attuned to, and fond of, nice things … I would probably say that my mother really enjoyed making things for me (and my dolls) and she liked making things to brighten the house – and it was a way to keep the fingers busy while listening to the radio. (Anita Seamons) (See colour illustrations 4, 6 and 27.)

Roger Smithells observed in the *Housewife*:

Few of us will have money to spend now on beautifying our homes, but long evenings by the fireside will give the housewife and her guests more time for all kinds of needlework. What cannot be bought can be made at home. The rag-bag can provide the raw material for new patchwork quilts, always amusing and now fashionable again. … Many other [ideas] will occur to the ingenious housewife who has set out on the important job of thoroughly and cheerfully adapting her home to new conditions.[5]

One 'ingenious idea' on the part of the wartime home-maker was to get the rest of the family to help, including husbands and sons, as well as daughters:

> … I can remember covering milk bottle tops (washed, I hasten to add!) – the ones that were made of a sort of cardboard and had a hole in the middle – with garden raffia or string using a looped blanket-stitch. These were then stitched together to make handy shopping baskets or table mats – they could be decorated further with scraps of coloured wool embroidery. (Anita Seamons)
>
> At some stage … we obtained some metal templates … that could be opened out like circular fans to make flower and leaf shapes. These were stitched over in layers of different coloured wools (on a fairly strong fabric). When you cut up the middle of the shape and pulled out the metal template the wool sprang back to make a multicoloured 3D flower – somewhat like the pom-pom balls we used to make using cardboard circles. This fascinated me and formed the basis of several sets of chairbacks and arm rest covers. The stitching was straightforward for a child and had the added bonus of a surprise at the end! (Anita Seamons)
>
> My grandmother also had friends in occasionally to make 'friendship quilts', each one bringing their own bright pieces. They were attractive but I can't remember who was the lucky recipient! (Audrey Hussey)

When the use of furnishing fabrics was restricted by inclusion in the coupon scheme, home-makers had to make do with whatever materials came to hand:

> I bought a second-hand sofa at a house auction sale, and it badly needed recovering, but by 1946 it was impossible to get suitable material. But a shop in Eton, near to where I was then living, got in a huge bale of off-white floor-cloth cotton, being thick and soft, and this made … a really excellent loose cover. I piped it with coloured piping, and it lasted for several years. (Virginia Leonard-Williams)
>
> Making quilts. Using an old sheet. Cut garments and lay flat on the sheet – like a jigsaw. Use the same type of garments, e.g. all wool or all cotton. Tack all the pieces in place then cover with another large piece of material. Tack well. Then quilt the pieces together. (Christine Goldie)
>
> … my mother [managed] to get hold of some flour bags. She unpicked them, washed them then dyed them green for me to make them into curtains, and [I] decorated the bottoms in different colours which improved the windows. (Anon)
>
> Cushion covers were made from old curtains or skirts. (Stroma Hammond)

I remember my grandmother's kitchen tablecloth made from a flour sack and trimmed with bands of bias binding. (Janet White)

In an article for *Embroidery*, the journal of the Embroiderers' Guild, Phyllis Platt recommended using the 'good parts of an old shirt' to make tablemats: 'Pad with an old linen towel, quilt with odd strands of DMC and finish with a needleworked edge. Such things as these cost practically nothing, yet the fact that they have been "schemed" to get the best effect makes them a real diversion of mind.' She also recommended the use of joining stitches when adding a border to lengthen curtains, or 'to piece together good parts cut from some worn object into a cushion cover'. She pointed out: 'to join small padded quilt squares with an open joining stitch greatly enhances the effect, as well as providing the ventilation so desirable in quilts'.[6]

When the Government realised that consumption of sheets had risen as a result of their use as dress fabric, they also had to be rationed,[7] and as the war progressed, even the most basic household essentials such as towels, face-cloths, tea-cloths and curtains had to be rationed severely. The public was instructed:

> Leave all washing up, particularly china, to drain instead of drying it, so as to save wear on your tea towels. If you have to go away to stay take your towel with you. If you are a billettee you must provide your own towels. It isn't fair to expect the housewife to be the only one who gives up her coupons. Everyone in the household must contribute coupons when new towels are needed. If you live in permanently in a hotel or a boarding house you must contribute your share to the proprietor if new towels have to be bought. Take your towel with you to the hairdresser.[8]

Old towels were cut up and the good parts used for face flannels – blanket stitch was used as edging to prevent fraying. (Anita Seamons)

By 1945, new sheets were virtually unobtainable and 10,000 women queued from the early hours of the morning when Pontings on Kensington High Street received a consignment. Households which had to replace everything due to bombing were given priority, although even they had to be put onto a six-month waiting list.[9] It was essential to make sheets last as long as possible, and the Mrs Sew-and-Sew leaflet 'Your Household Linen Has Got To **LAST!**' explained how. It was recommended that not only should worn sheets be cut down the centre and the less-worn edges joined to form a stronger middle, but that when *these* sheets began to wear thin they should be layered onto other similarly worn sheets by joining two together with running stitches down the centre; then, after smoothing carefully, sewing lines of running stitch 12in apart across the sheets top to bottom, oversewing the edges, and finally darning or patching any particularly worn areas. This method was also recommended for extending the life of worn tea-towels and dusters, making sure that any holes did not coincide; and for joining the fronts and backs of worn pillow-cases together, with the addition of a 'false back'. If a sheet was just too far gone, the best parts could be turned into handkerchiefs or torn up for bandages. Mrs Sew-and-Sew also advised:

> One fair-sized sheet can be made to do the work of two by cutting a line about 18 in. long down the centre of the top – these edges should be hemmed. The sheet can then be used double on a small bed, the slit allowing the top to be turned back over the blankets without difficulty.[10]

Of course, the scarcity of soft furnishings made it difficult for newly married couples to set up home – if they could find somewhere to live – particularly in the years of post-war austerity, even though there was an allowance of coupons to buy the very barest essentials and Utility pillows and quilts could be bought at a third to a quarter of the usual shop prices.[11] Even Princess Elizabeth and Prince Philip received a gift of 'towels and kitchen clothes' made by Lord & Taylor, as a wedding present from an ever-thoughtful Mrs Eleanor Roosevelt, in November 1947.[12]

Just as the war had finished I got married and I seem to remember we were allowed coupons for 3 sheets and 4 pillowslips. (Jean Hooper)

Dockets were issued to newlywed couples by the Government [for furniture]. Also issued were priority dockets to buy 15 yds of curtain material, 20 sq. yds. of linen, one mattress, two blankets and three sheets. (Evelyn Taylor)

I was married in 1948 … Bedding allowance was basic, so we made a bed cover from a parachute. It was a single layer, no lining, quilting or filling. This was not a silk parachute but a heavier weight one, used for dropping supplies, in a blue/green rayon fabric. We used the tapered panels to effect by creating a 'sun' pattern… We also bought an ex-Army blanket which we cut into strips, bound the edges, and put down for a stair carpet. (Barbara Saunders)

Those who were not so honest managed to buy items 'acquired' from Ministry of Supply storage depots and stolen Army sheets sold at £5 a pair in 1941.[13] However, the penalties of such thefts were severe and the thieves who had persistently stolen from the Advance Linen Services Ltd in 1945 found themselves on trial at the Old Bailey.[14] Yet the profits were high and, in 1946, black marketeers even plundered the bedding, towels, refrigerators and washing machines which had been left behind by the US military.[15]

However, it was maybe carpets and rugs which were the most valued items of home furnishing during the freezing winters of the war and early post-war years as houses were heated only by coal fires in the sitting room or kitchen – when coal was available – and it could be painful to walk with bare feet on the cold linoleum floor of an unheated bedroom. Carpets became so valued that in 1947 thirteen new Wilton carpets were taken during the re-fit of the liner *Queen Mary*; however, the thief who attempted to remove carpets from the Albemarle Hotel in Brighton spent six months in prison.[16] 'Simple HOUSEHOLD REPAIRS and how to handle them' described how to keep any carpets going as long as possible by inserting a patch or replacing the pile with tufts of wool – a heavy and difficult job on a large piece.[17]

To cope with draughts in the bedroom, *Home Chat* recommended hanging a heavy curtain over the unused fireplace, and, in the dining-room, keeping the feet warm with a foot-muff, or a 'garden mattress laid under the table with a rug or eiderdown to cover the feet', or by adding a 'deep flounce' reaching from the chair seats down to the floor.[18]

Every evening we all helped to make rag rugs, prodding strips of old clothes through a potato sack (hessian in those days). There were doormats, kitchen sink mats and posh ones for the sitting room. I can still remember the joy of finding a bright colour to use. Mostly things were drab greys, blues or brown. (Enid Mason)

Across the country, each area had its own names and methods for rug-making:

In Hawes, Yorkshire: The action of rugmaking was called 'stubbin'. The base of the rug was a kind of sacking or hessian. The strips of material were cut from old clothes. A tool with a wooden handle was used to push the pieces through the base. Sometimes the smaller ones were put across one's knee, larger ones were done on a framework.

Todmorden, Lancashire: They were called chippy mats, made the same way.

Slaithwaite, near Huddersfield: called rag rugs, again strips were cut from old clothes. ... a loop was made.

Some rugs were 3ft x 1ft to put at the base of every door to keep out draughts. Larger ones, some for a whole room were done on a kind of frame on 2 A shapes 7ft apart and the base material (made of old sacks from the farm) was wound round as the rug was made – like a roller at the top. This 'contraption' took up a lot of room! (Sheila Brown)

We were given clothes, including dance dresses, by a well-to-do person, which my grandmother would unpick, wash and cut into small pieces for her 'pegged rugs'. She made these on coarse brown potato sacks, did simple designs in lovely colours, and for two generations we had a hearthrug, bedside rug and one to-stand-at-the-sink rug. These were replaced, time and fabric permitting and were taken outside to shake, daily, and hung on a line or over a wall to be beaten and sun-dried-aired regularly. (Barbara Parsons)

After the war but still during the rationing period mother would go to house sales. On one occasion she bought a billiard table surround carpet two feet wide. She and father unpicked the seams and stitched it together again to make a stair carpet. There was enough for a hall runner. (Sheila Brooks)

Everything was re-used in some way – any clothing beyond use was given to two of the aunts who were making rag rugs. One even made a stair carpet this way! (Audrey Pevy)

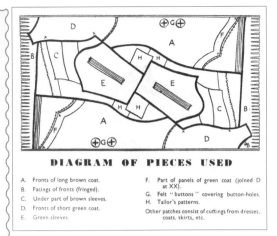

DIAGRAM OF PIECES USED

A. Fronts of long brown coat.	F. Part of panels of green coat (joined D at XX).
B. Facings of fronts (fringed).	G. Felt "buttons" covering button-holes.
C. Under part of brown sleeves.	H. Tailor's patterns.
D. Fronts of short green coat.	Other patches consist of cuttings from dresses,
E. Green sleeves.	coats, skirts, etc.

In her 'Thriftcraft' series for *Art and Craft Education* 1939–40, the textile artist Lilian Dring gave instructions on making a 'Thrift Rug' from old clothing by cutting as close to the garment's seams as possible and then moving the pieces within the required shape until they fitted snugly and formed a pleasing design.[1] This 'Thrift Rug' measures 3ft x 6ft and is made from two old velour coats stitched onto a length of backing fabric. (By kind courtesy of Matthew Dring)

In 1943, a Mass Observation survey discovered that to the British: 'Home means a place to go to when in trouble.' ... 'A place to glorify when away and rely on always'[19] and stitchers were performing a vital service to the country when they doggedly maintained their own family home while battles raged across the globe, cities were destroyed, and lives were lost. Every quietly stitched item kept normality alive and created a little comfort, beauty and colour, in readiness for the time which everyone had been looking forward to and fighting for: the return to rest and privacy in their own comfortable home. Although, by the time the war ended, 30 per cent of Britain's homes had been destroyed by bombing,[20] creating a desperate shortage which some families solved by moving into vacated military Nissen huts and thousands of prefabricated homes were constructed as rapidly as possible. From the end of the war until 1949, some 156,623 families were able to move into 'temporary' two-bedroom 'prefab' bungalows complete with hot water, a bath and even a refrigerator[21] – for many, a dream come true.

five

Blackout and the ARP

The Air Raid Wardens' Service in Britain was started in April 1937 when Local Authorities were instructed by the 'Air Raid Precautions Act' to organise the protection of 'persons and property from attack, injury and damage in the event of hostile attacks from the air'[1] and by the middle of 1938 there were some 200,000 volunteers,[2] one in six being women.[3] Across the country's built-up areas there were usually ten wardens' posts to the square mile, which were divided up into sectors each patrolled by a warden who was familiar with the locality. Air Raid Precaution (ARP) units were set up by large organisations, including Harrods of London which raised a force of 700 wardens.[4]

The British Blackout came into force from half-an-hour after sunset on Friday 1 September 1939, when every household or commercial premises had to ensure that no light could be seen from the outside which might lead enemy bombers to their targets. For this, the stitchers of Britain were quickly mobilised to produce a major national defence – the blackout curtain. The Government-recommended heavy black sateen cost 2s a yard, and when this ran out one had to improvise with other fabrics such as blankets and bedspreads, or even paper and paint. For some, the Blackout was a costly exercise, especially poorer families and large firms such as the City of London textile firm which had fifty skylights needing some 8,000 yards of material'.[5]

Indoors, the effect of the Blackout was dramatic, for the dark, funereal curtains instantly created a sense of gloom and vulnerability – home no longer felt like a place of security. Darkened rooms seemed to be isolated spaces in which to wait for the sound of enemy bombers outside

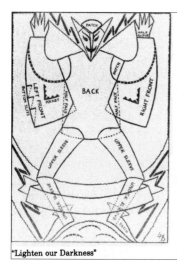

"Lighten our Darkness"

"Darken our Lightness"

Women's magazines recommended methods of cheering blackout curtains by pinning on shiny tinfoil stars and ingenious stitchers invented their own methods of overcoming the problem such as sewing on fabric numbers and letters for children's rooms, or flowers cut from printed material. *Art and Craft Education* gave two witty designs from the graphic artist Lilian Dring which cleverly utilised worn-out garments; a demon says 'Darken out Lightness' and an angel prays 'Lighten our Darkness'.[1] (© 1939 Scholastic Ltd)

in the encircling night sky and depressingly, the Board of Trade *Make Do and Mend Leaflet No. 11* 'Simple Household Repairs and how to handle them' hinted that the Blackout could last for years. The leaflet stressed that blackout material should not be washed as it would be:

> …more apt to let the light through. Instead, go over your curtains regularly with a vacuum cleaner if you have one; if not, take them down at least twice a year, shake gently and brush well. Then iron them thoroughly – this makes them more light proof and also kills any moth eggs or grubs which may be in them.[6]

In December 1939, *Housewife* magazine asked:

> Is Your House a Gloom-hole?' and encouraged: 'Don't let black-out curtains and dimmed lights turn your home into a dug-out. … Gloom is the great enemy to be routed. We cannot keep cheerful in dingy, disjointed homes. Consider your black-out arrangements. Perhaps they can be improved. If you substituted your gay curtains with yards of funeral black-out material then put your gay curtains up again and use the dark material to line them. Your home would begin to look itself again and your black-out would be just as efficient. Are you sick of taking elaborate precautions every night to make sure there are no cracks of light? Simplify the process by securing the curtains with tacks or drawing pins down the sides of the window frames and where two curtains meet fasten rings on one side and hooks on the other, allowing for a good overlap. A deep pelmet in a plain shade taken from the pattern of your curtain will dispose of possible leakage at the top and will also make your windows look more trim.[7]

Officially blackout fabric was to be used solely for making regulation curtains and blinds, but, of course, as it was unrationed, inventive stitchers found all sorts of other uses, of course, including costumes for amateur dramatics and dancing schools such as the Perth School of Dance. Stitchers preparing for an entertainment revue at Britain's top secret Bletchley Park even managed to transform blackout fabric into can-can dresses by adding frills of dyed bandages.

> When I was six or seven I joined a dancing class/troupe learning ballet and tap dancing. Our 'uniform' was made from (mostly) blackout material – a short pleated skirt topped with a bolero-top, a small piece of red material provided a mock 'blouse' under it. We used to go all over the local area putting on concerts in village halls in our spare time. One of … [mother's] brilliant successes, though, was the costume she made for one of my solo dances as a Golliwog.

Pupils of the Perth School of Dance dressed in their blackout fabric costumes. (By kind courtesy of Christine Goldie)

Trousers and jacket were fairly straightforward in blackout material with ribbon stripes, and bits of coloured material for the waistcoat – on my head I wore a complete hood, with eye, nose and mouth holes cut and outlined with paint like a 'black and white' minstrel.' (Anita Seamons)

The national Blackout was also applied to streetlights and vehicle headlamps:

We lived in a farm in Yorkshire and I always went, with my mother, to the Make Do and Mend classes in the village school, in the 'Blackout'. Not a chink of light was allowed from behind the curtains or the ARP man would be knocking at the door. So we often fell over on grass verges and bumped into trees as we walked the full length of the village. (Enid Mason)

Sometimes it could be amusing to hear people bumping into each other outside in the dark,[8] but by January 1940 there had been over 4,000 deaths due to Blackout accidents[9] and one in five members of the public had suffered injury.[10] People took their own precautions such as painting satchels and briefcases white, leaving pale-coloured shirt tails hanging out, wearing white buttonholes or handkerchiefs tucked into the breast pocket[11] and obtaining white-stitched covers for bowler hats.[12] Women bought white coats and were recommended to carry a white Pekingese or, failing that, hold a white handbag. White accessories were purchased or stitched at home, such as wide white organdy collars, white cuffs and corsages of rather glamorous luminous white fabric flowers.[13]

Understandably, in November 1939 a *Daily Mail* survey found that the Blackout came second in things which people hated most about the war[14] and as it was the responsibility of the ARP to enforce the regulations, maybe using their famous command 'Put that light out!', many neighbourhood ARP Wardens suffered much resentment and criticism, particularly during

Luminous accessories could make the wearer visible in the darkened streets of the Blackout. (Courtesy of the Imperial War Museum, London D 77)

the quiet months of the 'Phoney War', when bombing raids by the German *Luftwaffe* did not materialise and the Blackout regulations seemed unnecessary anyway. Around 300,000 persistent offenders were reported to the police, some having to appear in court and pay a heavy fine.[15]

Unfortunately, until May 1941, there was no ARP uniform to lend the volunteers an air of authority, except a tin hat, armband, silver badge, whistle for warning of an imminent air raid, and a large rattle to warn of the presence of poisonous enemy tear gas or blister gas – which, fortunately, was never used. It was not long before some wardens came to be seen in their neighbourhoods as self-important busybodies, for it was their duty to list the names of

" *It's gone to old Brown's head a little—catching the first chink of the season.*"

(Reproduced with permission of Punch Ltd, www. punch.co.uk)

every person resident in their sector and know where they would be sheltering in the event of an an air raid so that they could be rescued from bombed buildings if necessary. They also had to know the location of gas and water mains and any stores of inflammable materials.

Once issued, the uniform of both full- and part-time wardens was a deep navy-blue serge blouson battledress with a printed or embroidered yellow badge, the colour being changed to red from 1941, a coat displaying 'ARP', a blue armband printed with 'ARP', shoes or boots and thick socks, a blue beret and steel 'ARP' helmet and, for women, a scarf to buffer the weight of the helmet; also, a large green canvas gas-mask holder with front pocket, which was attached to a band passing across the chest and over the shoulder.

However, when the bombs *did* begin to fall, neighbourhood ARP Wardens became a welcome and reassuring sight and were soon accepted as some of the bravest members of the community. Thomas Alderton, ARP Warden in Bridlington, Yorkshire was the first to be awarded the George Cross medal for 'gallantry' and by the end of the war ARP Wardens were among the 535 decorated with the George Medal for 'good military conduct and valour'.[16] Their task, once the sirens sounded, was to quickly make sure that everyone within their sector was sheltering safely, including the drivers of any vehicles passing through, and to tie up any horses in the nearest protected space. Then, until the 'All Clear' was sounded, it was their duty to patrol the streets in the deafening noise of enemy bombers and exploding bombs, exposed to falling masonry, flying shards of broken glass, fire and smoke. Whenever possible, they looked in at their local air-raid shelters to check that all was well and give what information they could.

As one of the first to arrive at 'an incident', the ARP Warden was trained to deal with small fires, administer first aid for minor injuries, assess the situation and send back reports to the local Wardens' Post by messenger with requests for the appropriate emergency Civil Defence services. Searching through rubble and falling masonry for survivors or the dead whose bodies were often blown to pieces, with acrid smoke burning their eyes and clouds of brick dust filling their lungs, it was at these times, maybe crawling through cavities in the rubble, that female ARP Wardens were grateful for their uniform-issue of trousers instead of skirts.

The Blackout in Britian was in force from 1939 until dim-out in the autumn of 1944. It had been a long and dangerous five years – but at last the ARP Wardens could dispense with their uniforms and the nation's stitchers could take down their gloomy, inconvenient blackout curtains and use the fabric to make something else … or even take great pleasure burning them on the VE-Day bonfire!

six

Gas Masks and Bombs

'I think it is well also for the man in the street to realize that there is no power on earth that can prevent him from getting bombed. Whatever people may tell him, the bomber will always get through.' (Stanley Baldwin, MP)

Now that bombs could be dropped by aeroplane, it was not just the British forces who were open to attack: civilians had to be trained to deal with bombs also. If caught in the open, they were instructed to quickly lie on the ground, arch the back and scream so that blast from the explosion would not damage their eardrums.

The *Red Cross* of January 1943 answered the question: How does Blast act?

This is best studied by its effect on buildings, especially those of the brick type. When a bomb bursts there is a strange momentary silence, before the houses collapse. This silence is the pause between the compression and the suction wave. The walls are momentarily pushed in and then sucked out, so that the entire structure falls down. You will no doubt have observed how windows bulge outwards after a raid, and that where these have been sucked out, the streets are strewn with articles of clothing and the like which have been drawn out by the blast.

The internal organs, particularly the lungs, of those within the range of blast would be similarly affected. 'Casualties are often found dead, without showing any signs of external injury, though blood-stained fluid may be seen trickling from the mouth or nose.'[1]

At 8 p.m. on the evening of 7 September 1940, the first of 318 *Luftwaffe* bombers began a Blitzkrieg raid on London which continued until 4.30 a.m. the following morning. This was repeated for fifty-six consecutive nights – as a beginning – and on the evening of 14–15 November 1940, the city of Coventry was bombed for eleven hours. The Blitzkrieg of Britain's industrial centres, ports and docks did not cease until 10 May 1941. In 1942, Hitler turned his attention to the destruction of Britain's historic cities, using a tourists' Baedeker guide as an aid.[2]

Public air-raid warning sirens, 'Wailing Willie' or 'Wailing Winnie',[3] as they came to be known, gave people time to run for shelter, and householders took refuge in their basements, cellars or other places within the home which they felt would offer protection, or beneath the corrugated-iron arch of their Anderson air-raid shelter which they had assembled and erected over a carefully dug hole in their garden – the soil from which could then be heaped over the curved roof and used for growing vegetables. Families without a garden could obtain an indoor Morrison shelter, like a steel cage with a flat metal top, which was often used as a table.

Spending the night sheltering from enemy bombers soon became a way of life in London: some 177,000 people slept on the platforms or escalators of the London Underground.[4] Sheltering in the basements of large department stores could be quite comfortable, with music, soft drinks and biscuits, and the opportunity to buy a book or a piece of embroidery to stitch as one waited for

'Old Nick': RSM G.H. Nicholson standing outside his badly damaged shop, Gravesend, 7 September 1940. (Courtesy of Kent Messenger Group Li24246)

the 'All Clear'[5] – all of which caused not a little bitterness in poorer neighbourhoods where the public shelters were crowded, dark, damp, unsanitary, noisy and filled with cigarette smoke.

The Government advised people to take an extra outfit of clothing with them, or to leave a suitcase containing a change of clothes with a relative – just in case nothing was left of home and possessions when they emerged in the morning:

> My mother's old brocade curtains I made into a most beautiful sea-green housecoat for my mother. She was wearing it when her house in Plymouth was bombed and next day it was the only thing she had left to wear … (Luckily she and my father and sister got out unhurt). (Virginia Leonard-Williams)

The siren suit, as worn by the Prime Minister himself, which could be stitched at home using one of the readily available patterns, was a useful garment to put on quickly over night-clothes as the warning sirens sounded for it was warm, kept clothing clean, and preserved an all-important appearance of respectability; perhaps with a Kangaroo Cloak over the top, to hold essential possessions in its capacious pockets.[6]

> Winston Churchill had a siren suit which was a piece of clothing consisting of legs, arms and top all in one with a big zip up the front. My mother made me one out of my father's old grey trousers so that I could put it on over my pyjamas when there was an air raid in the night and we needed to go to the shelter. I hardly ever wore it as I was lucky and did not experience many raids. I was very proud of it but outgrew it very quickly. (Heather Fogg)

Sleeping in the London Underground. (Courtesy of the Imperial War Museum, London D 1582)

However, even in an underground air-raid shelter there was no safety from a direct hit and it was almost impossible to sleep through the menacing noise of enemy bombers with their powerful, deep, throbbing engines, the ear-splitting screams of the sirens attached to the wheels of their escorts, the *Stuka* and *Heinkel* dive-bombers, and the terrifying screaming sirens on the tails of the falling bombs before the earth-vibrating sounds of their explosions.

Yet, everywhere people tried to remain calm and keep up morale, and stitch helped to steady the nerves:

Many hours were whiled away in the family Anderson shelter as we stitched pinafores, peg-bags, embroidered handkerchiefs to give as presents for our relatives and friends. (Doreen Buchanan)

I have a firescreen worked in Jacobean embroidery that my mother did. She has signed and dated it 'Gladys Mason March 1941' and told me that she worked it by candlelight in the air-raid shelter. (Rosemary Culshaw)

Our neighbours organised sewing parties in the shelter during the winter evenings. It started with spill holders and pot holders for Christmas presents. I have a chair back made at one of these sewing bees, made out of a flour sack – the printing never washed out. (Susan Reynolds)

It [a tablecloth] is stitched in a fairly thick single strand thread from a transfer that I believe was from the William Briggs range. ... I can remember my mother taking this embroidery with her when we used to go under the stairs at home when the siren sounded in what we called 'doodlebug corner'! Under the stairs was considered to be the safest place if the house was damaged. A direct hit and it didn't matter where you were! .... I can remember Mother being very determined to finish the tablecloth before the war ended. (Susan Lindley) (See colour illustration 6.)

Shelterers never knew what would be left of their familiar streets and homes when they emerged upon the sound of the 'All Clear'. If their home still stood, it might be badly damaged and the contents, including clothing, blown out into the street, to be covered in acrid dust and rubble. Washing left out on the line would be shredded with shrapnel or broken glass.

The mobile baths and laundries, such as the National Emergency Washing Service, which drove through the streets of blitzed areas, allowed people to wash away the dust and leave their dirty clothes and linen to be washed and ironed before collection later. (See illustration page 134.)

'Bombees' who had lost all their clothing were given an allowance of clothing coupons for the purchase of replacements and, when necessary, were also provided with an outfit of clothes in which to go to work. At Dudley House in London, a committee of American ladies sorted the clothing which had been generously donated to the British War Relief of the United States into bags labelled with size and sex, to make distribution easier in heavily blitzed areas.

In 1944, the first of the V-1 *Vergeltungswaffe ein*, German pilotless flying bombs of 'revenge', called 'Doodlebugs' by the British, began to destroy London and surrounding counties, particularly along the 'bomb alley' stretching from London to Dover. 'The noise of their flight was hideous. It was coarser, louder, more blatant than the regular pulsation of ordinary aircraft, and

Ladies of the Dudley House Committee sorting clothes donated by the 'British War Relief' of the United States. (Above left, courtesy of the Imperial War Museum, London HU3615. Above right, courtesy of the Imperial War Museum, London D 2084)

was very like the clattering harshness of a cheap and gigantic motor bike.'[7] 'The long flame of the exhaust gave to the whole ugly structure a fiendish kind of life.'[8] Arriving at any time of the day or night, the bombs fell at over 349mph once the rocket engine had cut out and there was no chance to take cover in those few seconds of terrifying silence.[9] The blast travelled like a tornado for miles.[10] 'As many as half a dozen would come roaring over together on parallel tracks separated by about a mile. The noise was fantastic',[11] for it included the deep roar of coastal ack-ack guns which could be heard and felt twenty-five miles inland.[12] One hundred and forty-two of these V-1 'Doodlebugs' landed on Croydon alone.

In early October 1944, the V-1 was replaced by the faster-than-sound V-2 which approached silently at 5,000ft per second[13] at altitudes of up to sixty or seventy miles,[14] hitting the ground at a speed of 1,600km an hour and causing craters 10ft deep and 50ft across. The 'blinding blue flash'[15] of the explosion was followed later by an 'ear-splitting' double bang, a sound so 'vast' that it could 'be heard for distances of at least sixty miles'.[16] Just one V-2 killed 160 people out doing their Saturday shopping at New Cross, London. Fortunately, many of the launch sites of the V-2 in Holland were destroyed within ten days of the start of their active use.[17]

Fearing that the enemy would use poison gas, the British Government had issued 44 million gas masks by September 1939[18] to civilians, war workers and the forces, accompanied by advice on their use with glasses, wigs, beards or mascara. Everyone was required to practice wearing their mask for fifteen minutes every day,[19] including children who sometimes found that wearing them was 'very frightening indeed'.[20]

This massive number of gas masks had been manufactured in Respirator Assembly Factories, such as those in Blackburn and Leyland, near Preston[21] or in smaller factories, such as Crysaed's in St Ives, Cornwall, which had previously produced high-quality women's dress fabric and clothing. Betty Davey, one of the dress-makers, remembers 'boxing in' or adding the sides to Army khaki gas-mask holders after the buckles and webbing had been stitched on. The thick fabric demanded the use of heavy industrial electric machines working at 362 stitches per minute and it was hard work for fingers which had been used to much finer work.[22]

The horses and mules serving with the Army in the Middle East had also to be provided with their own gas masks: the Animal Anti-Gas Cover Mk 1/L which came in three sizes, large, small and extra-small. It consisted of 'a proofed drill cover and a detachable impregnated lining with two eyeshields and 12oz of ointment. To maintain this gas protection, 100 animals required two yards of drab shade 1 inch webbing cotton, thread, cotton, and 18/3 cord each month, plus "suitable needles"'.[23]

Civilian gas masks were contained in a khaki-brown cardboard box attached to a canvas shoulder strap and it was a sign of one's wealth – or stitching skill – to have a more pleasing gas-mask holder. Required to carry a gas mask at all times, women quickly transformed their gas-mask cases into smart fashion accessories.[24] One could buy luminous 'Genuine Crocodile' holders and briefcases or handbags with gas-mask compartments;[25] Elizabeth Arden hid the gas mask within a white velvet vanity case; Aarge Thaarup's masculine version combined gas masks with poker dice and brandy flask in cases covered with lines from his favourite poems[26] and a fashion started for shoulder bags which could hold both gas mask and the contents of a handbag.[27] Ladies could also buy a hooded, oiled silk gas suit in a choice of amethyst, rose, eau de nil, soft pink and apricot from Harvey Nichols which could be rapidly slipped on over one's clothing, which, it was claimed, would give protection from mustard gas for a sprint of 200 yards to a shelter.[28]

Home stitchers could find a pattern and instructions for making a gas mask cover in the useful book *101 Things To Do In War Time 1940* and 'CASES FOR GAS MASKS' informed readers:

Protection must be provided for the cardboard container issued by the ARP authorities, if, as advised, it is to be available at any time. Although the box is made of stout strawboard, it will soon drop to pieces if allowed to get very wet. … it is certainly advisable to provide a case which should be made of waterproof material. White American and Lancaster cloth are

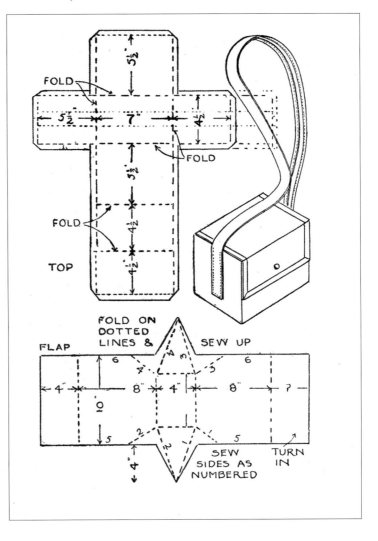

Pattern for a gas mask cover to be stitched at home, from *101 Things to do in Wartime*, 1940. (By kind courtesy of Batsford Book Imprints of Anova Books Ltd)

particularly effective and comparatively inexpensive materials. Willesden canvas is suitable for heavy wear, but leather is the most durable although more costly. Glazed calico is another suitable material.[29]

However, the public soon began to leave their gas masks at home when the feared enemy poison gas attacks did not transpire.

At 5 p.m. on the evening of 1 April 1945, Mrs Ivy Millichamp, the last victim of enemy bombing, was killed as she stood in her kitchen in Orpington, Kent.[30]

The years of gas masks and bombs were over.

seven

Sandbags and Blankets

Ubiquitous: *adj.* Having or seeming to have the ability to be everywhere at once.

In the Second World War, sandbags and blankets were ubiquitous. They were, perhaps, the most useful, widely used, simple, and quickly stitched items of the British war campaign and were manufactured in their millions.

Sandbags were an answer to the British Government's greatest fear – enemy bombing – and by the end of 1938 massive orders were being sent out to factories. Measuring 16in x 24in[1] and filled with sand, soil or even the sifted ash from household coal fires, sandbags could be used as emergency building blocks in trenches, or blast-walls and revetments to absorb the flying glass and debris of bomb blast around private air-raid shelters and houses, public buildings and monuments.

Homeowners were advised to build a sandbag blast wall to protect the entrance to their Anderson shelter in the garden, making sure to taper the walls down from a wide base to 2ft 6in at the top so as to avoid collapse, and also construct revetments around their windows with an overlap of 12in to prevent the glass from shattering. Sandbags could also be used to help construct a gas-proof 'Refuge Room' as described by the Air Raid Defence League, which required a ceiling reinforced with concrete or steel sheeting supported by wooden or steel props if necessary and, if the walls were less than 1ft thick, they also had to be reinforced with a 30in-thick lining of boxes or sandbags made out of 'any bags or sacks of stout paper or fibre' filled with earth, gravel or sand.[2] This was a massive undertaking, but well worthwhile if the room offered the possibility of a comfortable night's sleep.

Britain already possessed some 8 million second-hand sandbags, but this was just a fraction of the 475 million sandbags which, it was predicted, would be required by October 1939. To determine the number of bags needed to protect public buildings throughout the country, areas were graded according to the likelihood of bombing – Grade A areas needing eight sandbags per head of population; Grade B – six; and Grades C and D – three. In preparation, stores of empty sandbags were started at Alperton, Nottingham, Glasgow and Blackburn. However, the Government could not commit to providing sandbags to the 'general public' as it was estimated that this would raise the number needed by a further 1.5 million.[3]

The Scottish Jute Industry's factories around Dundee in Scotland could provide some 4 million sandbags a week, but as this was nowhere near the estimated number needed, 200 million were also ordered from the Indian Jute Mills Association of Calcutta, India.[4] In addition, seven of His Majesty's Prisons entered into a contract with the Government under the National Scheme for the Employment of Disabled Men, to sew another 4 million bags for delivery over a period of three to four years. Experienced female factory machinists in Dundee could stitch three bags in fifty seconds on their American 'Union Special' sewing machines, but it was calculated that men in prisons such as Wormwood Scrubs could only complete twenty per hour 'comfortably'.[5] After stitching, mechanical compressors reduced the volume of the

Sandbagging Rochester Cathedral.
(Courtesy of Kent Messenger Group
PD 605782)

Filling some of the 475 million
sandbags which were predicted to be
needed by October 1939. (Courtesy
of the Imperial War Museum,
London HU 55686)

Photograph of Mrs Marchant (front) who repaired 850 sandbags in one day. (Courtesy of the Imperial War Museum, London D16868)

completed bags before the bundles of 200 bags were hand-stitched into canvas wrappers ready for delivery.

The problem then arose, who would fill this vast number of bags, for the Ministry of Supply calculated that only three sandbags could be filled every ten days per head of population. As for filling materials, the War Office believed that it could rely on local supplies, stating that 'sand is not the only, or even the best, filling for protective sandbags' and plans were made to send excavating plant to 'rub up' the soil of public open spaces, which would then be transported to adjacent boroughs where the empty bags would be filled by volunteers.[6] Government instructions stated that: 'Sandbags should be ¾ filled with earth or sand so that when beaten with a shovel to a rectangular shape they measure about 20in x 10in x 5in.' In situations where the bag would not need to be moved again, the flap of excess hessian could be folded under to close the opening, for the weight of the filling would hold it in place. This method of closure also applied to the Army pattern sandbag, which measured 33in by 14in when empty.[7]

By November 1939, it became necessary to ship an additional 10 million sandbags to the British Expeditionary Force in Europe, and by March 1940 a further 20 million were needed in Marseilles and 'defended Ports Abroad'. Another 2 million were also needed in Finland, half a million in Turkey and 1.5 million in Switzerland[8] as well as those sent to Australia and Canada, where other items made from jute-hessian were also needed, such as fire-hose and lines for winter aviation suits and parachute harnesses.[9]

By September 1939, the War Department was facing a desperate shortage of sandbags,[10] for empty bags were stock-piling in Calcutta due to shortage of shipping and the machines in the Dundee factories were urgently needed for the production of camouflage cloth and tarpaulins. Additionally, the Scottish Jute Controller had become seriously concerned over loss of export revenue for factories in both Dundee and Calcutta due to the demands made by the massive Government contracts.

To make matters worse, by April 1941, there was 'a very great shortage of jute',[11] and the price had shot up – from £18 17s 6d per ton in December 1938 to £55 in December 1939.[12]

Then, when the sandbag defences within Britain were finally completed by May 1941, it seemed that the sandbag crisis was over.[13] However, the enormously increased British agricultural production had created another problem: the Food Ministry was making 'a considerable demand ... for hessian wrappers for all kinds of foodstuffs'[14] and such was the emergency that servicemen had to be released to make willow baskets; redundant banana boxes were brought out of store and second-hand sugar bags had to be used to transport cabbages and cauliflowers: but even so, thousands of sandbags had to be issued to farmers, particularly for the transportation of potatoes, carrots and onions.[15] Damaged sacks were darned in recovery plants, and one worker, Mrs Marchant, set a record of 850 sacks repaired in one day (see photograph opposite).

After nearly a year of concentrated enemy bombing, in June 1941 the Home Office approved the Fire Prevention (Business Premises) Order under which Local Authorities were allowed to sell sandbags to small businesses at 4½d per bag and a new form of sandbag, the 'sand mat', was devised for the purpose of extinguishing the many fires caused by incendiary bombs in commercial premises and private houses. These had to be stitched by 'the occupiers of premises' themselves and instructions stated that they should be made by cutting the regulation-sized sandbags to make bags measuring 16in by 14in, which then had to be sewn across the bottom before filling with about 20lb of soil, sand or sifted household ash, and the opening sewn up. 'This forms a loose cushion which can easily be grasped at the centre with one hand...'[16]

Street Fire Parties were quickly organised under Defence Regulations 27B,[17] each member being equipped with one sand mat and on the alert to cope with incendiary bombs. However, the correct 'operation' of the sand mat required nerves of steel, for the Government advised that: '... it should be placed accurately on the bomb, <u>not</u> thrown'. Sand mat 'operators' were also instructed to shake the heavy (20lb) contents regularly to keep it loose, and above all, to keep their sand mats dry, for experiments had revealed that 'the contact of wet sand causes violent scattering of the burning magnesium ... causing the operator to run the risk of being burnt'.[18] Leeds Fire Brigade also discovered that if one of the thousands of emergency sandbags which had been tied, in readiness, to lamp-posts in the north-east of England and frozen during the winter, should be placed on an incendiary bomb, it could cause fragments of molten magnesium to spray out 'to a height of 20ft or laterally 40ft'.[19]

Over-zealous stitchers were deterred from putting in any more than the most basic work on their sand mats:

The sand mats may, if desired, be tufted, i.e. the two surfaces may be drawn partially together with two rows of three or four loops or tufts at regular intervals, 3in to 4in from each side of the mat, which then looks like a miniature mattress. The tufted sand mat is adequate, but to place it on a bomb the operator must stoop and use both hands, which are then partially exposed to the bomb, whereas the untufted mat can be placed on the bomb with one hand, without stooping, and without exposing the hand. The tufting of sand mats also clearly takes time and trouble. For these reasons the tufted sand mat is officially not recommended.[20]

'Well, it was for A.R.P., but now I think it's something to do with the Grow More Food campaign.' Joseph Lee. Smiling Through Burst Sandbags. *Evening News*, 2 April 1940. (Courtesy of Solo Syndication, London)

Unfortunately, during the winter of 1939, it was found that the sandbags which had been used so extensively across the nation for the building of revetments were quickly rotting within three or four months of cold, wet weather, spilling their contents, and even causing damage to the buildings that they were supposed to be protecting.[21] It seemed that the answer must be rot-proofing, and the directors of the Willesden Paper and Canvas Works Ltd set about conducting experiments to prove that rot-proofed sandbags would last considerably longer, cost less in the long run and demand far less maintenance. However, when they resolutely lobbied the Ministry of Supply for the rot-proofing of further supplies of sandbags they were to find their results blocked by a solidly entrenched beaurocratic opposition and it was not until the matter was raised in Parliament that rot-proofing by Creosote, Cuprammonium, Tectal, Copper Cutch or Copper Soap[22] was finally allowed to go ahead. Indeed, it was understandable that the Treasury was concerned by the extra cost which would be involved in rot-proofing the hundreds of millions of sandbags which were estimated to be needed, for Scottish sandbags cost 2½d per bag and Indian bags 2d, and rot-proofing would add between another 1d and 3d per bag. However, the new supplies of rot-proofed sandbags were found to last over two years[23] instead of just a few months, and even by November 1939 savings from rot-proofing were estimated at around £28 million.[24] By May 1941, the Explosives Department of the Home Office was writing wistfully, 'What a pity we could not have rot-proof bags in the early days'.[25]

In the summer of 1944, the humble sandbag reached its height of usefulness, quite literally, during last-minute preparations for the D-Day landings in Normandy, when paratroopers who were sent on ahead to land behind enemy lines and hamper German response by sabotaging roads, bridges and railway lines were accompanied by scores of 'Ruperts', which were dummy sandbag 'troops' simultaneously dropped by scaled-down parachutes to decoy enemy fire, enhance the apparent number of landing paratroops[26] and divert the German troops who were sent to search for them.

While the sandbag played an important role in public defence, the blanket usually played its part in much more personal circumstances. On the Home Front, a blanket was essential when spending the night in an air-raid shelter and, due to beaucratic form-filling, blankets were also desperately needed in the Government-controlled Rest Centres to which 'bombees' were directed. However, the American and Canadian Red Cross generously met this need by supplying some 50,000 blankets and 30,000 quilts,[27] and as soon as local councils were allowed to take over the organisation of Rest Centres, blankets and camp beds were ordered 'in immense numbers'.[28]

Supplies of blankets also had to be rushed to hospitals in May 1940 for the care of the thousands of exhausted, shell-shocked and injured men who were brought back across the Channel from the evacuation of Dunkirk within a period of just a few days. Upon arrival, they were stripped, washed and taken to a bed where the comforting warmth of blankets aided the process of recovery.

At the beginning of the war, British housewives who remembered how useful blankets had been in the First World War, bought up whatever blankets they could find before prices increased – which they did, rapidly – and as a consequence of soaring prices, thieves began to raid military stores; however, the penalty for civilians who stole blankets could be six months' hard labour, and for soldiers, a court-martial.[29] By 1942, the Government was forced to take control of the spiralling costs and contracts were placed for 76.5 million blankets of three different sizes[30] with a maximum price set for each size and the manufacture of any other blankets was forbidden.[31]

One of the many uses for blankets in the home was in the protection of animals and infants in the event of an enemy poison gas attack. The RSPCA booklet *36 Air Raid Precautions for Animals* described how sedated pets could be wrapped in dampened blankets[32] and a similar procedure could be used for the protection of children under five years before they were issued with their gas masks. Protection from poison gas within the home could also be ensured by hanging dampened blankets at windows[33] and blankets could also be used against bomb blast by draping them over a Morrison shelter.[34]

If blankets were invaluable to civilians, they were essential to the British serviceman: these soldiers have each been issued with a blanket in preparation for the Normandy Landings. (By kind courtesy of *The News*, Portsmouth 2859)

Another use for the wartime blanket was in the stitching of the warm garments which were so essential during the freezing winters and there was even a form of snobbery attached to the colour of the 'edge to edge' blanket coat (which wrapped over at the front and tied with a self-fabric belt), for those made from grey-blue RAF blankets were regarded as definitely 'superior' to that of Army khaki.[35]

My wedding going away coat was made from a blanket, a horrible grey Army blanket. (Jean Brown)

I also remember her making a coat out of a plain blanket – very hairy round the neck! (Audrey Hussey)

One of the most successful coats she made was a blanket dyed a lovely turquoise colour. I was quite envious! (Nanete Anderson)

We made a dressing gown out of a blanket. Made it up as we went along. (Jim Broyad)

Even small pieces of old blanket came in handy for the soles of home-made slippers when they became virtually unobtainable.

The blanket played an essential role within the British Army and they were in particularly short supply after the Normandy landings as the men pushed across Europe in the freezing winter of 1944–45 and they were also vital for warmth in the jungles of Burma during the three-month winters; for not knowing that the temperature in the jungle could suddenly drop by ninety degrees at night, some British prisoners of the Japanese had been tempted to sell their blankets to villagers, only to discover that they would have to sleep naked on bamboo slats in temperatures just above freezing.

Many of our men sold their Army blankets to the Siamese villagers on the march from Ban Pong, thinking that they were not necessary in the tropics. They must regret it now; it's no joke being naked when the night temperatures are little above freezing point, sleeping on bare bamboo slats which rattle audibly as the men shiver.[36]

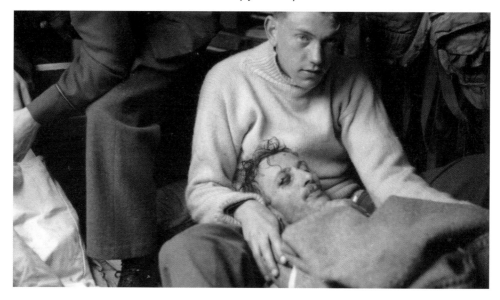

The blanket was an essential aid in the recovery of body temperature for men who had been recovered from the sea. (Photograph of Flying Officer Lord courtesy of the Imperial War Museum, London CH 9393)

The blanket also played an important medical role in Burma when the tropical summer temperatures and humidity caused heat exhaustion in the prisoners of war. Men had to be wrapped in blankets soaked with cool water before they could be carried on stretchers through the jungle to a medical aid station.[37]

However, if these under-nourished, exhausted prisoners of war suffered from tropical ulcers, they were to experience a much more painful relationship with the Army blanket in the only treatment available for the stomach-turning tropical ulcers, for after cutting away the rotting, dead tissue to expose healthy, raw, bleeding flesh the wound was then covered with a piece of Army blanket just removed from a four-gallon can of boiling hot water to draw out any remaining infection:

> The pain must be shocking, and the men's faces show it. These bits of blanket have to be reused continually. They cannot be thrown away because there is nothing to replace them. There is no soap to wash them clean after use, no disinfectant, and they are sterilised only by prolonged boiling. Every one seems to have old pus patches clinging stiffly to the fabric – boiling does not dislodge them and they cannot be scraped out. The foments are left in place, gradually cooling, until the next morning's torture session.[38]

Blankets could also save lives at sea, when wrapped around the survivors of torpedoed ships, newly rescued from the bitterly cold ocean, maybe covered in blood, vomit, excrement and spilt oil. Clothing had to be stripped off immediately and the sailor wrapped in warm, clean blankets before hot tea and rum were administered.

Yet another use for the wartime blanket was devised by MI9 as an aid for prisoners of war intent upon escpe. Seemingly innocent blankets were sent via the unknowing International Red Cross to be immersed in water and reveal the pattern of a civilian coat, just ready for cutting out and stitching in secret camp workshops. However, the POWs of Stalag Luft III found a further use for their blankets when digging tunnel 'Harry'. 'Railway tracks' of adapted Red Cross food tins allowed sand to be removed from the excavated face in boxes carried on trolleys

After surviving a forced march, a blanket tent is the only shelter for a British prisoner of war in Germany. (Courtesy of the Imperial War Museum, London BU 7104)

over lengths of track designed to meet at 'half-way houses' where the boxes could be transferred onto the next trolley and length of track. Blankets were nailed down over the tracks at the 'half-way houses' to keep the tunnellers' clothes free from dirt and 6in-wide strips of blanket were folded in half and nailed down over the 50ft of track near the entrance and exit to muffle any sound. In addition, a set of two blanket curtains were nailed 3ft apart at the 'half-way house' nearest to the exit shaft to hide the light and absorb the sound of the final escape.[39]

Blankets even made tents, when, in the last months of war, the Red Army penetrated into Germany and prisoners of war were force-marched to camps deeper inside the *Reich* on freezing roads without adequate clothing, shoes or food. Arriving at the overcrowded Stalag VII, a blanket could provide their only shelter.

Blankets still retained their value at the end of the war in newly liberated Europe when soldiers who managed to 'disappear' in the melee joined together in gangs to 'play' the black market by selling blankets which they had stolen from Army Stores in Brussels to the tailors of Paris who then transformed them into much needed, and highly priced, coats, sports' coats, dressing gowns, hats and bags for Parisians grown shabby under Nazi occupation. Unfortunately, it was possible for the Military Police to trace the source of garments so obviously made from such a very familiar fabric.[40]

The wartime blanket – rough and dull-coloured though it may have been – was nevertheless a source of comfort and a place to find rest, and it was appropriate that, throughout the Army, a man's blanket was wrapped around him by his comrades at his burial.[41] The blanket was also one of the first stitched items to bring comfort in one of the most unimaginably inhumane places that the world has ever seen – the Nazi concentration camp at Bergen-Belsen when Coldstream Guards visited every house in the neighbouring town of Celle, demanding from each an outfit of clothing and a blanket to be given to the 30,000 pitiful inmates.[42]

Just the barest minimum of stitching was needed to form these simple rectangles of jute-hessian or wool. Yet the millions of simple and quickly stitched sandbags and blankets were life-savers. They protected buildings and livelihoods, relieved exhaustion, gave reassurance of safety, allowed the injured body and mind to heal, and were an invaluable support to Britain in its long, hard slog to victory.

eight

'Blimps'

If any of the military equipment of the Second World War was loved by the British public, it was the barrage balloon – the LZ (Low Zone) Kite Balloon A Series, or the later B Series. Affectionately known as 'Blimps' (perhaps because a deflated B-Series balloon came to be described as a B-Limp?)[1] barrage balloons were the biggest military structures to be made with fabric and stitch in the Second World War. They formed what the Air Ministry termed a 'Roof Over Britain' by floating at an altitude of 5,000ft[2] trailing long taut steel cables which would damage any low-flying planes coming into contact or send them spinning out of control, thus forcing enemy mine-sowers and dive-bombers up into the target range of anti-aircraft guns. Britain was the only nation to use barrage balloons on such a large scale[3] and the sight of these silver-grey shapes floating reassuringly in the sky above areas vulnerable to enemy air attack became an iconic image of Britain at war.

Across Britain, barrage balloons became such a familiar and comforting sight that neighbourhoods and crews gave names to 'their' balloons, such as 'Waltzing Mathilda', 'Student Prince', or 'Flossie' and 'Blossom' – which protected the Chelsea area of London. Story-books, cartoons and films were filled with the adventures of the friendly silver-grey balloons, and one could even buy fabric printed with skies full of their chubby image. When civilians could 'acquire' the balloon fabric itself, it proved ideal for stitching shopping bags; and newspapers in the Orkneys reported children appearing at school in silver-grey coats and trousers, in addition to: 'Island Farmers Cut Up and Shared a Barrage Balloon' to cover their haystacks.[4] Another use was also jokingly attributed to the barrage balloon – that of keeping the British Isles afloat when 3.5 million troops were assembled in readiness for the D-Day invasion.

Balloon Command had been established in 1938 under the operational control of Fighter Command, using series 900 Squadron numbers; and eighteen Balloon Centres were built to support thirty-seven balloon squadrons, each consisting of five flights of nine balloons which were initially crewed by two corporals and ten men. 'Regular Balloon Operators' were trained at RAF Cardington, who then trained their local airmen. Posters encouraged men aged twenty-five to fifty to enlist as paid volunteers, declaring: 'Join a Barrage Balloon Squadron, here is an OPPORTUNITY for YOU and YOUR FRIENDS to DEFEND YOUR HOMES.'[5]

These 'Silver Monsters', costing over £500 each to make, had been developed from First World War reconnaissance airships produced by Short Brothers at their Cardington Airship Works in Bedfordshire, and were constructed from around 1,000sq.yds of Egyptian 2-ply close-weave rubber-proofed cotton cut into 600 precisely shaped pieces.[6]

Twenty-four panels ran from bow to stern, each 'Gore' being named in order 'A-F'. In addition, there was a fabric rudder and two fabric fins attached to the stern to minimise rolling. It was a complicated, heavy and cumbersome process for the 'fabric bashers' in balloon factories who stitched and glued the fabric to form the 66ft long, 30ft high,[7] 25ft-diameter balloon envelope.[8]

These were 'doped' with a layer of black water-proof paint which was then covered by aluminium varnish[9] and the factory workers, who were usually women, had to drink a ration of

The 'Roof over Britain'. (Courtesy of the Imperial War Museum, London HU 3725)

Cutting the fabric. (Courtesy of the Imperial War Museum, London A 571 43)

'Fabric bashers.' (Courtesy of the Imperial War Museum, London HU 56011)

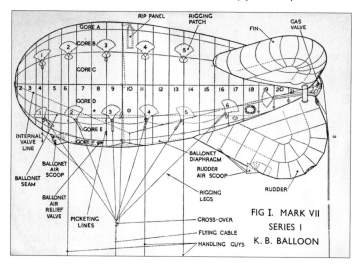

Diagram of the construction of a barrage balloon. (By kind courtesy of the Barrage Balloon Reunion Club)

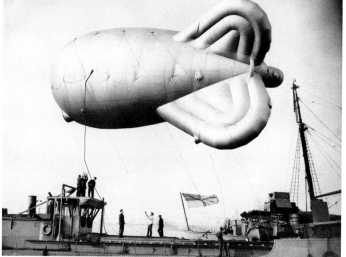

The Ellen B. Waterborne: one of the balloons flown by the Royal Navy Reserve to guard estuaries and harbours. (By kind courtesy of the Barrage Balloon Reunion Club)

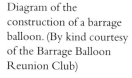

The smaller 'Waterborne Mark VIII' floated above slow-moving merchant ship convoys. (Courtesy of the Imperial War Museum, London A 6172)

one pint of milk a day as an antidote to the toxic fumes of the benzene solvents.[10] By 1945 the 'fabric bashers' had produced around 3,000 balloons, each painted with its own serial number and thousands had been sent, without charge, to the United States.[11]

Inside, the balloon contained a gas-proof diaphragm to separate the two horizontal chambers – the upper chamber, which was filled with 19,150cu.ft, or thirty cylinders, of lighter-than-air hydrogen gas which cost £50 for each balloon,[12] and a lower, air-filled 'ballonet' which acted as a reserve space to prevent the balloon from bursting when the hydrogen-filled chamber expanded at altitude. Once a balloon was launched, facing into the wind, nose slightly down, the 'scoops' at fins, rudder and bow took in air, filled the ballonet and forced the diaphragm downwards.[13]

Six cables, which were attached to the sides of the balloon, met at a 'crossover', and a steel 'Flying Rigging' cable ran down to a petrol-powered winch equipped with an altimeter[14] mounted on a Winch Lorry, thus allowing the balloon to be raised and lowered with the aid of hand lines.[15] It was this raising and lowering of balloons which always attracted much local interest – particularly from little boys – and armed guards sometimes had to be posted,[16] or the balloon kept up at a minimum height of 100ft.[17]

The need for the presence of barrage balloons was demonstrated only weeks after the war started, when, in November 1939, two German fighter-planes raided Harwich Harbour. Flying below the range of the Harwich heavy anti-aircraft guns, they dropped parachute bombs into the water and machine-gunned the observation post. Believing them to be British, ships' crews gave a friendly wave and the stunned harbour's light anti-aircraft gunners were too slow to open fire. Upon Churchill's insistence, a barrage of balloons was raised over the harbour within two days, closely followed by a larger water-borne barrage at the mouth of the Thames between Sheerness and Southend.[18]

'Water-borne' balloons tethered to pontoons, commandeered river barges, paddle-steamers, fishing boats and five converted cross-Channel ferries[19] guarded Britain's harbours and estuaries.

'Free Balloon Barrages' were also made using the small, spherical, top-secret Admiralty Type VI, filled with 320cu.ft of hydrogen-gas, from which were suspended deadly Air Mines set to self-destruct within eight hours. Floating in the sky where enemy aircraft were expected, 4,000 'Free Balloons' could foul an area of 10 x 30 miles – when the wind speed was correct. Taking seven minutes to inflate, they trailed 2,000ft of piano wire and launching involved operators first setting the fuse by winding it around nails driven into a piece of wood, then lighting it and running across the launch site holding the balloon aloft – which was a difficult and dangerous job over fields and rough ground particularly in the darkness of night, as was often required.[20]

By 1939, a DPL (Double Parachute Link) device was incorporated into balloon cables, so that when a plane hit the cable it caused a wave of tension to detonate automatic explosive cutters 150ft below the balloon and 150ft above the ground. As the cable severed, two 8ft drogue parachutes deployed which created a drag of 7 tons on a plane travelling at 200mph thus causing the plane to stall and then crash. Another device, the DPL/DR, used just one parachute plus a bomb, and as drag from the deployed parachute on the upper end of the cable pulled the lower end upwards, the bomb on the lower section of cable was detonated – the resultant explosion tearing off the plane's wing.[21]

The barrage balloon was not, however, regarded as being particularly effective by the military leaders of the Second World War: their behaviour was unpredictable and the conspicuously shining shapes led German planes quickly to their targets; also, they could cause damage to Allied planes as well as those of the enemy, so in order to avoid this problem, RAF fighter planes were fitted with a radio-transmitter device known as a 'squeaker' which gave warning of the deadly cables.[22] Yet the effectiveness of the presence of the barrage balloon was surely proved by the lengths to which the enemy was prepared to go to remove them. One August morning in 1940, a barrage near Dover lost its twenty-three balloons within just six minutes of enemy aircraft fire and when these were replaced, first by a single balloon within forty minutes followed by seventeen

A B-Limp. (Courtesy of the Imperial War Museum, London HU 36300)

more in the afternoon another fifteen were shot down by nightfall, but it had cost the *Luftwaffe* the loss of five planes in the attacks, including two brought down by the rifle fire of Balloon Command crews who had again increased the barrage to sixteen by the following morning.

In areas of heavy enemy attacks the ground would be covered with smouldering fragments of balloon fabric, but their destruction could be a spectacular and beautiful sight as the diving planes shot out their green or yellow tracer bullets into the shining silver shapes which then exploded in a mass of bright flames and drifted slowly down through the sky.[23]

The *Luftwaffe* soon developed high-altitude precision bombing in response to the balloon barrages, and also devices for the wings of the *Luftwaffe* fighter planes which pushed cables aside or caused them to slide into a recess where a cutter was activated by a small explosion. However, this weighed around 800lb and considerably reduced the performance of the plane.[24]

Yet it was not enemy fire which caused the most destruction to the barrage balloon: it was lightning, and to avoid these losses, meteorological teams were employed to advise on expected weather conditions, and lightning conductors were added to balloons;[25] also a copper wire encased within the balloon's cable which responded to the level of static electricity in the atmosphere and set off an alarm bell on the ground when a critical level was reached.

Passively defensive and softly rounded, the controlled, 'tame' barrage balloon was actually a wild and wayward beast just waiting to break itself free and take to the wind. The sharp, whipping steel cable end could easily injure or kill people on the ground, or dislodge chimney pots and tiles from rooftops. Within a day, thirty-nine of the forty balloons which had been newly launched to protect the British fleet at Scapa Flow in the Orkneys had snapped their cables in the strong gales[26] and in 1940, a group of 'rogue' balloons even made a North Sea crossing to

Denmark where they damaged power lines and church spires with their whipping steel cables: however, once captured, their fabric was turned into overalls for Danish workmen.[27]

… 27th June 1940 I could see 50 plus balloons from our bedroom window. [Redhill] 'Janet' our balloon ran wild during the early hours of the morning – broke branches from trees, swept chimney pots and chimneys from roofs of houses – five houses damaged on August Rd. and nearly all the houses down Wynfield Rd. suffered damage. Then the cable swept across and removed chimneys from houses opposite the cemetery and then had its final fling at the Ivan Hotel and some shops near it and across the road where the chemists at the corner sustained a deal of damage.

12th August 1940. A new balloon has arrived, and with it a crowded gallery of children watching it winched up for the first time. It is a smart new job. Janet was a shabby second-hand looking article. (Frank Taylor Lockwood)[28]

To counter this hazard, the DPL/DR, 'Double Parachute Ripping' device was installed, whereby, if the pull of a sudden strong gust of wind triggered the link below the balloon, it would simultaneously pull at the balloon and rip a patch off the balloon's envelope, revealing a

The 'young Amazons' of RAF Balloon Command. (By kind courtesy of *The News*, Portsmouth 2025)

Barrage balloon attached to a winch lorry. (By kind courtesy of Shaun Churchill)

Daily maintenance. (Courtesy of the Imperial War Museum, London HU 56007)

hole through which the hydrogen gas could escape, thus causing the balloon to deflate.[29] The small parachute which was simultaneously deployed at the top of the cable allowed the remaining long and heavy cable to fall gently and harmlessly to the ground. However, if faulty the DPL/DR device could itself fall down from the sky and in this event there followed a speedy and intensive search by the RAF to retrieve them before anyone was injured.

In the event of an inflated balloon falling to the ground, it was possible to deflate it by pulling a red cord which activated a length of cheesewire in a rip panel. Barrage balloons cost £500 to produce, plus cannisters of hydrogen gas for re-inflation at £50, so deflation was a last resort in life-threatening situations and only under orders from a senior officer. Whatever the circumstances, an official hearing had to be held to examine whether the action was justified and if so, those involved could be exonerated.[30]

During 'stand-by', balloons were kept low in a 'cradle' of short cables[31]; upon the order 'Alert Yellow' they were raised to 100ft in readiness; and upon the order 'Alert Red' followed by 'Fly 4,000' they were raised to full height to intercept fast-approaching enemy planes. 'Alert White' was the signal to lower quickly and clear the sky for chasing RAF fighters. When not active, they were 'bedded' or lowered down onto a ground-sheet which protected the fabric, then heavy bags filled with sand were attached and picket lines secured to large concrete blocks set in a diamond or star shape, or to screw pickets which had been twisted deep into the ground.[32]

In February 1941, when Britain stood alone against Hitler, and the men of Balloon Command were urgently needed for combat duty, a group of WAAFs volunteered to take their place, being referred to in the press as 'young Amazons' – i.e. unusually strong for *women* – *Picture Post* taking great care to point out that the brave men of Balloon Command had not been doing 'women's work', for women could only be allowed to take over this duty due to 'the simplification of balloon manipulation'; also, that it would still take sixteen women to perform the work of just ten men.[33] By 1943, women comprised some 73 per cent of Balloon Command[34] and Sqdn Ldr Diana Mary Barton, the first woman commander of a balloon unit in Grosvenor Square, London, went on to be awarded the 1939–45 OBE for her work in Balloon Command.

Despite the grave misgivings of the RAF, the women proved themselves completely capable of operating and maintaining both the 600lb[35] balloons and the Fordson 'Sussex' Winch Lorries. By 1942, WAAFs were competently running over 1,000 mixed or all-women Balloon Command sites[36] on remote sites or the open spaces of school playing fields, playgrounds and parks.

The routine of a balloon crew entailed night guard duty of two hours on and then three hours' rest, and all crew members were woken at 07.00 hours[37] for a day of continual operation, inspection, repair, maintenance, and topping up of the hydrogen. Despite the attachment of a windlass to aid the raising and lowering of balloons, it was still a demanding and exhausting job to keep the nose of a huge, tugging balloon headed into the wind or gale and it could take eighteen women hauling together to bring the balloon round to face a gale in a storm. Turning a 'bedded' balloon into the wind was particularly difficult in the dark therefore the winch itself had to be perfectly maintained. In addition, WAAF balloon crews had to be trained in manual handling in the event of the winch failing, with the risk of serious rope burns to their hands if the balloon was allowed to shoot back up into the air.[38]

Winching in a balloon demanded total concentration on the part of the winch driver if the cable was to be kept taut and the balloon remain under control, especially in gusting winds when a slack cable had to be winched in quickly, for if allowed to drift on a slack cable in the last 100ft, the enormous balloon could fall onto surrounding houses, squashing itself up against doors and windows, frightening people and blocking them in with its grey rubbery mass.

Rigorous daily maintenance of balloons was carried out by teams of WAAF in the repair sheds of Balloon Centres. Deflated, folded and carefully wrapped, balloons were taken in on trollies and once the envelope had been inflated with air, with the balloons resting on a perfectly clean floor to avoid further damage, the women, wearing dungarees, navy berets and soft-soled plimsolls, clambered inside and were sealed in to do their painstaking work – sometimes having to plead with teasing airmen to let them out.[39]

Repairing a tear in a barrage balloon. (Courtesy of the Imperial War Museum, London CH 181)

The exact position of each area to be repaired, inside and out, was entered on a blue-print, then the paint and glue around the holes was removed. Tiny holes, rips up to 3in and those caused by birds' pecking were repaired by small glued-on circular patches; longer tears were sewn together using herring-bone stitch and long threads were used so as to avoid knots. Larger rents were repaired by sewing machine. Three coats of silver aluminium paint were then applied to ensure that the envelope was again water- and gas-proof, and as the fumes were highly toxic, it was essential to work for just half an hour, spend twenty minutes in the fresh air, and drink the daily ration of one pint of milk as an antidote.[40] To ensure that balloons were repaired and back up in the sky again as quickly as possible, WAAF repair teams worked twelve-hour shifts (after a morning session of Physical Training followed by Parade).

In 1944, barrage balloons accompanied the D-Day invasion, to hover over the Normandy beaches and then, in the quiet left by the troops' departure from Britain, they were suddenly needed as defence against a new German 'secret weapon' – the massively destructive, pilotless V-1 flying-bomb. Squadrons of Balloon Command from all over the country made their way between 11–17 June to RAF Biggin Hill, the rapidly established operational Balloon Centre, in order to launch a 'great glistening formidable wall of some 1,750 balloons'[41] over the North Downs from Cobham in Kent to Limpsfield in Surrey. It was accompanied by 1,000 anti-aircraft guns and searchlights, with banks of fighter-planes to both north and south,[42] yet it quickly became apparent that the barrage must be thickened. GPO engineers (General Post Office) hurriedly attached additional cables to the existing balloons and more squadrons were called in to eventually cover an area of some 260 square miles. Balloon Command airmen took control of the balloons and the WAAF Balloon Operators were given the task of keeping up a supply of hydrogen cylinders and food.[43]

Elsewhere, stripped of their familiar barrage balloons, skies seemed unnervingly empty; but when congregated en masse across the North Downs the nation's balloons produced a magnificent sight:

> ... the result dazzled all of us who saw it. To come up from the south country by train, through the long tunnel in the Downs, and emerge into the clear blue sky of early summer day and see overhead hundreds and hundreds of sailing white balloons, serene and glistening above the light ground mist of the hills, was the only pleasant experience the doodlebug ever gave. (H.E. Bates)[44]

However, no one could predict what would happen should a V-1 catch upon a balloon cable. In fact, the 'doodlebugs' exploded upon impact at around 2,000ft, or appeared: '…rather like a fish taking the bait from a gigantic hook below a gigantic float. The fish wriggled forward in a series of sideward darts, wagging its tail for a distance of about 400 yards and then gave up…' (H.E. Bates).[45] This was the barrage balloon's finest hour! However, every V-1 destroyed meant the rapid replacement of a balloon and one Balloon Command Squadron alone 'caught' thirty-seven of the terrifyingly destructive bombs.

The barrage balloon continued to serve in the defence of British operations overseas; but by September 1944, German technology had rendered it obsolete in Britain – for the next weapon to be launched was the V-2 rocket-propelled bomb travelling faster than the speed of sound, against which there was no defence except the destruction of its launching sites.

All balloons were withdrawn in the autumn of 1944, and Balloon Command ceased from February 1945.[46]

No longer could stitched fabric comfort and defend. The war had moved into the space-age.

nine

Factory Work

'We shall not hesitate to take every step, even the most drastic, to call forth from our people
the last ounce and the last inch of effort of which they are capable.'
Rt Hon. Winston Churchill, 19 May 1940

'A first class workman's ticket to Hayford,
please.'(Reproduced with permission of
Punch Ltd, www.punch.co.uk)

The summer of 1940, the months of the 'Phoney
War' were hot and sunny, and the British relaxed at
the seaside if they had the chance.[1] Older children
who had arrived on the *Kindertransport* trains from
countries under German rule were shocked to find
that little preparation was in hand for war: Britain
had no idea of the strength of Nazi Germany, its
horrifying brutality and fearful weaponry. Factories
were producing munitions, aircraft, military vehicles
and equipment, but at a steady rate, and keeping to
peacetime hours.

Very soon, the British beaches would be covered
with anti-tank defences, and factories working to
full production around the clock.[2] By the spring
of 1944, munition production was six times that
of 1940. By 1943, the number of aircraft leaving
Britain's factories each month had trebled from
730 to some 2,190[3] with many male factory workers putting in thirty-six-hour shifts when needed
and women working thirteen-and-a-half-hour days,
seven days a week in the two months following the
evacuation of Dunkirk.[4]

Britain' factories also supplied her allies including
the United States, the USSR, China, France, Poland,
Greece, Czechoslovakia, Portugal and Turkey with war equipment ranging from boxes of
matches, nails, boots, soap and camouflage netting to railway track, machine-tools, ammunition,
tanks, motorcycles, aeroplane engines, aircraft, mine-sweeping trawlers and 'enough greatcoat
cloth to stretch from the White Sea to the Black Sea'; much of this free of charge.[5]

Such was the need for anti-aircraft, field, medium and heavy artillery equipment, telephones
and cables, machine- and sub-machine guns, small arms' ammunition, 20mm guns, rifles
and wireless equipment that any available rooms, including church halls and the kitchens or
living rooms of private houses, were soon being used by 900,000 part-time women workers.[6] Additional workers were brought from the West Indies and India,[7] 40,000 from neutral

Northern Ireland and around 175,000 women were released to join the war effort by the closure of factories manufacturing what had become 'luxury' goods.[8]

When men were conscripted into the services, it was women who had to take over their jobs, although there was reluctance among factory managers to take on women, being of the opinion that any women workers would just prove to be 'a damned nuisance'.[9] But all this had to change, for the Government insisted, and by the end of 1945, women without home ties, who were classed as 'Mobile', were some of the 22.5 million Britons who left home to take work in another part of the country[10] and when younger women workers had to be transferred to the production of munitions or into the services, 'Immobile' mothers with children under fourteen years old or who had elderly dependants had to take their place within their own locality.[11]

Government propaganda would have women believe that they could be as much use to the war effort in an overall as in a uniform[12] but there was a deep sense among factory workers of being just one of the invisible millions who could not play a more important role. A 'typical' factory worker, Ruby Loftus, was chosen to be an example of a woman who had patriotically risen to the challenge of long hours of factory work whilst keeping up commitments to family and home.

A woman's entry into the masculine world of explosives and toxic chemicals, noisy, draughty, dirty factories and work such as ship-building and heavy engineering was a dramatic change from housework or domestic service, especially if living away from home with strangers in an unfamiliar part of the country and attired in the masculine clothing of industry instead of her usual clean, tidy, feminine clothes. However, the Minister of Labour, Ernest Bevin, made sure that factory facilities were improved[13] and that women were made aware of the clothing they must wear in order to avoid accidents. In support, magazines gave advice and dress-making patterns for clothing with no decorations, front pockets or belt fastenings which might catch in machinery.[14] Anything metal such as money or hairclips had to be left in the 'Contraband Place'.[15]

Despite the Government's best efforts, there was still the demoralising effect of not wearing the uniforms of the services, which were worn with pride, even designed by a couturier. Some factories supplied a uniform – the weekly laundering of which had to be paid for by the workers[16] and there was an 'iron ration' allowance of extra coupons to be shared out amongst workers whose clothing might be burnt by sparks or acid,[17] or the 'industrial ten' for manual jobs involving heavy work, which included the Women's Land Army. In November 1941, boiler suits and bib-and-brace overalls were rated at a low points value or could be bought coupon-free upon presentation of a Factory Inspector's Certificate.[18]

These stitched work-garments would be just part of a dramatic change in self-identity for millions of 1940s women who were used to clear differences between male and female clothing. The enormous numbers who had to leave domestic service, maybe having worn neat, tidy, spotlessly clean uniforms, often had to adapt to jobs in which boiler suits were essential as protection against dirt, acid, sparks and grease. Many women had never worn a pair of trousers, 'slacks' or dungarees, as they were called, and had to overcome the strongly held prejudice that trousers were only for men or women of questionable morality.[19] Yet draughty, dirty factories demanded warm, protective clothing. There was one advantage, however, for women who wore trousers did not need to wear stockings, which were virtually unobtainable.[20] By 1944, the sales of trousers to women was five times higher than in 1943.[21]

Long factory shifts made it difficult to queue for food and children had to be left in the care of others, perhaps a neighbour. There were other reasons for women to avoid factory work: factories were obvious targets for enemy bombers and each had its own Home Guard unit and, to maintain the Blackout, doors and windows had to be tightly sealed, which, of course, produced airless, stuffy uncomfortable working conditions in which accidents were more likely to occur.[22] Working in a munitions' factory was particularly dangerous. Producing explosives and filling cartridges, bombs, bullets or sacks with cordite could result in fingers and hands being

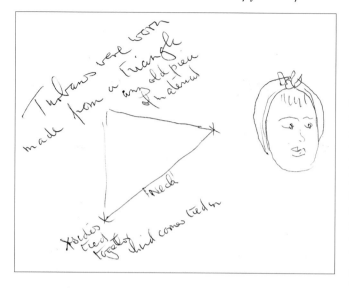

Turbans were worn
made from a triangle
any old piece
of material

Neck

Folded
tied together

Shoulders
tied to waist

How to make a turban. (By kind courtesy of Pat Salmon)

blown off – or worse, and exposure of the skin to the toxic powders required the application of a thick barrier cream, which actually caused problems in itself.[23] TNT turned hair red and skin yellow, and women suffered from nose-bleeds and eye infections.[24] Even though they had to change into protective suits, chemicals polluted under-clothing, making the washing water turn red.[25] Women stitching para-chutes often suffered from 'acute eyestrain' after gazing continually at the white, light-reflecting silk.[26] The smells of the day's work could follow a woman home in her clothing, particularly the stench of a liquid named 'suds' which was used to stop drills overheating.[27] However, as everyone was 'in the same boat', friendships blossomed as did a sense of sharing – workers perhaps contributing clothes to each other on special occasions.[28]

To make the noisy, gloomy, grimy factories a little more cheerful, loud-speakers played Home Service radio programmes of music to sing along to[29] and women took the opportunity whenever they could of bringing in a little colour and individuality, maybe in their wrap-around overall, the housewife's standby,[30] with its brightly coloured, easily washed, floral-printed cotton, and as there was always a high risk of fashionably long hair becoming entangled in factory machinery, women workers adopted the snood, or turban, which could be brightly coloured and tied in a variety of ways. However, covering the hair only served to increase a factory worker's sense of inferiority compared to members of the services who were able to freely show their hair, for shining, glossy, well-groomed hair was a woman's pride in the 1940s and an expression of her feminity. But snoods (crocheted or stitched net, pinned on at the front to enclose the hair), head-scarves and turbans could be easily and inexpensively made by hemming around a piece of fabric, and the turban had featured in recent Paris collections, which was a boost to the morale, and these *did* bring a sense of individuality and gaiety.

A wide choice of patriotic scarves could be bought in the shops, and even though they were not included in the Utility Scheme, the price was subsidised by the Government.[31] Turbans covered neglected hair, 'hid a multitude of pins' kept hair clean longer, and throughout the war there were notable society champions of the turban and the headscarf such as Clementine Churchill and the royal Princesses.

By the end of the war, thousands of women had demonstrated the adaptability and physical strength needed for a dramatically changed daily life, which even challenged their sense of womanly feminity. Dressed in protective clothing, their appearance had none of the glamour of their service counterparts. Often expected to do heavy physical work, put in very long hours and master skills in months – or even hours – which had taken peacetime apprentices years to achieve, they were true heroines of the period and many suffered nervous breakdowns due to the pressure, especially the factories' constant din. Wearing 'depressingly utilitarian' clothing,[32] often balancing work with running a home, they were the reliable and stalwart makers of the supply of weapons and munitions without which the war could not have ended in victory.

ten

In and Out the Classroom

Everywhere, children sang:
Whistle while you work
Hitler is a twerp
Goering's barmy
So's his army
Whistle while you work.[1]

'One caught it even at that early age, that one had to be enormously brave.'[2]

The Second World War was a total war, and it included children, many of whom rather enjoyed the excitement, but for thousands it was a time of exploitation, abuse, starvation, loss and even death.

Fearing the devastation of enemy bombing, the British Government planned 'Operation Pied Piper' – the evacuation of 4 million children, pregnant women, mothers with babies, blind and disabled people from designated 'Danger Zones' into safer 'Reception Areas' where house-holders with room to spare recieved an allowance for their upkeep. Fifty purpose-built school camps were also built for refugees and hard-to-place evacuees. Evacuation began at around 4 a.m. on Friday 1 September 1939.[3]

'Rule Britannia', Perth School of Dance. (By kind courtesy of Christine Goldie)

Evacuated boys and teachers of Kings School, Canterbury at Scotney Castle in Kent. (Courtesy of Kent Messenger Group. PD800514)

Rehearsal for evacuation by Barnsole School, Gillingham, Kent. (Courtesy of Kent Messenger Group PD800562)

An evacuee waits to be taken to the home of
strangers. (By kind courtesy of St Ives Trust
Archive Study Centre)

1940s city child. (Courtesy of the Imperial War
Museum, London HU36143)

Sometimes, children were allowed to take a toy with them. However, the parents of the
very poorest inner-city children, in their damp, cockroach-infested houses, had hardly enough
money for food and clothing and none to spare for toys and children might be sent to the local
shoe shop to ask for empty boxes to play with.[4]

Despite intense pressure from the Government, many mothers decided to keep their children at home and when less than half the expected number of children arrived at the railway
stations, the whole well-planned four-day operation was upset. Children who were expected in
each Reception Area were put on the wrong trains and when they arrived there were often too
many, too few, too late, and of the wrong age or sex – which was not a good start to this massive
mixing of the rigid 1940s' social classes, town and country. For their part, neither the evacuees
nor their parents knew where they were going or when they would return. Attached to each
child's clothing was an identification label and they carried items from the Ministry of Health
list which their mothers had been given – including a bag of food to last two days, which was
usually eaten on the train – plus a small suitcase, haversack, pillow-case or brown paper parcel
containing indoor shoes, stockings or socks, a spare set of underclothing, pyjamas or nightdress,
comb, toothbrush and toothpaste, soap, face-cloth, towel, and a warm coat or water-proof.[5]

Private schools and wealthy families arranged their own evacuation to places of relative
safety within Britain or overseas, thus causing great resentment in the poorer classes which was
addressed by the Children's Overseas Reception Board's organisation of transport overseas for
the children of less wealthy families in which each child was given sixty-six coupons for the
purchase of necessary clothing or clothing could also be obtained from the WVRS.[6] However,
when the SS *City of Benares* was sunk in September 1940[7] with the loss of seventy-seven of
these children's lives,[8] the scheme was discontinued.

The arrival of tired, hungry, disorientated evacuees from the cities often provoked anger: people in country districts felt as if they 'were being swamped by a "barbarian invasion"'[9] and one of the first problems concerned clothing. Most of the children were well cared for but many were ragged, their skin riddled with scabies, hair and clothes teeming with nits, lice and fleas. To add to their unhappiness, upon arrival many were stripped naked and plunged into baths, maybe for the first time in their lives, and their familiar clothes were burnt. Children also arrived in thin summer clothing, or stitched into brown paper to keep them warm until the spring: '… you could tell those ones a mile off!'[10]

Evacuation had exposed an unsuspected level of squalor. Immediately, a national campaign appealed for children's clothing and shoes, and a radio broadcast by the Ministry of Health resulted in donations of clothes and money from within Britain, parcels from Canada and America, and even a generous lakh of rupees from the Maharajah of Gondal;[11] the National Union of Teachers and voluntary organisations were to keep up the work of clothing the poorest evacuees for the rest of the war. Eventually, the Government made financial contributions, but the scheme was shrouded in secrecy so as not to be misused by parents who could afford to supply the clothes themselves.

Warm clothes were essential to every 1940s child in the country: 'They always had to walk to and from school, even if it was four miles away, even in blizzards. The boys wore shorts and the girls very short skirts and their legs bled from cold in winter.'[12] There were to be some of the most bitter winters that Britain had ever known, and to make matters worse, the Government demanded that boys should continue to wear short trousers until the age of eleven or twelve in order to conserve the nation's resources of raw materials.[13]

It could be a lonely, miserable life of physical assault, isolation, even starvation and sexual abuse for evacuees who were not accepted by the school children and families of their new and unfamiliar country neighbourhoods. Clothing which was sent by parents or charitable organisations might be spirited away by their 'foster' mothers to be given to their own children. Some children who had been sent into homes where they were ill-treated managed to let their parents know and were immediately taken home. However, others received a warm and understanding welcome and their new 'families' were generous in their support, which could later become a problem when the children had to return to their poorer city homes.

When the feared bombing did not materialise, an estimated 90,000 children returned home for Christmas 1939.[14] However, when the bombing *did* start in 1940, evacuation resumed, and in 1944, when the Nazi V-1 and V-2 rocket bombs arrived, almost 1.5 million children were again moved to safer areas.[15] For these, and various other reasons, evacuated children might be moved from one foster home to another, remain with one family, or be evacuated for a short time only.

With all this upheaval, their schools requisitioned for Civil Defence needs and male teachers serving in the forces, it was a patchy education for many Second World War children – which some thoroughly enjoyed, playing on bomb sites or working on farms for part of their school days. Black cloth diamonds were stitched onto the coat sleeves of those who had lost a member of their family.[16] Fortunate evacuees were enabled to enter further education through the generosity of their 'foster' parents, when their own families could not afford to provide the uniform and this would change their lives. But even if one had the money, school uniforms were difficult to obtain, especially if the school was keeping rigidly to pre-war standards. Most schools understood the problems that parents were encountering and overlooked infringements[17] but many parents had to use the whole family's entire coupon allowance on school uniforms[18] – or resort to the black market.

'… I can remember being told off by the headmaster when I had to wear a blouse with a Peter Pan collar to school because the one in the photo was in the wash.' (The blouse was made from a nylon parachute.) (By kind courtesy of Valerie Watson)

'Dress on left was blue floral, with three bands of bias binding at the neck. We went to Southgate County Grammar School and could wear any *blue* summer dress.' (By kind courtesy of Frances Wilson)

Under all circumstances, girls were taught to sew! (Courtesy of the Imperial War Museum, London D 989) (See colour illustrations 4, 7 and 8.)

When I went to County School … school uniform was strictly enforced. We had to buy from the school the material to make our blouses – tussore silk in wartime! It was impossible to buy them ready made and I had to make my own. (Delcia Miles)

Despite the difficult conditions of evacuation and shortages of school supplies, teachers still made sure that girls learnt to sew, even if it was with paper instead of fabric.

When I was about twelve years old and in my first year at senior school we were told that we were to make a pair of knickers because all types of seams and stitching were used. Well, we all got ready to start, wondering who was to wear these articles when completed. Pink and white squared graph paper was distributed to the class. We thought that we were to design them – OH NO. This was our material! And they were in miniature, might have fitted a toddler. We had to make run and fell seams, hems to take elastic at the waist and legs etc. All stitching had to be tiny and of course done by hand, no machines for us. Remarkably, they turned out fine and mine passed in a sewing exam with an A! … We had a very strict needlework mistress who taught us to make button-holes both bound and sewn, to sew tapes on. Pretty well anything in the correct way, all on paper. (Margaret Woods)

I am … certain that I did the small needlecase, which is cross stitch in stranded cotton on flannel with blanket stitch edge at junior school… The larger needlecase was done in my first year at grammar school … Also worked on flannel with decorative stitching, and edgings. It contained two extra 'pages' which were meant to demonstrate two different types of hems. Also in that year I made an apron and learned how to darn …' (Jean Brown)(See colour illustrations 7 and 8.)

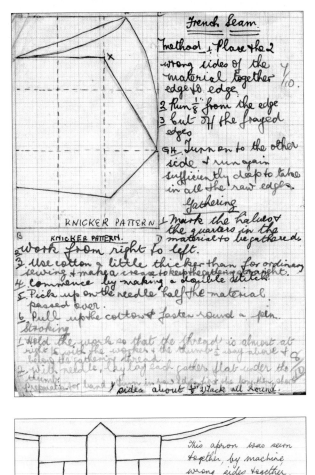

Page from a typical 1940s school exercise book. (By kind courtesy of Frances Wilson)

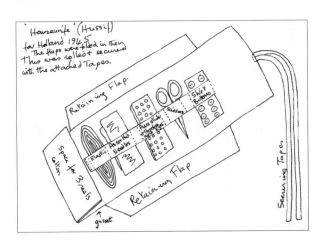

'At school we made pinafores in "Domestic Science" lessons out of 3in strips of material.' (By kind courtesy of Frances Wilson)

In 1945, girls were asked to make 'Hussifs' or 'Housewives' to send to the newly liberated Holland where, after Nazi occupation, sewing materials were almost non-existent. 'It was a good exercise for us in our Domestic Science needlework class and made a change from learning about four kinds of patches. ... We had some lovely thank you letters.' (By kind courtesy of Sheila Brooks)

[At primary school] We had to design and make our own 'Pockette' [7 ½ x 4 ½ ins] from a piece of 'tapestry' canvas and a cotton lining and we could choose our own colours of raffia. I chose black and purple and a design made out of black squares, and purple diamonds, outlined in bright yellow. The flap and the lower part of the bag [had] cross stitch borders in alternating yellow and black crosses.' (Hazel Sims)

… School Certificate needlework demanded a renovated garment. Another neighbour came to the rescue with a large pair of navy trousers she had worn in the ambulance service … I constructed a pair of slightly flared shorts which were a great success.' (Valerie Green)

Our needlework classes at senior school started in the first year by covering our Hymn books in navy serge. This we decorated with rows of chain stitch plan, broad, twisted, whipped and threaded and if we were deft with a needle, magic chain. We then went on to drafting our own patterns for wrap around cookery aprons, and gym dresses, which were a tabard type affair in parachute silk which must have looked charming over our navy knickers – we hated them! (Susan Reynolds)

In year 1 we made 'wrappers' for our needlework – a 2ft square of fabric, hemmed with the edges embroidered and our names chain-stitched across one corner. We also made our cookery aprons – stiff white cotton fabric in a bib style with our initials chain-stitched on the bib. In year 2 we made an afternoon apron decorated with patterned braid and in year 3 we made a blouse. I remember struggling with mine and having to take it home to finish.' (Sheila Westall)

Needlework was included in domestic science and our first lessons were spent working on making an overall which we should eventually wear when we started cookery lessons. The garment used a great deal of material and I think we started them before clothing coupons were introduced. There was a full gathered skirt and a sleeveless bodice.' (Heather Fogg)

Girls stitched smocked babies' dresses and summer dressing gowns for themselves (Zoe Rains); cotton knickers with 'thick French seams and a double gusset!' (Angela Davies); dressmaking included collars, cuffs, and buttonholes (Anne Blakeney) and they were also asked to stitch items which would be of value to the community:

On a Sunday afternoon we would go into school to do our bit for the war effort. As well as rolling bandages and filling pads with moss we made pyjamas. Stripy winceyette – French seams and with sewing machines. Another group made bedroom slippers. A simple pattern with a tongue – they were made from samples from a tailor's pattern book. Using three layers of tweed they were bound and attached to soles. Really tough work! All for hospital use.' (Zoe Rains)

Then, upon entering higher education, girls were taught more about stitch, including various sewing processes and upholstery. They made: hand-sewn 'undies and blouses', using 'No.10 betweens to sew fine lawn material for our specimens at college' (Doreen Newson); a 'bra out of a nylon parachute' (Sybil Cross); '… a child's dress with smocking front yoke, gathering at the back and buttons and buttonholes. One sleeve was set in and the other puffed – one into a band and the other gathered' (Joan Trethewy); and 'Lots of make-do and mend.' (Zoe Rains)

As usual girls were also taught to sew at home from an early age by aunts, grandmothers, godmother, uncles and mothers:

These boys, whose clothing has been lost in an air raid, are wearing new clothes purchased by the Lady Mayoress of Portsmouth, Lady Margaret Daley, from money given to Her Majesty Queen Elizabeth by four Scottish girls. Lady Daley set up clothing depots in Portsmouth and organised the distribution of more than 180,000 garments to 34,321 people. (By kind courtesy of *The News*, Portsmouth)

I learnt to darn aged 4! (Diana Trotter)

I learnt to embroider before I learnt to write, from mother. At 4 years old, I gave an embroidered needlebook to my Grandmother. (Jean Panter)

My Aunt taught me to embroider…. Sitting embroidering whilst looking after me on a wet afternoon and I wanted to 'have a go'. Becoming irritated, she picked up a little cotton bag full of a tangle of coloured threads. 'Here,' she said, 'Sort this lot out.' I did. I was hooked. … I started to embroider aged 4 ½. … I made a needlecase from velvet and flannel, one for my Mum (monogrammed), one for me (monogrammed) when I was about 5 years old. (Hazel Sims)

My uncle did embroidery at sea during quiet periods and he really encouraged me to sew. He provided me with tray cloths with crinoline ladies ad nauseum. He supplied me with all the materials … (Delcia Miles)

At home, girls stitched: 'handkerchiefs, table runners, tray-cloths, cushion covers, chair backs and tablecloths for anyone who wanted it done' (Stroma Hammond); or, aged six, blanket stitched around pieces of towels that had 'gone'. 'I must have been about 8 when I made a handkerchief with shell-stitch hemming. … At least the radio kept me entertained while I

The Tale of a Shirt!

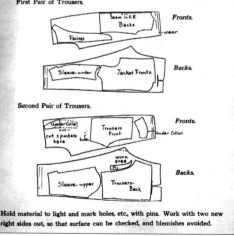

Dark blue stripes on light blue. Dark blue Rick-Rack Braid (narrow). Buttons to match Braid.

White broadcloth. Narrow Rick-Rack Braid — one row blue, one maroon.

Navy and bright blue stripes on light blue. Two rows crimson Rick-Rack Braid, point to point, forming diamonds.

McCall Pattern 5433

Size 4

Back View

The pattern was shortened a little by a tuck. Braid put on sleeves to cover joining.

This shirt is now embarking on its third life, having been worn out twice already. One side had been raised to remove worn spot at neck.

More Shirt Tales

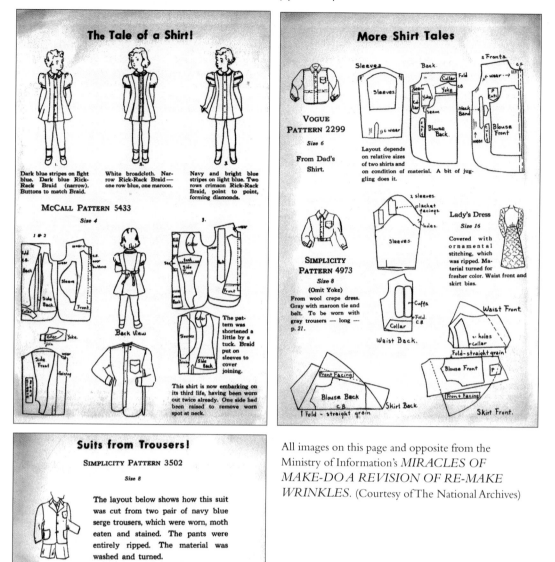

Vogue Pattern 2299

Size 6

From Dad's Shirt.

Layout depends on relative sizes of two shirts and on condition of material. A bit of juggling does it.

Simplicity Pattern 4973

Size 8

(Omit Yoke)

From wool crepe dress. Gray with maroon tie and belt. To be worn with gray trousers — long — p. 21.

Lady's Dress

Size 16

Covered with ornamental stitching, which was ripped. Material turned for fresher color. Waist front and skirt bias.

Suits from Trousers!

Simplicity Pattern 3502

Size 8

The layout below shows how this suit was cut from two pair of navy blue serge trousers, which were worn, moth eaten and stained. The pants were entirely ripped. The material was washed and turned.

First Pair of Trousers.

Second Pair of Trousers.

Hold material to light and mark holes, etc, with pins. Work with two new right sides out, so that surface can be checked, and blemishes avoided.

All images on this page and opposite from the Ministry of Information's *MIRACLES OF MAKE-DO A REVISION OF RE-MAKE WRINKLES*. (Courtesy of The National Archives)

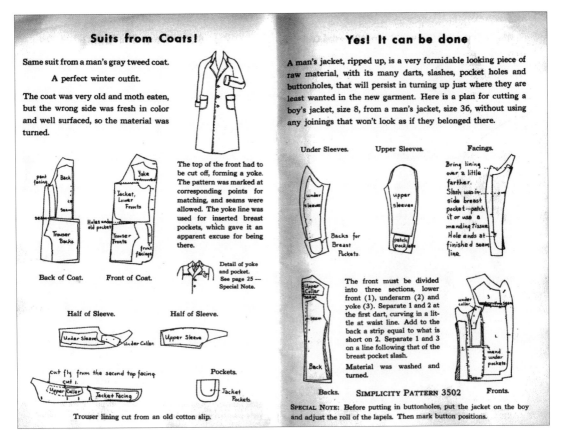

Suits from Coats!

Same suit from a man's gray tweed coat.

A perfect winter outfit.

The coat was very old and moth eaten, but the wrong side was fresh in color and well surfaced, so the material was turned.

The top of the front had to be cut off, forming a yoke. The pattern was marked at corresponding points for matching and seams were allowed. The yoke line was used for inserted breast pockets, which gave it an apparent excuse for being there.

Detail of yoke and pocket. See page 25 — Special Note.

Back of Coat.   Front of Coat.

Half of Sleeve.   Half of Sleeve.

cut fly from the second top facing   Pockets.

Trouser lining cut from an old cotton slip.

Yes! It can be done

A man's jacket, ripped up, is a very formidable looking piece of raw material, with its many darts, slashes, pocket holes and buttonholes, that will persist in turning up just where they are least wanted in the new garment. Here is a plan for cutting a boy's jacket, size 8, from a man's jacket, size 36, without using any joinings that won't look as if they belonged there.

Under Sleeves.   Upper Sleeves.   Facings.

The front must be divided into three sections, lower front (1), underarm (2) and yoke (3). Separate 1 and 2 at the first dart, curving in a little at waist line. Add to the back a strip equal to what is short on 2. Separate 1 and 3 on a line following that of the breast pocket slash.

Material was washed and turned.

Backs.   SIMPLICITY PATTERN 3502   Fronts.

SPECIAL NOTE: Before putting in buttonholes, put the jacket on the boy and adjust the roll of the lapels. Then mark button positions.

learned to darn my dad's socks. I don't think I ever "enjoyed" darning – but a nicely woven darn was very satisfying when it was finished.' (Anita Seamons)

I was coming up to school age when war broke out. I was sent to live with my grandmother in Pembrokeshire. She was of the firm belief that the devil made work for idle hands. The first thing she taught me was to hem dusters from pieces on their last legs and hankies from any small squares. (Audrey Hussey)

How to provide children's clothing, including garments for evacuees, was one of the main anxieties of the war. The WI set up groups to mend evacuees' clothing[19] and a series in *Home Chat* showed how 'Jane' used Bestway patterns and '…'dodges' of stitchery to make clothes for 'the kiddies staying with her'. *Make Do and Mend* leaflets instructed: 'Make very large hems and turnings in children's clothes to allow for growing. Also make tucks across the shoulders and at the top of the bodice so that the shoulders can be widened, or the frock or coat let down later.'[20] As the war progressed, children became quite used to wearing passed-down or shared clothing and in large families there was a saying that whoever was up first in the morning was the best dressed – they could take their pick from the limited choice of clothing.

When I joined the Royal Navy I was given the first real clothes I ever remember as being mine alone.[21] (Charlie Workman)

'I particularly remember a lavender-coloured coat with attached hood that she made for me from a neighbour's cast-off coat. The front of the hood was trimmed with rabbit fur (the rabbit had been the family dinner). Similar rabbit furs made gloves for my aunts and a lined hood for my cousin. This coat with attached hood was similar to the lavender one, but without the rabbit fur trim.' (By kind courtesy of Sheila Westall)

Everyone who could stitch rallied round to keep wartime children clothed:

Make do and mend was my star turn. I got great tufts of below-standard sheeting and made them into little jackets for all the children I knew. Every blessed scrap of anything was sewn on to them, and padded with all sorts of nonsense. (Derbyshire woman)[22]

My father would do any alterations to my brothers' clothes and I remember he made my summer dresses when I was small. (Evelyn Taylor)

I well remember my grandmother making knickers for my sister and I from any clothes that could be cut up – and they had lace round the legs. (Valerie Crooks) (Girls' knickers had elastic round the legs, with a pocket for handkerchiefs.) (Jean Brown)

Even men who were away in the services contributed to their children's clothing – often unknowingly! Their shirts, especially, came in very useful:

… stripey men's shirts made nice little summer dresses (I think my mother was lucky to have a girl!) (Anita Seamons)

When it came to clothes she could make something new out of any old blouse or shirt. (Pat Crocker)

A gentleman's gaberdine mac made two macs for my friend and I and we even had a beret to match. My father's ancient Harris tweed jacket made a lovely coat for me with leggings if I remember rightly. (Gill Garratt)

Men's trousers came in *very* useful:

The first garment I remember my mother making for me in the war was a lovely edge to edge cream coat and pleated skirt. This was made from my father's cricket trousers! They were rather baggy as was the fashion, so there was plenty of material. (Gill Garratt)

All the girls wore pleated skirts with stitched-on cotton tops (like a vest top). These were easy to make from the best pieces of women's skirts or men's trouser legs and the cotton tops were from old pillowcases. (Sheila Westall)

I used the legs and any other reasonable pieces of his Dad's trousers to make him day wear trousers. (Wyn Trevitt)

Mothers also contributed their own clothes and had to be ingenious with whatever fabrics came their way. *Pearson's Complete Needlecraft* advised: 'The mother of a growing family or the aunt with small nieces and nephews can always find a use for her out-of-date, shabby clothes. Some may be too adult in colour or texture or not washable easily enough for children, but most will convert delightfully into miniatures of themselves for a little girl or boy.'[23]

'Sunday best.' (By kind courtesy of Anita Seamons)

My parents had friends in the 'rag trade' in London and who regularly passed on remnants of fabric left over from garment cutting in the factory. My mother's best challenge was to make me a dress when I was about 6 … from 29 pieces of the same fabric pieced together. (Jean Brown)

My mother's bottle green, black fur trimmed, coat became a coat with attached hood for myself, trimmed around the face and hem with the fur! (Rosetta Price)

… my friend had a lovely slip, as her mother had blanket-stitched round holes to make them look like flowers. (Frances Wilson)

My 'best' dress was a very old pink organdie bridesmaid's dress where the skirt was re-cut and gathered at the waist, and the top was a white parachute nylon blouse which had the organdie in a pie frill around the Peter Pan collar and short sleeve cuffs. My! Did I cause a stir when I went to church! (Valerie Watson)

My grandmother wore cotton 'chemises' and for some reason decided she would wear them no longer, so my mother unpicked them, dyed them blue and made me some pleated sorts which I thought were really good. (M.E. Harris)

His pyjamas at this time were made from his Dad's pyjama jackets. Dad did not feel the cold, in fact he never wore pyjama jackets again.' (Wyn Trevitt)

As an only child and reading a lot, I was often pretending to be a certain character in a book. Rupert Bear was a favourite. I begged for a red jumper and yellow and black skirt (we didn't wear trousers) from my mother. She managed to knit a red jumper from donations of wool and dyed a piece of blanket yellow, using onions, to make a skirt. She embroidered the black lines on it. What dedication!' (Gill Garratt)

Clothes and shoes were available from WVS stalls and their mobile clothing exchanges for which second-hand clothing had been generously sent from America and 'the Dominions',

Birthdays in the 1940s were usually celebrated with special dresses, and wartime mothers even rose to this challenge. 'This dress was yellow satin and the flowers on the chest were hand-embroidered in 'lazy-daisy' stitch in pink and blue with green leaves.' (By kind courtesy of Sheila Westall)

including Canadian 'Bundles for Britain'; or customers brought their own: '... many mothers take the trouble to add small new trimmings, such as binding or a collar, so that garments will look fresh and attractive. In some cases clothing is altered or remade by working parties attached to the exchange.[24] Each item was awarded points which could be spent on something 'new'. *Housewife* (1948) commented: 'The WVS clothing exchanges are doing a wonderful job, appreciated by all mothers who use them, but I believe they are doing something more which is of equal importance and value. In every family throughout these islands the hand-me-down is accepted cheerfully and as a matter of course by children. It is part of life as they have known it for the last eight to nine years. But when the hand-me-down comes from a clothing exchange it is new to the child who wears it. To the small girl of eight who has seen the blue jersey coming slowly but surely in her direction for *years* it must be suffocating happiness to have a bright red one which nobody at home has *ever* seen before.'[25]

I remember some sort of clothes exchange we used to go to in Newmarket, some of the clothes were rather grand. In particular there was a party dress of pale grey chiffon trimmed with red ribbon over which I refused point blank to wear a cardigan! – as my mother said 'Pride will have to keep you warm then!' – but I did love that dress. (Anita Seamons)

Schools sometimes sold second-hand clothing, as did greengrocers, and one mother received a pair of curtains in return for a toddler's coat through one of the many exhange advertisements in her local newspaper.[26]

There was also the option of 'renovation'. Magazines offered tips, the WVS ran classes,[27] and Mrs Sew-and-Sew advised 'A Too-small Frock. Take the bodice off the skirt, open it down the front, and convert it into a bolero to wear over the skirt with a blouse or jumper. A Too-short skirt. Add a band of colour at the hem, or a series of bands alternating with the material. Enlarging a Frock. ... insert a band of contrasting colour to form the lower bodice, and bands of the same colour to widen the shoulders.'[28]

I cannot recall ever having new clothes and those we had were altered to fit; as a growing girl my oatmeal coloured Princess style winter coat was first lengthened with a dark brown fake hem, and then later cut round the skirt and different fabric inserted. I was very proud of my clever Mum to make my coat fit! (Susan Reynolds)

'There were party dresses in organdie – there must have been a lot of it around then, or perhaps my mother had a store of it – trimmed with flower braid and rick-rack.' [Organdy was not rationed as it was used for straining paint.] (By kind courtesy of Anita Seamons)

Young girls also stitched clothes for themselves and their siblings:

> Apart from school uniforms we only had one 'best' outfit each, my sister and I, so I soon learned how to stitch my own clothes on the hand sewing machine. The first skirt I made was out of a pair of my father's trousers. He was a big man, so I was able to make what we called a six-gored skirt. Others followed. Then I found I could cut up aunt's dresses and make blouses. (Enid Mason)
>
> As growing girls we were always short of dresses. I think I remember having three to wear in the evening [after school] and so we were delighted when a parcel came from my cousin in Canada. I don't remember wearing any of the garments as they were not what we wore in this country, but I cut up quite a few of them. Of necessity they were usually gored because I had unpicked each piece, washed and ironed the pieces and then made them up. (Gwen Jones)

Factories were allowed brief periods before Christmas for toymaking, but materials were limited and the toys were shoddy and expensive.

> As a teenager I used to go and help a neighbour who made soft toys, she took clothing coupons to buy cloth for Teddy Bears and we all emptied our Bit Bags for suitable material for other animals and dolls. … The neighbour made the soft toys to sell … There was a constant request for toys and if she was making any profit no doubt it was given to the Red Cross or similar as she was the daughter of the chief industrialist in the town. (Doreen Newson)
>
> My grandmother … used scraps of fabrics for making Suffolk puffs which also turned into mats and 'clowns' which were hanging toys. (Jean Brown)
>
> An aunt worked in a factory making all sorts of utility and some luxury goods for the large London stores. This aunt made me a toy rabbit – it had a blue satin body and ears but the inside of the ears and the tummy was made from a lovely brocade covered in tiny butterflies, this was my favourite toy. (Irene Hearl)

By 1941, Selfridges found that they had 'no teddy bears at all – and everyone seems to want a teddy bear'.[28] So they had to be made at home:

As factories had to cease toy production, stitchers used whatever materials were available and made them by hand. This photograph shows a group of WRNS busily making toys from old clothing, to be given at a Christmas party for the children of sailors at the Liverpool Naval Base. (Courtesy of the Imperial War Museum, London A 13420)

I was 10 when [a teddy bear coat] was given to me and in 1945 it was made into a teddy bear … it had a lot of use but the material was still quite good. (Mary Thomas)

Our teddy bears were home made by an aunt and just had a fur fabric head. The palms of the hands were felt and the backs were fur fabric. The feet were felt and made to look like shoes. Clothes covered the rest of the body and you could undress it. The body was coarse cotton. (Wilma Raumati)

Again, everyone rallied round; one little girl received her first doll as a Christmas present from the Lancaster Police Department[30] and children in evacuee and refugee camp schools who had not received a present or message from their parents received their Christmas gifts from America, via the British War Relief Fund.[31]

… my mother begged scraps of material from her friends and made twelve rag dolls with lovely clothes sewn on to them and hair made from wool. I can't remember whether she sold them cheaply or was given things in return … The dolls were part hand and part sewing machine stitched. I was allowed to choose one for Christmas and chose a ginger plaited haired doll and called her Sally. (Gill Garratt)

Christmas and birthday presents were also stitched at home using whatever materials were available. (See colour illustration 9.)

I remember one Christmas when I woke up in the night and because of the blackout I couldn't see a thing. I crawled to the end of my bed to feel my presents and was most upset as I could only feel four round things in a box and I thought I had been given four pieces of blackout curtain. When morning came it turned out to be a gorgeous brown corduroy elephant with a howdah on its back. My Mother had made it out of my Father's old cycling shorts. It was a favourite of mine for many years. (Pat Crocker)

My mother joined a queue and bought a canvas doll's face, a strip of doll's hair and a papier mache doll's head. From this she made my Christmas presents. The canvas face and strip of hair had a bonnet sewn on the back to hide the doll's bald head! The useful material drawer came into its own, supplying sheeting for dolls' bodies, with other material for dolls' clothing. A worn leather glove supplied the ends of two fingers to be turned into leather shoes for the face and hair doll. Mother even stitched pink fingernails on the doll's hands. (Rosetta Price)

Peggy and Golly – I think they were one of each, Christmas and birthday. I am sure I took Peggy to bed with me. (Janet White) (See colour illustration 9.)

And children made toys for themselves: (See colour illustrations 10 and 11.)

My eldest sister … had a pattern for a toy Scottie Dog and she made several dogs out of scraps left over from the [blackout] curtains. (Clare Williams)

When I was 11 years old my toddler sister had outgrown a pale pink corded coat with hood. Toys were difficult to come by. I used the coat to make Jennifer a doll using a moulded face purchased from a shop. I stitched yellow strands of wool onto the head and made two plaits.' (Valerie Green)

I started sewing when I started school and I remember that I had a 'new' second-hand dollshouse when I was 7 or 8 to replace my first dollshouse I had had at the age of 3. For that second dollshouse I made the bedding for the dollshouse pram. [Sheets, pillow and quilted cover.] My grandmother had given me a small wooden box which would hold postage stamps, the same size as a stamp and this I turned into a dollshouse sewing box, for which I put threads on cards and made a needle case in woven thread over card. (Jean Brown) (See colour illustration 11.)

[My] sister and I learned to use a Singer sewing machine at an early age. We both loved sewing and I made a rag doll when I was seven years old. (Gloria Barker) (See colour illustration 10.)

'I did love all my dolls and spent hours dressing and undressing them. Of the two big dolls the only one I made clothes for was Bubbles – she was only quite small, and I was an impatient child! … her party dress – pale lilac organdie with a pink ribbon trim and bonnet.' (By kind courtesy of Anita Seamons)

Just like 1940s adults, boys and girls usually had quite separate interests and occupations. Boys re-enacted battles and kept a close eye on the unfolding events and military equipment of the war – including collecting shrapnel and live bombs – while most girls loved their dolls:

> I had a very special doll called Suzy. She was … a rag doll, very soft and made of velvet. … Her face has been re-embroidered as one of the soldiers stationed on the gun-emplacement pencilled over it. I was very upset but he made up for it and 'found' me a two wheel bike and painted it red and taught me to ride it …. My father risked life and limb to retrieve her from next-door as I forgot to grab her when the siren went. Shrapnel was everywhere but I cried so much, he retrieved Suzy for me. (Gill Garratt) (See colour illustration 12.)
>
> I was just nine and I carried my best baby doll when we travelled down to South Wales by train in May 1940. A week or two later, one of my kind aunts, aware that it was a very trau-matic time for me and wanting to cheer me up, sent a little doll and some pieces of material with which to make clothes for her. She had thoughtfully realised that my mother did not have her 'rag bag' with her. … It was always useful for doll's clothes and I loved looking through it. (Heather Fogg)
>
> Another time my grandmother gave me two little mascot dolls – china, jointed but with clothes of felt stuck to their bodies. … I used to have great fun devising clothes for them from scraps of material and anything else I could find – the girl became a 'flower
>
> fairy' once, using a deconstructed rose flower that must have adorned a twenties flapper dress at some time! (Anita Seamons)
>
> I was always sewing dolls' clothes … Although I had some really beautiful doll's clothes (knit-ted) by a lighthouse keeper who lodged with a lady I called Auntie Phyll. I had the smartest dolls' clothes and my big Teddy bear had a lovely sailor suit complete with collar. (Gill Garratt)

Two very special dolls which gave valuable war service were 'France' and 'Marianne'. Presented to the Princesses Elizabeth and Margaret Rose by the children of France on the occasion of the King and Queen's State Visit to Paris in 1938, they excited enormous public interest when exhibited in Britain at St James's Palace in December 1938 and January 1939. Around 1,600 visitors paid to see them on display each day, with their breathtaking wardrobes of French cou-ture clothes and accessories of the finest French craftsmanship. Sadly, there was little time for the Princesses to play with them, for after the outbreak of war, the dolls, with their magnificent trousseaux were sent to tour Canada to raise funds for war refugees. (See colour illustration 13.)

Designed by Jumeau, they could be dressed either as young girls or as sophisticated aris-tocratic young ladies and their wardrobes included 360 garments and accessories including sewing kits by Keller, fifty pairs of exquisitely stitched Hermés and Pierre Masson gloves, embroidered table linen by L. Rouff, doll-size embroidered handkerchiefs, jewellery by Cartier, furs, perfumes by Coty and Lanvin, a Citroen car, a flower shop and 'Marianne's' ermine cloak worth around 200 guineas. The couturiers who provided the clothing included Worth, Vionnet, Rochas, Paquin, Paray, Lanvin, Lelong, Patou and Piguet, employing their most experienced seamstresses to hand-stitch the outfits, for only the finest, most perfect stitching could be used on the 2ft 10in doll-size clothing.[32]

Just like the 1940s' adults, the children of the Second World War also had uniforms and could play their part in the nation's war effort. Both boys and girls wore the uniforms of their cadet or training corps whilst in training for one of the forces or working with the JWO, and they proudly took part in local morale-boosting parades with the Red cross, WVS and Home Guard.[33]

Guides and Scouts helped the Civil Defence and Guides were awarded Crosses for 'acts of bravery or fortitude'.[34] Scouts over the age of fourteen received a National Service Badge and were trained in some 180 jobs, such as how to 'deal with an emergency and control panic' or act as messengers for the ARP, courageously cycling through the streets under enemy bombing attack.[35]

On Fridays you wore uniform, Brownies and Guides, and you saluted the flag as you walked round the field. Guides and Brownies played ever such a big part in the war, you know. You got a war service badge. I've still got mine. What I did was mix up cocoa for the air-raid warden and fill sandbags. You had to notch up so many hours to get this badge to sew on your uniform. (Cynthia Gillett) [36]

Wartime shortages had most impact, perhaps, on the fourteen year olds who were leaving school to start work, or students entering college and university; for suddenly, they needed adult-design clothing in the styles of their fathers and mothers. [37] Leaving home, girls might have just one skirt, blouse and jumper, two dresses and a coat; and for balls, would have to be ingenious, maybe making a gown out of sheets or curtains, or a long petticoat under an old black chiffon nightdress. [39]

It was very difficult during clothes rationing for teenagers when they left school and started work. Not having any adult clothes, just school uniform they couldn't 'make do and mend'. Utility clothing … was used but young people did not think them very glamorous … (June Simper)

I recall (being a teenager at the time) sending away for a panel or two of white parachute nylon and making a blouse and petticoat.' (Mary Cole)

…as a 'teenager' kitted out for college in 1942 … Two outfits were real 'Make Do'. One, a woollen dress in a bronzey brown and deep grassy green was made from two of my mother's … skirts. The other one for summer, was a skirt of pretty patterned curtain fabric – a flowered skirt with a pale blue linen blouse made from the curtains at the landing windows.' (Denise Cochrane)

At college I was lucky to have an uncle who worked in a woollen mill in Yorkshire. He sent me a length of grey worsted which my mother, an accomplished seamstress, made into a shirt-waister dress with pleats falling from the hips. It did marathon service for years. My aunt was nanny to a Jewish lady doctor who sent me three wonderful garments – a black boucle wool suit, a black georgette longsleeved dress and a raspberry-pink linen dress. Together with the grey worsted shirt-waister, I was ready for anything. (Denise Cochrane)

The dangers, evacuations and shortages of the war had a lasting effect on many children's lives, maybe for the worse, maybe for the better. Their own wartime stitching, or that of their relatives and parents, not only played a part on Britain's road to victory, but also created memories – and habits – to last a lifetime.

Instead of regretting these Make Do and Mend years, I am actually very proud to have been brought up in that way. (Enid Mason)

eleven

Royal Navy – Royal Naval Reserve – Merchant Navy

For centuries, Britain's strength had been founded upon her domination of the seas. At the outset of the Second World War, she proudly possessed the largest Navy in the world and believed it to be unconquerable. Unfortunately, Adolph Hitler realised that if these ships were sunk, or the shipping routes blocked, it would expose Britain's greatest weakness – that of dependence upon her Royal Navy and Merchant Navy for food, oil, and the raw materials with which to wage war.[1] Thereore, upon declaration of war with Germany in 1939, Britain found herself in the position of having to blockade the enemy whilst simultaneously defending her home waters and the vast shipping routes upon which she depended.[2] Stitch would supply the clothing, flags and aircraft covering which was essential to this enormous task.

Germany had secretly been assembling a *Kriegsmarine* of newly designed, aggressively armed warships and a fleet of efficient killers: the fast E-boats and S-boats, and the *Unterseeboote*, or U-boat submarine, while Britain's Royal Navy had been seriously neglected. Enemy action rapidly caused appalling losses of both ships and men, and very soon more warships and merchant ships were urgently needed. In May 1941, under a 'Lend-Lease' agreement, American shipyards rose to the challenge and by 1943, production exceeded the depradations of the enemy – including the British-designed[4] 'Liberty' ships which could be constructed in just forty-two days using assembly line production.[3]

To increase British naval resources, the Government had immediately requisitioned all British ships upon the outbreak of war, from fishing trawlers to luxury liners and merchant 'tramps', to serve the Ministry of Supply and, in 1941, the Ministry of War Transport.[4] While the ships remained the responsibility of their owners, their crews, cargoes and destinations were organised by the newly established wartime Merchant Navy Pool and they were adapted for such duties as troop carrying and mine-sweeping – detonating underwater enemy mines from a safe distance. Merchant ships were provided with First World War guns and the crews trained to use them; however, by 1944, this task had been taken over by some 35,000 DEMS (Defensive Equipment Merchant Ships) gunners, including 13,000 soldiers from the Marine Regiment of Artillery.[5]

Catapult-Aircraft Merchant Ships (CAMS) allowed Sea Hurricanes to be catapulted off their decks to repel the German Focke-Wolf Condors flying out from Norway, but, as they could not land again, they had to be 'ditched' into the ocean; however the sacrifice was deemed worthwhile for the protection of such urgently needed supplies. It was only after CAMS were no longer needed that a proper life-jacket was designed for the pilots![6] In the North Atlantic, Royal Navy personnel also flew planes of the Fleet Air Arm such as the Albacore and Swordfish torpedo bombers which operated from short runways on the decks of aircraft carriers.

Stitching repairs to the fabric skin of an Albacore torpedo bomber. (Courtesy of the Imperial War Museum, London A 22313.)

Naval 'whites'. (Courtesy of the Imperial War Museum, London A 5826)

The design of the Royal Navy-stitched 'White Ensign' flag itself evokes an impression of cleanliness and order. (Courtesy of the Imperial War Museum, London A 13622)

The Royal Navy prided itself upon the perfect maintenance of ships, equipment and clothing, which included the frequent washing and blanco-ing of Tropical Whites, and this could sometimes be turned into a source of income for the two young Royal Marine bugle boys, aged between fourteen to eighteen years or Royal Navy buglers aged sixteen and over, whose task it was to run through the decks of capital ships spreading orders with bugles and drums before tannoy systems were installed.[7]

My other bugler, Curly Regan, and I had a 'dhobi' firm as we lived in with the band on HMS *King George* and we had constant demand for clean laundry, starched shorts and shirts every day. How we managed this when we had no electric iron remains our secret, but it was a lovely little earner![8] (Charlie Workman)

Every Royal Navy sailor was required to have a 'hussif' or sewing kit and its first use was often the stitching of his uniform scarf. The ends of the 50 x 12in fabric had first to be sewn together to form a loop which was then placed under the uniform collar with the end of the loop caught in the tape which threaded through two slits in the jumper. This tape was then tied in a bow, leaving a bight of 2in. The fabric also had other uses: 'Suitably embroidered, the old squares could be converted into heart-warming cushion-covers, much appreciated by the recipients.'[9]

In 1939, a further 12,000 men joined the Royal Navy from the Merchant Navy[10] and received their Royal Navy uniforms – which closely resembled that of the enemy, for across

Seaman Tommy Prynne. (By kind courtesy of St Ives Trust Archive Study Centre)

Royal Navy Officers. (Courtesy of the Imperial War Museum, London A 13855)

Stitching a rubber dinghy. (Courtesy of the Imperial War Museum, London A 571 48)

Europe, sailors' national 'square rig' could only be differentiated by the design of scarf, collar and lanyard.[11]

In Britain, the sight of bell bottoms always sparked a sense of patriotic pride in the Royal Navy's long and glorious history:

> We could always hitch anywhere in bell-bottoms. Almost everyone, not only the nice girls, really did seem to like a sailor ... especially if he were standing at the roadside. Elsewhere we were bought drinks, people called us Jack and dear old ladies came smiling up to us – 'Touch a sailor's collar'. ... As far as anyone knew we were on shore leave after months of reckless daring at sea. It was only other sailors who could tell at once we hadn't been in the Navy a dog watch from such giveaways as the colour of our collars (not yet faded), the swing of our bell-bottoms, the way we wore our caps. But there was a shop in London where you could buy nearly faded collars ... they also sold cap ribbons with the legend FLEET AIR ARM ... completely unauthorized but some thought them a better line than plain HMS, switching ribbons as we left the airfield.[12]

These were the more pleasant aspects of wearing a naval uniform. At sea, during the Second World War, the enemy might attack at any moment by bombers and dive-bombers, mines and – particularly in the dark of night – torpedoes. Death could be by fire, fire-flash, explosion, or drowning. If one survived a sinking ship, there was then the possibility of slow death in a life-boat from exposure, starvation and thirst. Of necessity, sailors kept their abandon-ship supplies, extra clothing and life-suit with them when on watch, ready for immediate use.[13]

The first British deaths from enemy action in the Second World War occurred at sea, on 3 September 1939, before war was actually declared, when a German U-boat torpedoed the passenger liner *Athenia*. The 'success' of the Nazis continued:

The Red Ensign. (Courtesy of the Imperial War Museum, London E 433)

> The losses of ships and men of the merchant navy in those first years of the war were beyond belief. They were nothing more than sitting ducks.[14] (Charlie Workman)

The entrance to the English Channel was quickly blocked by Nazi patrols, and when Germany gained Italy as an ally, British merchant routes through the Mediterranean were all but closed, causing a detour of some 20,000 miles on journeys to the Middle East for vital oil supplies. Then when France fell to German occupation, Britain also suffered the loss of support from its powerful war fleet: her survival now depended upon the Atlantic crossings to America and Canada, primarily to Halifax, Nova Scotia.[17] The 'Battle of the Atlantic' had begun, like a lethal game of hide and seek. More than 30,000 merchant sailors would lose their lives,[16] from Britain, India, China, Norway, America, Greece, Holland, Denmark, Belgium, Australia, New Zealand, South Africa and Canada, plus thousands of sailors from neutral or other allied countries.[17] As European Navies sought shelter in Britain, their distinctive appearance was gradually lost, for the only replacements for worn-out uniforms were those of the British.[18]

At first, the owners of merchant ships preferred to sail independently; however, as U-boat attacks intensified towards the end of 1940 with the Nazis adopting a strategy of forming submarine 'wolf packs', they joined slowly moving convoys of forty or more ships[19] escorted by six heavily armed Royal Navy ships. These were kept in formation by RNVR Convoy Commodores, their ship being identified by a white stitched flag displaying a blue St George's Cross,[20] while the flag of the Merchant Navy was the 'Red Ensign' or 'Red Duster'. These valiant and much-appreciated escorts, plus those of the Fleet Air Arm, could only go part way across the Atlantic, where an unprotected stretch of ocean known as the 'mid-Atlantic gap' or 'the graveyard' had to be crossed before the resumption of escorts, from Canada or America.[21]

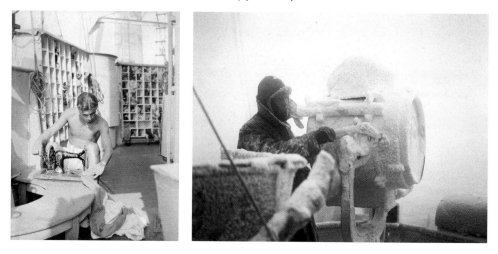

Above, left Stitched flags were a vital part of a convoy's ship-to-ship communication. (Photograph of repairs to bunting courtesy of the Imperial War Museum, London A 30461)

Above, right Deck duty on a Russian convoy. (Courtesy of the Imperial War Museum, London A 6872)

North Atlantic seas could be mountainous, with days of thick fog on the approaches to the Canadian seaboard and warm clothing was essential; however, there were no waterproof outer garments and even if a sailor's thick layers of clothing were soaked through he had to finish his watch.

It was in these mixed Royal Navy and Merchant Navy convoys that the issue of clothing could become a problem, for the typical attitude of a seaman on a 'tramp' steamer to the uniform of the Royal Navy would probably have been: 'What, wear fancy dress for going to sea? Not likely, mate.'[22] (Charlie Workman.) As a civilian he would have to buy his own clothes:

Captain Pedreaux then made us sign a document, after which we were told to present ourselves at Tooner & Denisons Outfitters in Ramsden Dock road where a line of credit had been opened up … We were to equip ourselves with what are now known as jeans, but were then called dungarees, plus thick sweaters, thick long-johns underwear, socks, a pair of wellington boots, and a full-length oilskin coat. Our bill for all the gear was just over five pounds each. Apparently the ship's agents would foot this, and then of course it would be stopped off our wages at the end of the voyage.[23] (Charlie Workman)

One of our shipmates who alternated watches with me, had a magnificent royal blue top coat almost down to his ankles; some relative of his had been a commissionaire at a cinema. It still had the huge shoulder epaulettes on it and 'Gaumont Cinemas' in gold braid on the lapels. The first time he went on watch dressed in it the rear admiral [Royal Navy] almost had an apoplectic fit. He must have thought he was hallucinating. The quartermaster who was at the wheel at the time, told me that he didn't stop spluttering for an hour. … The seaman himself had no idea that anyone could take exception to what after all was a good, warm coat, even if it was somewhat garish.[24] (Charlie Workman)

If a Merchant seaman survived the bombing, torpedoeing or mining of his ship, his pay would be stopped from that day with just a week's survivors' leave and an allowance of £13 15s plus

The crews of British submarines in their small, enclosed communities, under minute-by-minute risk of attack and working with greasy engines, broke free from any attempt at Parade Ground standards. (Courtesy of the Imperial War Museum, London A 16270)

The 'Jolly Roger' flags of submarine crews, which recorded the number of their enemy sinkings, were an indication in fabric and stitch of their independent spirit (Courtesy of the Imperial War Museum, London A 28198)

extra coupons to replace all his lost clothing.[25] However, he could claim extra clothing coupons. The lower ranks of the Royal Navy received Government-issue uniforms with an annual allowance of ten coupons to cover wear and tear; but, like the merchant sailor, Commissioned Officers in the Royal Navy were also required to provide their own clothing.[26]

On 21 August 1941, the first of the British convoys set sail across the North Sea carrying supplies to Russia for its Red Army,[27] and these slowly moving Russian convoys were to be among the most dangerous and challenging of the war. In summer, they were easy targets for the enemy and in winter the cold was almost unbearable. Ice-breakers led the way with the merchant ships following close astern before the sea froze over again[28] and sea-spray froze instantly on superstructure and deck cargo, having to be constantly chipped away to avoid the ship capsizing from the weight.

With temperatures around 10 degrees below freezing,[29] men had to wrap themselves in their warmest garments. Swept into the freezing sea, it was estimated that a sailor would survive the cold for only around three minutes.[30] Frozen fingers could not negotiate icy buttons and the wooden toggles and loops of duffle coats solved this problem.[31] Under these conditions, the usual Royal Navy standards of dress were abandoned, which could cause problems when ships returned to Britain. As HMS *Beagle* tied up in a Scottish port, her sailors exhausted and thankful to be safely back after a long and harrowing escort duty to Russia, their attire was noticed from the bridge of a nearby battleship which quickly signalled: 'WILL YOU KINDLY WEAR THE RIG OF THE DAY_STOP_YOU LOOK LIKE A CROWD OF PIRATES_END.' Suffering from prolonged lack of sleep, the Chief Yeoman of Signals found it necessary to ask his Number One, 'Sir, how do you spell "BOLLOCKS"?'[32]

In 1944, ships were sent to join the British Eastern Fleet and the American naval forces in the 'Battle of the Pacific'. Then, on 7 May 1945, the final British deaths of the war occurred at sea, just after Germany's official surrender, when a Norwegian 'tramp' and a Canadian steamer travelling in convoy from Edinburgh were torpedoed, with the loss of twenty-three lives.[33] The ships and boats of Britain had all played a vital role in the achievement of victory from the very beginning to the bitter end.

At sea, the Second World War produced an enormous contrast in clothing as Royal Navy and civilians worked together for victory. In a variety of attire, the Royal Navy and Merchant Navy had kept a nation fed and its war machine supplied, both at home and overseas. With outstanding courage and under heavy enemy fire, they had rescued tens of thousands of men from the beaches of France, Greece, and Crete and maintained the 'suicide run' to and from Malta. They had transported hundreds of thousands of troops to destinations across the world, including the beaches of Normandy in the crucial D-Day invasion, and then ensured that they were constantly supplied. They endured the some of the harshest conditions in the world to take tanks, aircraft and other sorely needed supplies to the Russian Red Army. This courage and commitment to others, whether in immaculate or dishevelled clothing, did not go unnoticed:

My journey across London via the Underground from Euston to Liverpool Street Station clad in a salt- (not to mention vomit-) stained uniform and still jealously clutching my orange-coloured life jacket was more of an ordeal than the whole of the western ocean, with the masses of people sheltering from the nightly Blitz all wanting to crowd around me and slap my back or shake my hand.[34] (Len Deighton)

twelve

The Royal Air Force

Per Ardua ad Astra

In 1939, flying was a new and glamorous activity and both male and female aeronauts were as idolised as film stars. The Royal Air Force was just twenty years old,[1] under-funded, short of aeroplanes and personnel, and acting rather as an elite flying club.[2] The original 'French Blue' uniform had been changed to slate grey, and a grey battledress was to be issued in 1940, identical to that of the British Army except for the three points on the breast pocket.[3]

The bomber had become the most feared weapon of war after its use in the First World War and horrified cinema audiences watched cinema newsreels of the appalling devastation, injury and loss of life caused by the German *Luftwaffe* in the Spanish Civil War. Adolph Hitler had just to threaten to bomb a treasured capital city and a country would capitulate.

When war was declared in 1939, Britain had some 2,500 Royal Air Force Volunteer Reserve pilots and another 4,500 men were sent by British Training Command to train as pilots in the southern states of America.[4] By 1943, the Empire Air Training Scheme had brought in a further 11,000 pilots in addition to the 17,000 aircrew each year from South Africa, West Africa,[5] Canada, Australia, New Zealand, and Southern Rhodesia.[6] Britain's wartime squadrons included forty-two Canadian, twenty-seven South African, sixteen Australian, nine Indian and six flown by New Zealanders. They were joined by 6,000 volunteers from the West Indies,[7] a handful from Brazil, the Americans who formed the 'Eagle Squadron',[8] and pilots in exile who made up fifty-one squadrons which fought ferociously for the freedom of Norway, Poland, France, Czechoslovakia, Holland, Greece, Yugoslavia and Belgium.[9] Four of the eight 'Ace' Second World War pilots (who had shot down five or more enemy planes) were from the Empire.[10] All of these airmen from overseas retained their national uniform, but in action wore the standard issue of the RAF.

Trainee pilots had to master the techniques of extreme aerobatics in the de Havilland 'Moth' and Miles Magister training planes and learn how to deal with 'G' forces which made limbs a dead-weight, 'crushed pilots' heads down on their chests, and turned the blood in their veins to the weight of molten metal'[11] also causing the plane's light controls to become almost too stiff and heavy to operate.[12] Blood forced away from the brain caused misty vision (or grey-out), or even complete black-out.[13]

> The force on the pull-out [when dive-bombing] was so great that all the zip fasteners on my flying suit were undone by it. (P/O Bamford)[14]

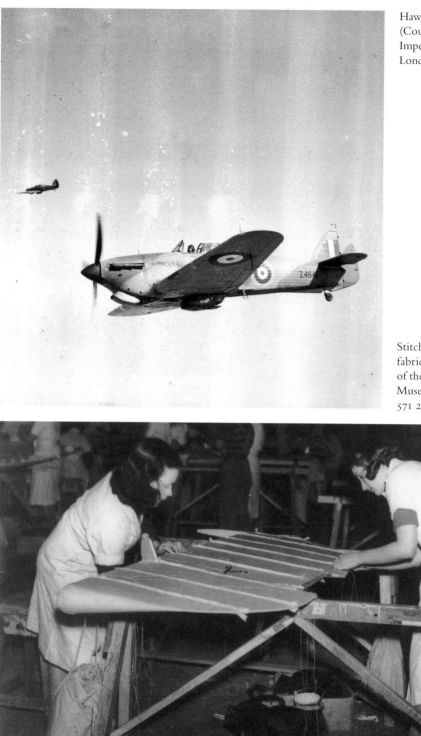

Hawker Hurricane.
(Courtesy of the
Imperial War Museum,
London CM 2116)

Stitching on a plane's
fabric skin. (Courtesy
of the Imperial War
Museum, London
571 23)

However, Flight Training School offered luxurious accommodation: the food was superb and each young officer had his own personal batman or batwoman,[15] although this was to be gradually curtailed. The daily routine was still ordered according to the RAF's exclusive traditions – officers dressed for dinner, either in mess kit, dinner jacket or lounge suit depending on the day of the week, and 'dressed-down' in blazers, flannels and ties on Saturdays.[16]

In the final two weeks of training, the Government allowance of £50 was spent at the RAF Depot, Uxbridge, to purchase individually tailored uniforms, the fabric of officers' uniform being less scratchy than their sergeants'[17] and including a dark blue shirt to be worn with a black tie, black socks and shoes; their field service cap bearing a black mohair band with gold embroidered insignia.[18] As usual, the uniforms of the lower ranks were provided by the Government.

Initially, it was not thought necessary to train pilots to shoot at moving targets or practice the tactics of combat;[19] instead, upon the outbreak of war planes were sent off on 'gentlemanly' reconnaisance missions or to drop propaganda leaflets and pilots sent to support the British Expeditionary Force were in for an enormous shock when they first encountered the ruthless and experienced tactics of the German *Luftwaffe*, arriving quickly at the opinion that the *Luftwaffe*'s superiority in the air was unbeatable.[20]

In the nightmare hell of the evacuation of Dunkirk, thousands of men – and a few women – who formed exposed lines stretching across the sand and into the sea whilst being constantly bombed and strafed by enemy fire could not see any proper response from the RAF and public opinion as to its effectiveness was so low that the sight of an airman's uniform in a pub could result in violence.[21] In fact, 4,822 sorties had been flown, but out of sight, inland or high in the sky.[22]

The several hundred types of planes which would be used to defend Britain were constructed from a mixture of metal, wood and fabric and they were produced in their thousands. Stitched fabric was a useful cover for control surfaces, the ailerons and rudders on planes with

The Irvin sheepskin and parachute.
(Courtesy of the Imperial War Museum, London C 420)

Mosquito. (Courtesy of the Imperial War Museum, London CH 18305)

Squadron Leader R.W. Oxspring, Commanding Officer of No.91 Squadron Supermarine Spitfire Vc, Hawkinge, Kent. One of the first Spitfire pilots to fly in the Battle of Britain, and then serve in North Africa; he destroyed twelve enemy aircraft.

a metal fuselage, such as the Spitfire; it was a cheap 'skin' for the Horsa glider, which could not be retrieved once landed, and Barnes Wallis found fabric to be the most suitable skin for the metal geodetic structures of his 176 Vickers Wellesley bomber and the 11,461 Vickers Wellington bombers.[23]

Stitch was also essential to the construction of the fabric-covered Hawker Hurricane series designed by Sidney Camm, with a complete fabric skin of Irish linen, sewn at 8 stitches to the inch and stretched taut over the tubular high-tensile steel frame by the application of several layers of 'dope'.[24] Such an easily repaired skin and frame could withstand even the most intense enemy fire since bullets passed straight through the fabric. However, this was quickly replaced by metal,[25] although the 14,231 Hurricanes which served during the Second World War retained their fabric-covered tail, including the Hurricane IIC 'Hurri-Bomber' and the Hurricane Mk X which was produced by the Canada Car and Foundry in Fort William, Ontaria, where the chief designer, Elsie MacGill, was known as the 'Queen of the Hurricanes'. In action, Hurricanes destroyed more enemy planes than all other fighters or bombers combined.[26]

However, the Hurricane was soon upstaged by the beautiful Vickers' metal-skinned Supermarine Spitfire designed by R.G. Mitchell, who was reported to have remarked 'Just the sort of bloody silly name they would choose.'[27]

Unfortunately, it was intensely cold in the Spitfire cockpit at high altitude; however warmth was provided by the yellow-lined sheepskin jackets and trousers made by the Irvin Parachute Company, which incorporated a high fur collar or hood; they also supplied electrically heated gloves and socks.[28] Additional warmth under this 'Irvin clobber' could be gained from the Frock White polo-necked sweater, which was replaced by an air force-blue version in 1941–42. Another option was the 1940s issue gabardine flying-suit with quilted lining and detachable brown fur collar[29] worn over the basic 1940s' design service-dress uniform[30] plus three pairs of gloves.[31] A flying helmet could be attached by press-studs, and over this, an oxygen mask, goggles and maybe a microphone. Sheepskin was also used to line the 1940s' flying boots and 1936-pattern black-leather life-saving waistcoat.[32] However, 'The layers of warm clothing needed against the intense cold of high altitudes, the oxygen mask that enveloped half the face, became horribly restricting in the intense physical exertion of a dogfight and pilots climbed out of the narrow cockpits soaked in sweat. Almost everyone lost pounds during periods of action.'[33]

Flying gear had to be kept perfectly dry in heated cloakrooms, for any moisture could freeze at high altitudes and result in severe frostbite.[34] Particular care had to be taken with boots, which could easily become wet in the dewy grass of an early morning 'scramble'.[35]

An exception to the problem of cold was the efficiently heated cockpit of the Mosquito light bomber, where pilots could comfortably wear a lightweight serge 'Suit Aircrew' battle-dress with wool-and-rayon underclothing, or even swimming trunks in hot summer weather. As silk inner-gloves provided enough warmth for the hands, there was far more sensitivity of control in the darkness of night flights.[36]

Designed for de Havilland by Arthur Renn, a manufacturer of musical instruments with extensive experience in the use of wood when supplies of metal grew low, the 'Timber Terror' or Mosquito was also constructed with a fabric skin. Parts for the monocoque frames of the 7,785 planes were produced by women in Australia and the Roddis Manufacturing Company of Wisconsin, America and then shipped to British factories such as the Lebus Furniture Factory to be covered in the fabric, Madapolam. After stitching, this was first shrunk with water then tightened and stiffened with a toxic red/silver 'dope', or plasticised lacquer which could cause vomiting if breathed in too deeply. Powered by a pair of Rolls-Royce Merlin XXI engines, stitch, glue, fabric and wood produced a plane so light and fast that it needed no defensive armament and could be used for reconnaissance and as a bomber or night fighter. With a top speed of 380mph, the Mosquito was 20mph faster than the Spitfire, suffering the least losses of any Allied bomber. Mosquitos allowed 250 French Resistance fighters to escape execution by the strategic bombing of the guardhouse and fences of their prison at Amiens and two Mosquitos destroyed the Gestapo Headquarters at the Hague in which were stored the

'Ace' fighter–pilot Wing Commander P.B. Lucas DSO DFC. (Courtesy of the Imperial War Museum, London CH 13644)

Coastal Command aircrew with their mascot. (Courtesy of the Imperial War Museum, London CH13725)

addresses of resistance fighters and Dutch Jews in hiding. However, the Mosquito could not be used in the tropics as the wood warped and glue dissolved.[37]

In July 1940, when Adolph Hitler commanded the German *Luftwaffe* to annihilate Britain's air defenses in preparation for invasion, British fighter pilots, some as young as eighteen years old, were again outnumbered by a formidably experienced enemy. For the first time the 'dog-fights', or air battles, were over England. Through the summer, autumn and winter of 1940 the British public would witness at first hand the courage of their 'Fighter Boys', particularly in 'Hellfire Corner' around Dover, in Kent, and these 'Battle of Britain' pilots were to become icons of wartime courage and national pride. Such were the massive losses of fighter-planes that when the largest Spitfire factory near Southampton was bombed, production from the Shadow Factory at Castle Bromwich near Birmingham[38] had to be hurriedly augmented by workers in sites such as car showrooms, hotels,[39] even kitchens and school classrooms. Due to the extreme shortage of materials, around one-third of the planes flown in the Battle of Britain were constructed from salvaged parts by RAF and Civilian Repair Units who were also repairing some 160 damaged planes each week at the height of the battle.[40]

Two planes flying at speeds of around 300mph[41] produce a combined speed of around 600mph which, in combat, demanded split-second awareness in three dimensions. Constant twisting of the head caused the rough fabric of uniform collars to rub necks raw, which pilots could relieve by wearing a silk or woollen scarf, or an Old School cravat; however, if scarf ends tangled in the aircraft's controls an airman could be strangled.[42] As a concession, the RAF allowed fighter-pilots to leave their top tunic button undone and this, with their silk scarves, became their famous trademark. Immediately recognised as 'Fighter Boys' when they went to unwind in the evening at their favourite pubs,[43] round after round of drinks were bought for them by an admiring and grateful public – a much-needed tonic to young men who could see no end to their days of intense fear and danger except terrible injury or death.

> Deep down we knew, but dared not admit, that we had little hope of existing much longer… So meanwhile, we made merry.[44]

Another way of coping with the constant strain was provided by stitch in the form of lucky mascots and talismans which were carefully taken by Second World War airmen when they departed on operations:

> At some stage I had been given an outsize Teddy as big as myself which, truth to tell, I didn't like very much. It was probably my Mother's suggestion that I raffle it. I took it round, sitting in my doll's pram to most of the houses round our side of the town selling raffle tickets for a few weeks, there was also a pair of nylons that someone donated. I had a bit of help from Mum and Dad but I did a lot on my own (at about 8 years old). The raffle was drawn at a dance at the Turner Hall where a final push to sell raffle tickets was made. The Teddy was won by an airman – apparently it became a mascot on a bomber and was last heard of dropping bombs on Germany. (Anita Seamons)

Imaginary stitch – or lack of it – also contributed to 'Jane', another talisman which was widely appreciated by all three services, sometimes known as 'Jane's Fighting Men',[45] particularly in the RAF. An invention of the cartoonist Pett for the *Daily Mirror*, she was based on the body of his wife Chrystabel and images of 'Jane' and her dachshund 'Fritzi' were painted onto submarines, aircraft and military vehicles, worn as tattoos, pinned up in bases throughout the world, sent out in the submarines' daily newspaper *Good Morning* and letters from home and carried in breast pockets.

(Courtesy of Mirrorpix)

A loveable, innocent, amusing and kind-hearted character was depicted in every woman's uniform of the war, however in each aptly named 'strip' cartoon she was increasingly revealed as the story-line progressed. So important was 'Jane' to the morale of the British Services that she even played a role on the eve of the crucial and dangerous D-Day landings by finally appearing without any clothes at all[46] and men attributed the power of good fortune to their image, including the crew of the submarine HM *Tallyho!* who chalked underwear onto their conning tower's painted Jane before leaving port, believing that good luck would follow if it had washed off by the time they next surfaced.[47]

It was understandable that men placed their trust in lucky mascots, personal talismans or rituals. During the 'Battle of Britain' the supply of trained pilots could not keep pace with the carnage and when training was cut down from six to four months, new pilots were without the skill to cope with the ferocious aerial battles. The death they faced might come from enemy bullets, the tearing splinters of cannon shells, drowning, or in the flames of their burning plane and thick, warm clothing and boots or an emergency parachute turned into a deadly weight in the cold sea. Or maybe worse, they might survive only to be permanently maimed, their face horribly disfigured by burns.[48]

You saw chaps who had really taken shock extremely badly. They'd come into the bar and they'd have a terrible facial twitch or body twitch.[49]

Bomber crew. (Courtesy of the Imperial War Museum, London C 415)

Standard-issue 1940s RAF uniform offered little protection from enemy canon or machine-gun fire and some fighter-pilots even took to wearing a pair of car hubcaps between the legs,[50] however splinter-proof linings for helmets and flying boots were issued from 1941, using sheepskin plus thirty layers of parachute silk; although the boots were 'noted for falling off when baling out.'[51] Each parachute and Mae West life-jacket had to be adjusted to fit perfectly; and, for 'baling out' over enemy-occupied territory, a civilian jacket was often worn under the battledress blouse, plus rations, money, revolver and knife, and a map in the boots.[52]

When, on 15 September 1940, Fighter Command threw every available plane into the 'Big Wing' to face the massive formations of Nazi bombers and fighter escorts which, it was believed by Germany, would be the end of Britain's air defence, Hitler discovered instead that the RAF could not, in fact, be conquered. Now he was forced to change his strategy and set about the destruction of civilian Britain and its morale by the intense bombing of cities, ports, factories, transport and communication links – the Blitz had begun and it was the turn of the RAF's Bomber Command to take over the crucial role with planes such as Blenheims and Beaufighters, Lancasters, Stirlings, Halifaxes and Wellingtons. In these planes crews of up to six worked as a team, and again stitch was part of the construction process, for every geodetic-designed bomber was covered with fabric.[53]

The experience of a bomber's crew was quite different to that of the pilots of Fighter Command, for they were sent out over enemy territory knowing that their destinations were heavily defended from ground and air and that at any moment they could become the target of enemy fighter planes. Sealed into the aircraft, with helmets, headphones and oxygen masks, they were only aware of the constant vibration of the engines, and the enemy fire which could cause disaster or death seemed to float past and explode silently with a strange beauty. Bombers forged ahead through the delicate white lights of strings of light flak, which either faded or whizzed up and past, while the explosions of heavy flak appeared as black, red and orange

Airspeed Horsa glider. (Courtesy of the Imperial War Museum, London CH 10891)

balls.[54] Once Germany had developed its radar to warn of approaching attack, their probing searchlights could lock onto a plane and encase it in a cone of deadly light, clearly exposing it to a barrage of anti-aircraft fire.

> There was nothing we could do in that nightmare situation, it was impossible to see outside our aircraft to any worthwhile degree because of the dazzle, and all sensation of speed seemed to vanish. The world had disappeared and we felt as if we were hanging motionless in space.[55]

But one problem was the same for both fighter pilots and bomber crews – intense cold – and the coldest positions in a bomber were the gun turrets.[56] If they were not to freeze to death, rear gunners, or 'Tail End Charlies', locked into their cramped turrets needed electrically heated glazed sheepskin Irvin suits, moccasins and gloves; combination underwear; layers of woollen socks; a Frock White pullover; a lined and quilted overall; leather gauntlets, mittens and silk gloves; and the Type B or C helmet lined with thirty layers of parachute silk. By 1943, the sheepskin 'Irvins' were replaced by yellow fabric kapok-padded Taylor buoyancy suits, which provided both warmth and a far greater chance of survival in the sea, but many men preferred to continue wearing their Irvins.[57]

Bomber crews' uniforms were of no particular interest to the British public, as had been the 'Battle of Britain' fighter-pilots', yet their courageous determination was not less than that of the fighter-pilot and in Europe, the sound of the bombers' engines was the sound of hope. If a bomber's crew had to bale out, their uniforms sometimes guaranteed that they would be greeted as heroes and given every possible aid to escape back to Britain by the people of Nazi-occupied countries, despite the terrible consequences if this should be discovered. However, by the end of the war the RAF would be responsible for sending the 'One Thousand Bomber' raids to Germany, causing the loss of some 600,000 lives, mostly civilian[58] and there naturally developed a deep and violent hatred of Allied bomber crews.

The RAF also utilised planes covered with fabric which had no engines – the fabric and Balsa wood Airspeed Horsa glider, designed by the Airspeed Aircraft Company in 1940 to carry a maximum load of twenty-eight fully equipped men or two jeeps, or their equivalent. Horsa gliders were towed into position by bombers such as the Whitley, Halifax or American Dakota and then released to silently enter enemy-occupied territory and throughout the war, around 3,655 Horsas transported thousands of paratroops and tons of urgently needed supplies, predominantly in the invasions of Sicily and Belgium and Normandy. Pilots wore the standard parachutists' smock over battledress trousers and, once landed, the famous Airborne forces' red beret. Unfortunately, the flight of the Horsa was influenced by wind-speed and direction; an uninterrupted landing site was needed if it were not to crumple upon impact; and paratroops had no protection from enemy fire, as bullets could tear the plane's fusilage to shreds.[59]

Development of RAF planes continued apace throughout the war, and in June 1944 they tackled the latest of Hitler's weapons – the V-1 rocket-bomb, or 'Doodle-bug' – with the jet-powered Hawker Tempest V, which 'flew with the sound of an immense and continuous whisper',[60] also 'stripped down' Typhoons, Spitfire XIVs, and the Mustangs of the Polish (City of Warsaw) 316 Squadron[61] which destroyed nearly 2,000 V-1s in eighty days and nights,[62] sometimes flying at speeds of around 400mph to flick them with a wing-tip, disorientate the guidance gyroscope and cause them to crash harmlessly over countryside.[63] When the V-1s were superceded by the faster-than-sound V-2, pilots who undertook the tremendously skilled precision bombing of their launch-sites found that they had been carefully positioned in heavily populated civilian areas or next to such buildings as hospitals.[64]

By 1945, the nation's stitchers had provided uniforms for the 1,011,427 RAF officers and men of Fighter Command, Bomber Command, Coastal Command and their huge supporting organisation of ground crews, amny of whom did not return.[65]

The Commonwealth Air Forces Memorial at Runnymede commemorates the 20,000 Allied airmen of the Second World War whose bodies have no grave:[66]

> If I climb up into Heaven Thou art there
> If I go down into Hell Thou art there also.
> If I take the wings of the morning and remain
> In the uttermost parts of the sea;
> Even there also shalt Thy hand lead me
> And Thy right hand shall hold me.
> (From Psalm 139)

Chapter 13

Parachutes

The only way to fall from the sky without sustaining injury is to use the canopy of a parachute, the fabric curved and shaped by stitch to catch the air, then securely attached to the body with rigging and harness. With a parachute it is possible to defy gravity.

Speed of fall is decelerated from 118mph within twelve seconds of jumping from a plane to just 14mph on landing.[1]

Parachutes had first been used by Germany as a new form of warfare – that of dropping armed paratroops from the air. The advantage was that the troops, with their support system of vehicles, supplies and medical aid could be dropped behind enemy lines or into territory which was inaccessible or could only be reached with difficulty on the ground. Such was the effectiveness of dropping men, supplies, bombs and mines from gliders or specially adapted bombers that by 1943 there was a world-wide shortage of parachutes.[2]

Realising the potential of this airborne warfare, Churchill demanded the assembly of ten units of 1,000 British paratroops to act as shock troops spearheading major invasions[3] and volunteers were invited to undertake the dangerous training. By November 1940, the No.2 Commandos was ready for action as the 11th Special Air Service Battalion (SAS), with Glider Wing and Parachute Wing and the 1st British Airborne Division was later formed in 1943. These 'Red Berets', whose badge showed Bellerphon riding the winged horse Pegasus, came to be renowned for their ferocity when under attack. They would 'jump' with an extra 100lb added to their body weight which included food and water to last three days, weapon, ammunition and ordnance.[4]

The role of the Airborne Divisions in the Second World War was exceptionally dangerous and in the assault on Arnhem in 1944 around 1,500 men lost their lives while some 6,200 were taken prisoner out of the 10,000-strong British 1st Airborne and 82nd American Airborne Divisions who were dropped into Holland in 'Operation Market Garden'.[5] Again, there was tragic loss of life when paratroops were dropped in the early hours of the morning of D-Day, 6 June 1944, to capture and then defend the bridges which would be on the left flank of troops leaving the Normandy beaches.[6] Eighteen fabric-covered gliders were riddled with enemy bullets; only one landed on target, and men were drowned by the weight of their heavy 60lb packs in fields deliberately flooded with water. However, in March 1945, the massive 'Operation Varsity' dropped 21,680 paratroops from some 1,500 aircraft to successfully breach enemy defences of the river Rhine, allowing the Allies to gain entry to Germany itself,[7] and in Burma only the Airborne Divisions were able to seize remote jungle airstrips and drop millions of tons of sorely needed supplies to the Allied ground forces.

Cutting and stitching some 100 yards of fabric to construct the commonly used RAF X-type parachute with a 28ft-diameter canopy[8] was a skilled and complicated process, especially as the curved panels and sub-divisions of panels were cut on the bias to minimise tearing. An elasticated 'puckered vent' was formed at the apex to allow air to escape correctly at varying speeds and bands of fabric reinforced both the apex and completed skirt, or lower circumference.[9] Silk was the ideal material, being strong, light and fine enough to be folded into the small volumes required by the constricted spaces of airmen's packs; however, when supplies of silk soon failed, it had to be replaced by cotton 'Ramtex', and then, when British factories started to produce nylon, it was adopted by the RAF.[10] Cellulose acetate yarn was also used for heavy supply-drops, and jute-hessian for dropping mines at sea.[11]

Newly stitched parachutes were numbered and rigorously tested before being packed into canvas bags. Upon issue, the names, ranks and numbers of their 'owners' were added – which could cause a problem when a plane was shot down over enemy-occupied territory, for if a parachute was found by the enemy, a determined search would result for its user.

Parachutes used in supply-drops were stored and packed by Air Despach Companies before skilful loading onto aircraft,[12] with colour-coded parachutes allowing for faster retrieval on the ground. Bright red parachutes dropped ammunition in 'Operation Market Garden'; green, rations; yellow, communications equipment; white, medical supplies; and blue, oil, petrol and lubricants. Black silk was also used from 1941, for the secret night-time drops of Special Operations Executive (SOE) agents and their supplies deep into enemy territory; and, from 1942, parachutes successfully dropped around 6,000 'Clockwork Mouse' (James ML) and 'Flying Flea' (Royal Enfield WD/RE) motorbikes, also 3,200 'parascooters' (Exelsior Welbikes weighing just 70lb).[13] The 'Singer' Model 31 SV 52 sewing machine was also dropped by parachute, with its stand, a table and sewing materials for use at the front line or remote outposts.[14] Heavy supply-drops of vehicles were achieved by the use of parachute clusters.[16] Parachutes were also used by both Allies and Axis to drop bombs and mines, although these drifted with the wind and were impossible to control[15] and a top-secret parachute-and-cable system (PAC) protected British ports, airfields and ships at sea with parachutes sent up by rockets to suspend the 100ft steel cables which deterred low-flying enemy aircraft.[16]

Much smaller parachutes with tiny harnesses were also stitched for a few 'para-pigeons',[17] and, from 1944, 24ft-circumference parachutes were used by the many 'para-dogs' which were trained at the War Dog Training School at Potters Bar London to work with the SAS.[18] In action, they were dropped by static line as the last of the 'stick' or line of paratroops, immediately after their handlers,[19] to carry messages in leather pouches, detect land-mines[20] and join patrols in North Africa and Italy. 'Para-dogs' also worked under American command against Japan[21] and SAS Rob was awarded the Dickin Medal after successfully completing over twenty 'jumps'.[22]

The two methods of parachute deployment, or canopy opening, were: 'rigging line first', in which the 'chutes were attached to a 'static line'; the weight of the falling man, woman, dog, or supplies causing the fastening line of the parachute's outer bag to snap. The line:

Parachutes dropping supplies for the Chindits in the jungle of Burma. (Courtesy of the Imperial War Museum, London AP 258601)

Stitching parachutes. (Courtesy of the Imperial War Museum, London A 571 127 L.N.A.)

Testing a newly made parachute. (Courtesy of the Imperial War Museum, London A 571 129 L.N.A.)

... then lifted the bottom [closed] end of the inner bag until it was inverted above the man's shoulders, when two further ties broke and allowed the bag to become free. The rigging lines were then pulled out from their stowages as the man continued to fall and when they were fully extended, a tie that had held the mouth of the bag closed broke, and allowed the canopy to be withdrawn. When the canopy and lines were fully extended, the tie connecting the top of the canopy to the end of the static line inside the inner bag snapped and the canopy was then free to develop.[23]

However, there was the danger that just after release from the 'line', the canopy would not fill with air and open sufficiently wide enough to cause the necessary amount of drag, or it might even invert. This was termed 'Blown Periphery Malfunction' which, of course, resulted in the parachute's load hitting the ground at speed. Fortunately, it was found that by sewing an extra ring of net around the circumference, or skirt, this problem was eliminated.[24] In this method, each 'stick' or line of paratroops had to leave the plane as quickly as possible, with the boots of one man almost touching the shoulders of the man in front.

A second method of deployment was by the manual operation of the parachutist: the 'canopy-first' system. This was a quicker method and allowed aircrew or paratroopers to safely 'jump' from planes flying at a lower altitude than that which the 'static line' system would allow. Canopy deployment was achieved by pulling the D-ring[25] attached to the rip-cord which opened the parachute pack. A 'reefing' sytem, which regulated the canopy opening into two stages, allowed the smooth dropping of devices sensitive to shock, or torpedoes designed to detonate on impact.[28]

Once stitched, all parachutes were labelled with a serial number, the Air Ministry's stamp of approval and the manufacturer's name. Airmen were instructed to 'bring it back if it doesn't work and bring it back if it *does* work': the penalty for not doing so – to treat the Parachute Section to a round of drinks.[26] Until the end of 1941, parachute packs were incorporated into 'combined pattern suits' such as the limited number of GQ 'Sidcot' flying suits and the Irvin Harnessuit which was used by Bomber Command, Coastal Command and a few Fighter Command units during 1940.[27]

Packs could be clipped on at the chest or be stowed on an aircraft's seat, and in some suits both options were provided.[28] However, the most commonly used parachute pack in pilot-only, single-engined planes during the Second World War was the *Parachute, Single-point, Quick-release with Seat pack, Type C-2 15A/197. Pack 15A/96* which fitted into the bucket seats and could be covered by a thin clip-on cushion accompanied by a further cushion for the back which attached to the webbing straps.[29] This pack was put in place in preparation for the pilot to quickly fasten parachute and aircraft harnesses as he took rapidly took his seat in the cockpit of his plane in a 'scramble'. The *Type C-2*, incorporating a dinghy and an emergency oxygen supply, later replaced the seat cushion.[30]

Airmen who needed to be able to move around in larger planes were provided with the *Parachute, Single-point, Quick-release with Two-point detachable Chest Pack (Observer Type) Harness 15A/137, Pack 15A/141* in which the harness only was worn and the parachute pack stowed until needed.[31] The air-crew of Lancaster and Halifax heavy bombers wore the *Parachute, Single-point, Quick-release, Back type pack 15A/512* at all times during a flight, with its non-detachable harness allowing for speedy 'bale-out'.[32] Airborne troops carefully checked the fit of each other's packs and as the harness passed between the legs it had to be carefully adjusted as, otherwise, the sharp jolt when the parachute canopy opened could be most uncomfortable.

Events leading up to the decision to leave a burning, out-of-control aircraft were always dramatic, and often tragic: members of the WAAF who were tuned in to pilot's radio transmissions would hear the desperate screams of the trapped men, knowing that their only hope was to use their parachute and 'bale out'. Yet, even when the decision was made, an airman could not entirely depend upon his parachute to take him to safety. Sometimes a parachute could catch fire. Sometimes the plane was too low in the sky for a parachute to open in time. Sometimes the parachute had been damaged by enemy fire, or maybe the 'pull' of the plane's slip-stream, which could be 60mph or more, would prove to be a final obstacle for it was possible for a man to be blown back in again.[33]

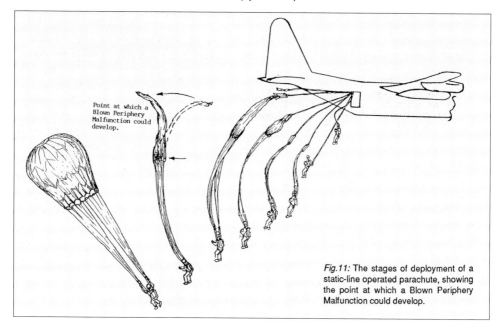

Point at which a Blown Periphery Malfunction could develop.

Fig.11: The stages of deployment of a static-line operated parachute, showing the point at which a Blown Periphery Malfunction could develop.

The 'static line' system. (By kind courtesy of G.M.S. Enterprises)

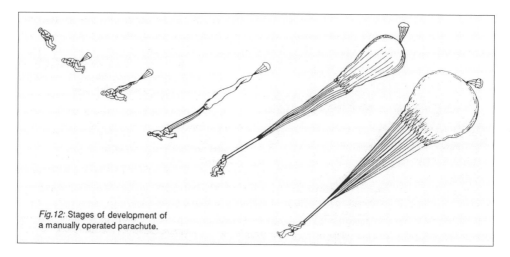

Fig.12: Stages of development of a manually operated parachute.

The 'canopy-first' system. (By kind courtesy of G.M.S. Enterprises)

Having left behind the noise, danger and chaos of a damaged plane, relief at the parachute's opening was followed swiftly by an experience of another more peaceful world, if only for a few brief minutes:

The atmosphere grew strangely silent as the engine noise quickly faded away in the distance … there was no feeling or impression of moving downwards at all, but only that I was spinning backwards and forwards as the lines above were twisting and untwisting. The open 'chute, like a gigantic silken umbrella, billowed out overhead and the cone of long cord lines tapering down to the harness, which pulled tightly around my cradled body, rendered me nearly helpless, suspended in the air. At intervals, loud cracking noises were evident aloft, when air was being expelled from pockets in the swelling silk canopy. (Pilot Officer Gordon J. Richie, Royal Canadian Air Force)[34]

The mind quickly filled with thoughts of what was in store on landing – if one was not to be shot whilst drifting down attached to the conspicuous canopy. Absolutely anything could happen; a man could be immediately captured by the enemy and spend the rest of the war in a prisoner-of-war camp, or receive a hero's welcome from grateful partisans and be helped to get back to Britain. The parachute might catch on a tree or church steeple where he could be left hanging helplessly in mid-air, or the landing ground might have been deliberately flooded so that paratroops would drown under the weight of their heavy packs, or they might land in a minefield.

The vision of plunging headlong out into the inky darkness of the night, at 2am in the morning, was a frightening thought and the only consolation and spur to going through with it, was the knowledge that it offered the best prospects for survival. (Pilot Officer Gordon J. Richie, Royal Canadian Air Force)[35]

Once returned to base, parachutes were inspected for damage and their use carefully recorded to ensure that they were not used too often. Within Britain, this was usually the work of some 2,800 WAAF repairers and packers.[36] After any necessary repairs, parachutes were stored loosely rolled and covered in air-tight bags[37] before re-packing, for the fabric would weaken at the creases if kept folded for long periods. Cotton or rayon parachutes had to be thoroughly dried and aired to avoid mould and dry rot,[38] and if a parachute had been exposed to salt water for more than twenty-four hours it had to be discarded.[39] Parachutes which had been unused for two months were unpacked and could then be used only twenty-five more times.[40]

Parachute packers worked under intense pressure. Whilst packing as quickly as possible, they were constantly reminded that men's lives depended upon their making no mistakes. Seven WAAF packed nearly 50,000 parachutes between them by 1944.

Parachutes were also highly valued by civilians on the ground for their fabric, and as a consequence there was a certain amount of 'leakage' to grateful and needy stitchers throughout the war. Most fortunate were the women factory workers whose job it was to construct the chutes, for they were sometimes allowed to keep any flawed pieces[41] when it was illegal to use large pieces and punishable by imprisonment.[42] At the end of the war they were sold off to a public eager for any fabric which might provide clothing during the severe post-war rationing. Leaflets described how parachutes could be used: 'out of 1/3 of a 24 panel parachute you can make two nightdresses, two slips, two pairs of cami-knickers and four pairs of knickers'[43] and the Board of Trade's 'NYLON NEWS FROM MRS SEW-AND-SEW' advised on the use of parachutes made from the new, synthetic nylon:

TOO HOT AN IRON IS DANGEROUS … Allow ample material so as not to strain the seams, and never make the garment too close-fitting. This nylon fabric is rather apt to slip at the seams. So make liberal turnings at seams and hems, and always tack very carefully before you start to sew. Set your machine at as low tension as possible. By machining with a loose, easy stitch, you will avoid puckering at the seams.

These are the memories of those who can remember the role that the military parachute played in the lives of civilians – either 'obtained' during the war or bought after VE-Day:

'This photograph was taken in 1942/43 of me aged about three years in a dress made by my mother from parachute silk. At that time living in a village in Kent over-looking the Straits of Dover parachutes frequently 'rained down' and the village womenfolk gathered up the silk 'chutes to make "cami-knicks"! But I had a silk dress!' (By kind courtesy of Penny Hodgson)

As a boy of seven, I had a jerkin made of parachute 'silk' (actually fine linen). I went picking whin berries in the mountains (near Swansea, Wales) and got sunburnt through the fabric. [It was] zipped up at the neck, short sleeves, collar, coffee colour. (John Williams)

The inevitable parachute came our way – we had a young German airman bail out in the farm next to us. His chute was caught in a tree with him attached. My mother went to free him but he thought she was going to kill him with her scissors! His parachute made me a crinoline dress for a local dance show. It was dyed pink and the rope sections dyed a deeper colour and looked effective. The young pilot who baled out was so fair and had the bluest of eyes. If I'd been older I'd have fallen for him! I'd never seen anyone so blonde. (Gill Garratt)

At one stage father got hold of half a silk parachute – it made us all underwear for ages. The fashion then was for French knickers so we were really up to date! (Audrey Pevy)

1947 An Orange Nylon Parachute produced a Dressing Gown embroidered on the back with a Chinese Dragon in black. (Sheila Fowles)

Parachute silk was also used and people did dye it – either using strong coffee or watered down redcurrants, my Granny even used Stephen's dark blue ink! (Muriel Pushman)

My mother, or was it my grandmother, got part of a parachute. All the material was used to make clothes and the nylon cord for stitching and darning. This nylon cord lasted for ages, drawing out threads from the end. (Valerie Crooks)

'When I was seventeen in 1948, three years after the cessation of hostilities, I wore a real silk parachute blouse, with lace on it, and a skirt from my father's trousers, when I sang "Rejoice Greatly" from Handel's Messiah as a solo in the Christmas concert at school.' (By kind courtesy of Frances Wilson)

[I remember] obtaining (by hook or by crook?) a portion of a lovely black parachute. Beautiful silk which I fashioned into a 'house coat' using a friend's machine and hand embroidering the back and front with smocking! Any spare bits were fashioned into knickers!! Then I received a part cotton parachute in orange colour which I managed to make into pyjamas – very functional but not exotic. … no chance of tempting the forces. (Mary Escofet)

The best thing I made from a panel of bright yellow cotton parachute material was a youth hostel sheet sleeping bag….made to a prescribed pattern incorporating a pillowcase. It did not matter that mine tapered at the foot end…. I also made a blouse from the same material, which was not a success … too easily creased and too thin. (Bettina Cohen)

When I was confirmed onto the C of E at age fourteen-fifteen [in] 1950–51, my confirmation dress was made of white (cream) parachute silk, made by my mother. (Betty M. Whenray)

After the war ended my father purchased some panels of parachute silk which he thught we could make into petticoats or nighties. The material was very fine, but there were so many panels and seams that we did not have much success with *that*. (Gloria Barker)

How many women and children were kept clothed and in good morale using parachute 'silk' through the years of rationing? How many airmen were saved from death by their carefully stitched, folded and packed parachute? How many men and women died during their descent into enemy-occupied territory, or were subsequently captured, tortured or imprisoned? What were the feelings of the starving civilians of Europe, the Middle East and South Pacific when boxes of food were dropped from the sky by parachute upon their liberation? The use of the parachutes which were stitched during the Second World War was always intensely personal, often dramatic, and completely essential for the achievement of victory.

Parachute inspection, repair and repacking. (Courtesy of the Imperial War Museum, London CH 10451)

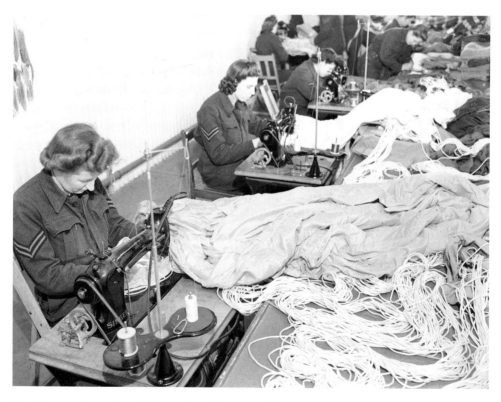

Repairing parachutes for a glider squadron. (Courtesy of the Imperial War Museum, London CH 9506)

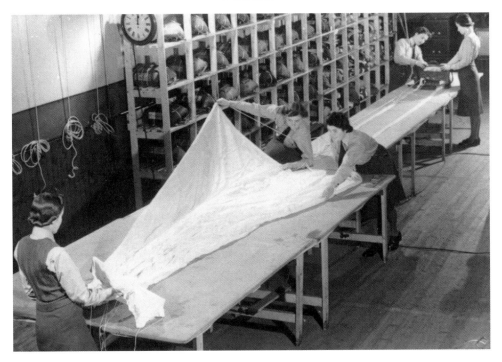

Folding parachutes was a highly skilled task. (Courtesy of the Imperial War Museum, London CH 5801)

Parachute packing. (Courtesy of the Imperial War Museum, London CH 13257)

fourteen

Army

There was a unique aroma of cordite that lingered over the battlefield after every explosion and every round fired. Its sickly sweet fumes seemed to hang at ground level, combining with the smell of dead bodies and phosphorus. Some men found the cocktail of odours was so revolting that they felt constantly sick. In addition to these were the smells of dead, and often rotting farm animals, the odour of dried sweat on unwashed uniforms and bodies, and the stench of unburied human faeces.[1]

The smell of death was totally in the air – like going into a morgue. But you got used to that smell. It got into your clothes and it was there continuously, so you didn't notice it in the end.[2]

The success of a wartime operation depends upon the infantry – each individual man in his soldier's uniform engaged with the enemy in a battle for the occupation of a site or a few more yards of territory. The complex organisation of the British Army during the Second World War existed to empower its divisions at the Front Line. Of these, just one in ten men were called upon to fight, kill, and take prisoners:[3] the remainder worked in their support and were ready to move into newly cleared territory.

From April 1939, all able-bodied twenty-year-old men were required to enlist in one of the British Armed Forces, and this was soon extended to men between the ages of eighteen and forty-one. Sergeant-Majors determinedly changing the raw recruits into soldiers and trying to instill the traditional Army standard of 'spit and polish': brass and leather had to be rubbed to a shine, trouser creases pressed to a knife-edge. As soon as they put on their Army uniforms, civilians were suddenly turned into targets for the enemy and it took enormous mental adjustment for men at the Front Line to understand that they should see the 'Teds' of the *Heer*, or German Army, as similarly uniformed targets. Many found that only comradeship, letters from home and a sense of humour would carry them through the horrors of what they saw and what they had to do and endure.

Musicians, librarians, gardeners, school-teachers, burglars, masons and carpenters – all had to conform to a life in uniform. Each man was identified by two numbered discs worn around his neck – the red disc to be detached at death, and with a typically ironic sense of humour, upon embarking on the stormy Channel crossing of D-Day, they were heard to 'baa' like sheep.[4] These were men who had probably never been outside Britain, maybe never left their home town, and in their heavy, foot-blistering Army boots, they would slog and fight their way across Europe, North Africa, the Middle East and Far East.

By 1945, there were some 3 million men and women in the British Army.[5] They had been joined by 4.4 million men and women from Canada, Australia, New Zealand, Belgium, Holland, Spain, Norway, Ireland, Yugoslavia, Romania, Hungary, Italy, South Africa, France, Poland, Czechoslovakia, Greece, Cyprus, Rhodesia, the Sudan; the legendary Ghurkas of Nepal; the Jewish Brigade; a volunteer army of 2.5 million from India; and the American Army.[6]

New recruits appearing as a cohesive force of soldiers, their civilian lives having to be abandoned as they donned their Army uniforms. (Courtesy of the Imperial War Museum, London F 3692)

Stitchers made uniforms for the 5 million members of the three British Services[7] from the 540 million yards of fabric obtained under a Government contract which had been placed as soon as war seemed imminent with textile factories having to rapidly adapt their machinery to produce the heavy-duty cloth.[8] The British Army uniform, which included eighty items of kit, cost around £20;[9] and when war was declared on 3 September 1939, around 420,000 uniforms were still urgently needed,[10] and many new recruits had to be issued with the First World War khaki service dress.[11] A light-weight denim summer Army battledress, or working dress, was also put into production.[12]

The 1937-pattern battledress in tough dull green-brown khaki wool serge was quick to produce and economical on fabric, but was universally disliked – for despite men's best efforts they felt that not only did they look untidy, but also pregnant and hunch-backed and the short jacket gathered into a waistband with integral belt rode up annoyingly when the wearer bent over.[13] Five front jacket buttons were concealed in a 'fly' front and the two box-pleated breast pockets were also fastened by concealed buttons; buttons also held the epaulettes to the shoulder. The collar fastened by two hooks and eyes which men in the lower ranks were obliged to keep closed, resulting in necks being chafed raw by the scratchy fabric and the straight-cut trousers also gave great discomfort at the crotch, especially in hot weather. However, it was possible to alleviate this by wearing a pair of pyjama trousers underneath and the design *did* allow ease of movement when hanging loose on tall, thin men or stretched by shorter, stouter men. The trouser left-hand hip-pocket was designed to hold a map and there was also a hip-pocket on the right and four loops at the waist to hold a webbing belt when the jacket was not being worn.[14] One item of the uniform which *was* appreciated was the double-breasted mid-calf length khaki greatcoat which provided welcome warmth in cold conditions. Men of the Scot's Divisions were issued with tartan trews, or kilts – despite the vulnerability of bare legs – and these 'Jocks' were accepted as the toughest soldiers in the Army.

Officers' uniform allowed considerably more personal expression: it could be standard-issue or bespoke tailored and 225 coupons were allowed for its purchase, plus a further eighty-eight coupons annually to cover maintenance plus extra coupons for tropical uniform.[15] Officers could also purchase a better-quality greatcoat from the Army, a light-weight khaki raincoat, or even wear a civilian beige 'British Warm' overcoat.[16] They were allowed to leave their jacket open at the neck to reveal the khaki-coloured shirt, collar and tie,[17] and it was also possible to alter the collar to hide the sand-coloured lining, or even replace the buttons with a zip and as

General Bernard Law Montgomery (third from left, front row) with Army officers. (Courtesy of the Imperial War Museum, London B 15688)

the Army struggled to drive out the Nazi occupiers from France after the Normandy landing, officers wore whatever served the purpose, including riding boots and breeches. However, it was an advantage for an officer to dress inconspicuously, so as not to attract the attention of enemy snipers, and when some even removed their badges and pips or stripes of rank, puzzled Germans were given the impression that no one was in charge.[18]

Soldiers' essential kit was carried in 'Large' and 'Small' packs, and personal items were kept safe in a roll-type bag. They also carried a 'Housewife' or 'Hussif' in order to repair the uniform or darn their socks – as they had been trained. The 'Hussif' consisted of a pouch or folded and tied fabric case containing darning wool and darning needles, buttons, press-studs, linen thread in khaki and black plus the appropriate needles.[19]

These Army uniforms could be the only clothes that many men would wear for the next six years and by March 1942, when they began to show wear and tear, ten coupons were allowed annually to renew both uniform and underwear. It was also possible to obtain coupon-free handkerchiefs by presenting a chit signed by a commanding officer.[20]

The first campaign for the British Army was to stem the movement of Nazi forces westward from Poland, and the British Expeditionary Force (BEF) which arrived at camps along the Franco-Belgian border in the bitterly cold winter of 1939–40 were issued with white snow suits for both camouflage and warmth (later to be eagerly transformed by the stitchers of Britain into civilian clothing). Unfortunately, it was assumed that the fighting would take place along fixed lines, as in the First World War, and Commanding Officers were not at all prepared for the new *Blitzkreig* strategy of the Germans which used fast-moving fighter-planes, bombers and tanks. By May 1940, the BEF, French, and Polish troops, and over 1,000 female nurses[21] had been driven back onto the beaches of Dunkirk in France, where 368,226[22] were rescued, from 26 May to 4 June 1940, by the Royal Navy, including ships commanded by the Royal Navy Volunteer Reserve and hundreds of civilian boat-owners in sea-going craft of over 30ft in length.

Upon their arrival in Britain, the shocked and exhausted soldiers were swiftly taken to hospitals where nurses were forced to cut away their tattered uniforms – if the men still possessed one – for many had abandoned their soaked and heavy clothing to swim out to the rescue boats and then accepted whatever they were offered, even 'a woman's blouse and a Belgian flag'.[23] During their re-cuperation, soldiers were issued with 'Hospital Blues': a 'badly tailored' jacket and trousers in royal blue serge, with a white shirt and red tie.

Royal Engineers at Portsmouth waiting for a landing craft to take them to Normandy following the D-Day invasion. (By kind courtesy of *The News*, Portsmouth 2945)

Realising that they had failed in their objective, the returning men were anxious that the sight of their uniforms would be met with scorn; however, Britain was overjoyed to have them safely back and understood, if only partially, the tremendous hardships which they had suffered. Sensing victory, Adolph Hitler began to assemble an invasion fleet and ordered the German *Luftwaffe* to destroy Britain's only defence, its Air Force. It seemed that this was Britain's 'darkest hour', especially as all the equipment of the BEF had been abandoned on the French beaches.

In April 1941, when Axis forces attempted to wrest control of the Suez Canal from Britain in order to gain control of supplies of oil from Persia, soldiers who were sent to fight in the Western Desert had to learn to endure lips and skin blistered by sun and blowing sand, the infamous desert flea, and thirst. Their desert uniform included a greatcoat for the freezing nights, plus regulation tropical dress – 'Khaki Drill' (KD), which required starching and ironing. However, when the fighting was prolonged, attention to uniform came second in priority to gaining ascendancy over the enemy and uniform regulations were waived. Officers adopted the legendary Eighth Army 'uniform' of corduroy trousers, suede 'chukka' boots and silk scarves[24] and lower ranks took to mixing civilian clothing with their battledress and tropical drill; but upon the arrival of Field Marshal Montgomery in August 1942, men resumed their regulation clothing.

By 6 June 1944, the Allies were ready to launch an invasion on Hitler's 'Fortress Europe' and once more enter France, as they had left, by the sea. Under the Supreme Command, of US General Eisenhower, 150,000 men and women were landed on the beaches of Normandy despite high seas and raging stormy weather in the Channel. It seemed that victory was, at last, in sight and that the war was all but over, but for the men of the 21st Army it was just the beginning of the long, hard, dangerous slog through France, Holland and Belgium, into the very heart of the Third Reich itself.

The French summer was plagued with biting insects which had visited the decaying corpses of both humans and farm animals, and dysentery was rife. The almost unbearable itching of the lice which hid in uniforms could sometimes be remedied by running the flame of a candle or match along the seams. Again, Commanding Officers were lenient as regards dress, understanding that personal 'adaptations' were an aid to getting the job done: 'The psychological advantages of going into battle with your tunic collar turned up and one hand in your pocket, when possible, cannot be overemphasised.' These shared transgressions also strengthened the bonds of comradeship which made men determined not to let each other down, and were

This battered and mended flag was given by a six-year-old girl to the Grenadier Guards whose tank was parked for a while outside her home in Portsmouth, preparatory to the D-Day invasion. It was flown on the tank as it battled all the way across mainland Europe and, in May 1945, into Germany itself. (Courtesy of the D-Day Museum, Portsmouth PMRS 2005/708)

each individual's statement that life was not all about war. Men of the Artillery Divisions fought on in swimming trunks and sunglasses and, in the intense heat inside the armoured tanks, soldiers of the Royal Tank Regiments stripped down to underpants or shorts beneath their denim overalls.[25] Marching regiments picked roses from the hedgerows to tuck into caps and berets, or shaded themselves under 'liberated' umbrellas.

A 'craze' started for scarves[26] made from such fabrics as strips of camouflage face veil, 'liberated' tablecloths and women's head-scarves, for the exhausted men were sick of the horror and ear-splitting noise of explosions, they were hungry for colour, and the most desirable, spirit-lifting scarves were those strips torn from brightly coloured discarded parachutes, both British and German. A scarf could also ease the chafing uniform neck, be worn as a mask against dust and smoke or decorate the dug-outs which were made when the advance halted. Even small pieces of stitched fabric such as a pink silk cushion from a brothel could help to keep a man going despite his trauma and exhaustion.[27]

The British and American Armies' liberation of the European cities saw scenes of joyful celebration and the soldiers deservedly received the welcome of heroes. However, their success led to yet another phase of the British soldier's relationship with his uniform: it had to be restored by 'spit and polish' to top condition in order to pass inspection by the Military Police. But even after careful attention it still did not appeal to the celebrating women of Europe when compared to that of the American Army with its collared shirt and tie, well-cut trousers and skirted jacket. So, with determined disregard for Army regulations, soldiers obtained shirts and ties for *themselves* – if only one, to be shared amongst a group. Collared shirts were created out of regulation issue by soldiers with tailoring skills, and civilian tailors made the unflattering trousers actually fit. Going for the ultimate effect, some managed to acquire the shirts and ties of British Army officers, or even those of the 'opposition'. This became such a common, unstoppable practice that the Army was eventually finally forced to change its regulations.[28]

In this photograph it appears that the 'Auk', or General Sir Claude Auchinlek (centre), is wearing the unpopular KD shorts, known by the men as 'Bombay Bloomers', with deep turn-ups which could be unbuttoned and let down to the ankles, where they were secured by threaded tapes.¹ (Courtesy of the Imperial War Museum, London AUS 745)

Stitched flags were of great importance for Army organisation across the world for the direction of troops and vehicles, and transmission of messages by Morse. Rank and signal flags were flown from the wireless aerials of vehicles of armoured units. (Photograph of the Western Desert Signalling Squadron courtesy of the Imperial War Museum, London E 173)

Regulations were also flouted by men of the 1st Airborne Division when they had to swim across the Rhine to safety in Holland after the disastrous 'Operation Market Garden', for stripping off their uniforms, they reached the other shore naked and quickly had to find what garments they could; many marched on in spare items of comrades' uniforms or scrounged civilian clothing, including women's dresses and coats.[29]

The 21st Army Group which battled with the Nazis in the French Ardennes also battled with the intense cold of the 1944–45 winter. Living in freezing dug-outs, inadequately fed and equipped, suffering from coughs and colds, frostbite and trench foot, they raided local homes for any items which would give warmth, even rugs, blankets or curtains and stitched clothes from the skins of the animals which they had killed for food. While the Army greatcoat provided warmth at night, the collar and cuffs could be unfolded over the face and hands and the short cape gave extra warmth to the shoulders, it was dangerous to wear in action for it impeded movement. Many men tried to acquire two, but when some cut theirs to jacket length, their legs were left exposed to the bitter night cold. Captured German clothing was also gratefully used, which had been destined for the Eastern Front: tiger-striped parkas, sheepskin jackets, fur hats and coats. Eventually, clothing arrived from 'Blighty': fur-lined RAF boots, duffel coats, rabbit-fur waistcoats, seaboot socks, Airborne smocks and windproof smocks, and tank crews' warm, wool-lined, waterproof oversuits.[30]

The 21st Army had come a long way, but the most bitter battles of the war were still yet to be fought – within Germany – in the last weeks of the war; some with the ferocious eleven-to twelve-year-old boys of the *Hitler Jugend*, or Hitler Youth, and supporting troops had to be brought up to the Front Line, including tailors, cooks, clerks and Scots' bagpipers. When victory was finally achieved, the 21st Army Group was once more required to look its best. Only the Guards had maintained parade-ground standards throughout the campaign,[31] but obvious 'adaptations' were common and these had to be changed.

No one had to tell us when the war ended – it was 'on parade', all brasses polished, marching her, there and everywhere – a very strict dress code enforced! (Harry Free of the 43rd Reconnaissance Regiment.)[32]

However, men who had always worn their uniforms reluctantly anyway soon tired of blanco-ing webbing, Brasso-ing buttons and polishing boots to a mirror shine – they just wanted to

Chindit. (Courtesy of the Imperial War Museum, London SA 7907)

The 'Full Jungle Head-dress'. (Courtesy of the
Imperial War Museum, London IND 2073)

get back to Britain and be civilians again, so in preparation for their appearance at home, some
asked tailors to make their uniforms more flattering by reducing fullness in the battledress
blouse and adding flare to the trousers by sewing in an extra triangle of khaki.[33]

The war may have ended in Europe, but the men of the 14th Army (the 'Forgotten Army')
still fought on in the humid, enervating jungles of Japanese-occupied Burma. For them, the
largest army of the war with nearly 1 million troops from Britain, West and East Africa, China
and India, the prospect of a return to civilian life was still three months away. Yet they took
inspiration from the guerrilla warfare of Charles Orde Wingate's company of 'Chindits', who
had proved that the seemingly invincible Japanese could be beaten.

Stitch provided the special clothing which was needed by men who were fighting wet-
through by jungle rains in the soft black mud and dense prickly bamboo thickets which cut
clothes – and skin – to shreds while attacked by ever-present stinging red ants, leeches, tics and
spiders the size of a hand. The 'Full Jungle Head-dress', which accompanied the 1942-issue
'Jungle Green', consisted of bush jacket, long- and short-sleeved shirts, long and short trousers,
all stitched from a green cellular material[34] that could withstand gnawing by rats and protect the
wearer from tropical disease-carrying mosquitoes.[35]

6 August 1945
The American bomber *Enola Gay* drops a 4 tonne atomic bomb onto the Japanese city
of Hiroshima, creating a ground temperature of 9,000 degrees Fahrenheit (5,000 degrees
Centigrade).

9 August 1945
The American bomber *Bockscar* drops an atomic bomb onto the Japanese city of Nagasaki.

15 August 1945 – 2 September 1945
Japan reluctantly surrenders. Japan signs a surrender document.

The war is over. The long days, weeks, months and years in Army uniform were ended.

An inscription carved into the memorial stone for the British 2nd Division at Kohima reads:
'When you go home, tell them of us, and say: For your tomorrow, we gave our today.'

fifteen

Home Guard

The uniform of the Home Guard was perhaps the most treasured and cherished of the war. Its stitched garments transformed men who thought they were no longer of use to the nation into members of a highly valued and potentially formidable fighting force. Was its importance to the wearer recognised by the British Government when the Home Guard were allowed to keep their uniform once the war was over despite the extreme national shortages of materials? The uniform of the Home Guard also hid one of the nation's greatest secrets.

In the spring of 1940, Hitler was sweeping easily across Europe and by mid-July it was known that a Nazi invasion of Britain was planned for mid-August. Paranoia swept Britain that, as in Norway, Holland and Belgium, there would be an initial invasion of German para-troops and rumours abounded that Nazis would at any moment be dropped from the skies disguised as nuns, monks, Red Cross nurses or dressed as women in skirts and blouses.[1]

Everything possible had to be done to hinder the enemy should they reach British soil by sea or air. Beaches on the south coast were mined and covered in barbed-wire; parked cars were disabled by the removal of rotor arms; old cars and agricultural machinery were brought out to obstruct possible landing areas for enemy aircraft; sign-posts were removed; even the destinations on trains and buses were removed. Church bells were kept silent, ready to be rung as an alarm,[2] and in June 1940 a booklet of instructions was given out to every household in Britain named *If the Invader Comes*, which demanded 'Think before you act. But always think of your country before you think of yourself.' A last-ditch defence force was required within Britain itself.

On 14 May, the Minister for War, Anthony Eden, sent out a call over the radio for men between the ages of seventeen and sixty-five who were not eligible for active service to be part of a new organisation – the Local Defence Volunteers or 'Parashots' as they were known, since their primary function was to deal with any Nazi paratroops.[3] Then, if the worst should come to the worst, they would defend the civilian population from Nazi invasion while the Army tussled with invading German tanks. Before the radio programme had ended, eager men were queuing to register at Police Stations and by the end of June 1940 they were said to number 1.5 million.[4] All over the country platoons were formed, including those of Buckingham Palace, Eton College, cricket clubs, factories, local hunts and Americans in London.[5]

Just twelve days after the broadcast the situation worsened: the British Expeditionary Force and the French Army had to be rescued by sea from the beaches of Dunkirk after being forced to abandon all their equipment on the beaches. Hitler now controlled France and was in a position to establish army, air and naval bases uncomfortably close to British shores. Britain's Army was demoralised, exhausted, barely equipped and stripped of its only ally, the powerful French Army. In such a dire situation, the Home Guard truly became an important new mili-tary defence force within the nation.

Until uniforms could be provided, the men – for women were not welcome – were only distinguished by a brassard, an 'LDV' stencilled armband,[6] and their only weapons were such as

Local Defence Volunteers. (Courtesy of the Kent Messenger Group PD 800660)

they could find for themselves – including axes, knives, bill-hooks, game-shooting guns[7] and even the boarding pikes taken from Nelson's *Victory*.[8] Unfortunately, the British public did not take them seriously, with their armbands and bread-knives, and they were nicknamed 'Dad's Army', despite the fact that a large number of members were energetically youthful. It was difficult to accept that men who had been classed as not suitable for Service were now in charge of the defence of the nation.

Three nights a week,[9] old and young, men of all social classes, educations and occupations learned how to defend their neighbourhoods; but unfortunately their efforts were undisciplined, without proper guidance and dangerous – for an 'LDV' volunteer was four times more likely to die in training than a regular soldier. Typically, the cartoonist Giles 'once arranged war games in North London causing absolute bedlam. Smoke bombs polluted washing for a square mile in Edgeware'[10] and public displays were staged in which the men threw potato 'hand grenades' and screamed aggressively. In June 1941, the War Office issued truncheons, and in July they put in an order for more 'weapons' – 250,000 knife blades welded to long metal tubes.[11]

On 23 July the Prime Minister, Winston Churchill, insisted that they should be re-named the 'Home Guard' and over a million new stencilled armbands were stitched, displaying the letters 'HG'. Then, in December 1941, upon Churchill's further demand that 'every man must have a weapon of some kind, be it only a mace or pike', home-made weapons were devised such as the 'Molotov Cocktail', the 'Woolworth bomb' and the 'sticky bomb', or the 8,000 'Northover Projectors' which used toy-pistol caps to fire grenades.[12]

Britain's Home Guard received more respect when, in August 1940, a system of ranking was introduced and units were allied to their county's Army regiments so that regular troops could be released from anti-invasion duties[13] and, when a uniform battledress of khaki serge was finally issued via the Territorial Army Association,[14] the men of the Home Guard began to feel more like *real* soldiers. It included an official-looking whistle and notebook and 'big boots which made a satisfyingly important sound when "patrolling" the quiet streets',[15] and could unfortunately be too much of a boost to the ego, for the Home Guard threw itself into its duties rather too enthusiastically when it came to checking Identity Cards and setting up road blocks; and on the evening of 7 September, by mistake, they rang the church bells of southern England as a warning of enemy invasion. Following this, they were instructed only to ring a warning after seeing no fewer than twenty-five genuine German paratroops descending.[16]

However, behind the scenes, using the Home Guard as a cover, a much more professional, top-secret resistance organisation was being established by Major Colin McVean Gubbins, and later, Colonel C.R. Major, the existence of which was never discovered by German Intelligence.[17] Three 'Auxiliary Units' were trained, ready to go into hiding in perfectly con-cealed and well-equipped dugouts[18] as soon as a Nazi force arrived, to carry out as much nocturnal sabotage as possible until they were caught;[19] which, they were warned, could be in just hours or days. They were men who knew every detail of their area in daylight and dark-ness – farmers and farm labourers, gamekeepers and ghillies, poachers and parsons, doctors and miners, council officials and publicans.[20]

These 'Auxiliary Unit' Patrol Leaders took the uniform of Home Guard Sergeants and Group Leaders appeared as Home Guard Captains,[21] their battledress blouse being subtly altered to incorporate much larger inner pockets in which to carry quantities of the new 'plastic' explosives activated by 'time pencils' with which they were issued even before the Commandos.[22] Their names did not appear on the Home Guard lists – in fact, their names were never recorded at all, and having no valid military uniform to protect them under the Geneva Conventions, they accepted that they would be shot if captured.

The regular Home Guard was also increasing in proficiency, for, witnessing the haphazard efforts of the regular Home Guard training, Major Tom Winteringham, an expert in guerilla warfare, set up a training programme which was later adopted by the Government and, after this, a volunteer could possess such skills as garotting with cheese-cutter,[23] bringing down a German Stuka with a .303 rifle – when the deafening, screaming noise of this dive-bomber was known to make men freeze with terror – or destroying a German *panzer* tank with a hand grenade or crowbar. A unit of armed Home Guard was posted to guard the entrance to the offices of the War Cabinet[24] and men of the Home Guard faithfully patrolled the south coast

The Home Guard.
(Courtesy of Kent
Messenger Group
PD 800575)

and rivers, sometimes using bicycles, horses and roller skates. Using their initiative, they trained dogs to disarm enemy paratroopers and captured Hitler's deputy, Herman Hess, when he flew single-handed to Scotland in 1941.[25] They were also ready to stretch cloth screens across streets to confuse and slow down the enemy, or scatter upturned soup-plates in the road to appear as anti-tank mines.[26]

Fortunately, by July 1940, some 200,000 .300 rifles had finally arrived by naval convoy from America,[27] because, on 7 September 1940 the Home Guard was placed on Invasion Red Alert, and it was their most testing moment: waiting through the night for the enemy to arrive at any moment; wondering if they would be able to kill; knowing that there could be a flood of 100,000 Nazi soldiers.[28] As dawn broke peacefully there was a deep sense of relief.

Then, much to their frustration, Hitler decided to turn his attention to the riches of Russia and invasion was no longer a threat.

However, the Home Guard had become such a valuable military resource that conscription was introduced in 1942 and Home Guard troops were trained in Civil Defence to join the men and women of the Auxiliary Territorial Service in the operation of 'ack-ack' (anti-aircraft) batteries[29] for which aircraft recognition and the use of the rifle were essential. Many instructors were members of the WAAF[30] – although very few women were actually allowed to join the Home Guard and only after April 1943[31] when they acted merely as unarmed Women's Home Guard Auxiliaries, their 'uniform' being just a Home Guard Auxiliary metal badge and an 'HG' armband.[32]

Then, when in June 1944 the Nazis unleashed their deadly V-1 flying bombs against Britain, the Home Guard were among the first to be informed, in order that they might take over from Anti-Aircraft Command regiments in the north of England which were urgently needed for round-the-clock defence at the 1,000 anti-aircraft gun emplacements along the south coast.[33] But this was to be the Home Guard's final role, for in September 1944 the organisation was stood down,[34] much to the sorrow of many of its members, although they *were* allowed to keep their uniforms.

On 2 December 1944, Home Guard contingents from across Britain paraded before the King and Queen in a three-mile-long procession through London, with Princesses Elizabeth and Margaret taking the farewell salute and it was a moving occasion, for the Home Guard had proved itself to be a valued and respected body of men – and just a few women – who had not hesitated to stand against the formidable might of Hitler's Germany, even with pitchforks and breadknives.

"Have you gone completely nuts? - standing there mumbling 'so you're not leaving us after all, Old Pal'"

NEB cartoon first published in the *Daily Mail*, 7 October 1944. (Courtesy of Solo Syndication, London)

sixteen

JWO

'I see the damage done by the enemy attacks,
but I also see, side by side with the devastation and amid the ruins,
quiet and confident, bright and smiling eyes.
I see the spirit of an unconquerable people.'
Winston Churchill, 12 April 1941

The Joint War Organisation (JWO) had been formed in the First World War from the volunteers of the British Red Cross and Order of St John. In the chaos and destruction of the Second World War, their stitched uniforms enabled these men and women to stand out as beacons of something which seemed to be threatened: human care for the health and well-being of others, for both the British Red Cross uniform and that of the Order of St John were protected under the Geneva Conventions as those of Voluntary Aid Societies[1] – in these uniforms, they could render humanitarian aid anywhere in the world.

The work of the JWO was breathtaking in its scope – administering medical care, supplying food, clothing, smiles, healing for the mind in letters and parcels from home and stimulating activities for those incarcerated by the enemy – even Christmas presents. Their uniforms could be seen in Red Cross hospital ships or planes, and in war zones, accompanying the advance of Allied troops in their 'White Angel' trucks.[2]

Volunteers had first to complete their training in First Aid and Home Nursing through either the Red Cross or Order of St John, including sixty hours of hospital experience in the stressful conditions of wartime wards where an attitude of fortitude, cheerfulness and compassion was essential and they could also attend courses in other subjects such as 'Infant and Child Welfare' or 'First Aid in Chemical Warfare'.

I was working at the hospital (Derby Royal Infirmary) and I was also working at the Air Raid Wardens Post … they were so short of people, you see. We did a lot of things we would not be allowed to do now, because there was nobody else to do it. I was even left in charge of the ward sometimes. There were very few proper nurses, because they were out in the forces. (Margaret Henry)[3] (Courtesy of British Red Cross Museum and Archives)

This was in addition to going to work and so it meant night duty. When not on call we slept fully clothed on bunk beds in a big shelter. (Betty Brampton aged eighteen) (Courtesy of Museum of St John and St John Ambulance)[4]

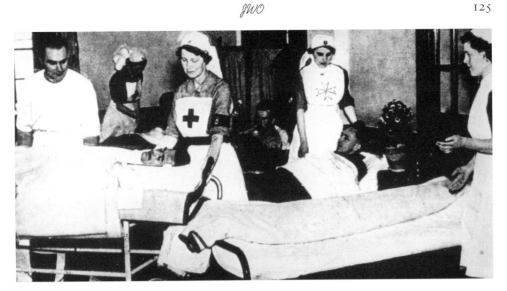

A nurse's clothing transformed her from an ordinary volunteer into a 'symbolic being' who was often thought of as an 'angel'.[1] The process of stitch allowed the men and women of the Joint War Organisation (JWO) to be seen as standing apart from the war and representing an unbroken care of human beings for one another. (Courtesy of the British Red Cross Museum and Archives 1105)

JWO volunteers iding the Civil Defence. (Courtesy of the British Red Cross Museum and Archives RC 384)

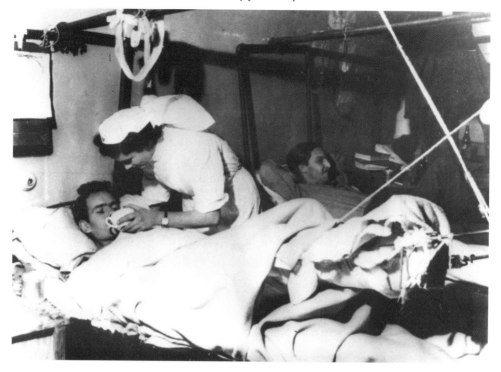

A service hospital in Italy.
(Courtesy of the British Red
Cross Museum and Archives
IN123)

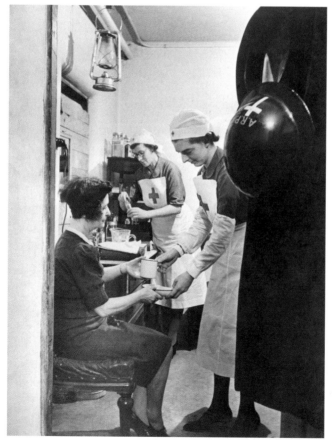

First Aid Post staffed by JWO
volunteers. (Courtesy of
the Imperial War Museum,
London D 1652)

We would work all day and then go fire watching in the evening. I mean you never had your clothes off hardly, and if you were at home you didn't want to take them off in case there was an air raid and you had to go down to the shelters. (Daisy Trzaskowski) (Courtesy of British Red Cross Museum and Archives)[5]

Such was the tremendous strain on these first aiders that a Country Hospitality Scheme was started where they could take a weekend off to recover in a more peaceful environment.

The training also allowed one to join the Voluntary Aid Detachment (VAD) to supplement the medical services of the Armed Forces at home and overseas and by 1945, about 15,000 VADs had served in Britain or travelled with troops to serve at the Front Line[6] as Welfare Workers or in Mobile Units.

By June 1940, over 90,000 JWO volunteers were involved in aiding the Civil Defence,[7] including caring for 'bombees', or victims of enemy bombing raids, who were taken to JWO-staffed First Aid Posts – maybe adapted single-decker corporation buses,[8] which were manned both day and night.[9] The JWO also provided hospitals and the bombees' Rest Centres with medical supplies, food, bedding, soap and towels, hot water bottles, hospital clothing and bandages.[10]

An essential part of their work was the maintenance of their uniform: 'Whatever happened, a nurse's uniform had to be neat and tidy at all times!'[11] for a fresh, clean, tidy uniform could inspire immediate trust and reassurance. In times of crisis the black and white uniforms of the

Order of St John nurse. (Courtesy of the Museum of St John and St John Ambulance)

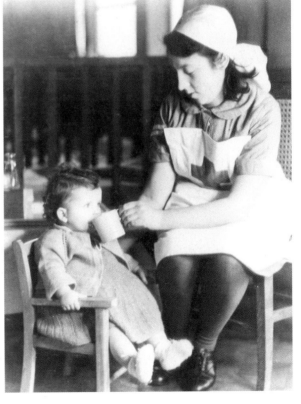

A JWO Day Nursery. (Courtesy of the British Red Cross Museum and Archives IN290)

Dockland air-raid shelter. (Courtesy of the British Red Cross Museum and Archives)

The Central Hospital Supply Service (CHSS) at work making hospital dressings. (Courtesy of the British Red Cross Museum and Archives IN1106)

Order of St John were seen as a rock of support, with the ancient Cross of St John, or Maltese Cross, stitched onto white aprons and armbands, or painted onto their helmets and vehicles. St John volunteers were assigned to an ambulance and driver, and with members of the British Red Cross they would drive nearly 9 million miles to transport nearly 1 million injured soldiers in support of the British Army. Within Britain they travelled more than 5 million miles to move more than 600,000 patients.[12]

The emblem of the Red Cross – a red cross upon a white ground – the symbol of an organisation of aid which reaches across all nations and religions, is a tribute to the flag of

Preston Hall Hospital near Aylesford, Kent, June 1940. (Courtesy of Kent Messenger Group PD 800578)

Nurses and servicemen at Zachery Merton convalescent home. (Courtesy of the British Red Cross Museum and Archives IN715)

Switzerland – a white cross upon a red ground – where the concept first originated and where the conference was hosted in which the Geneva Convention was established in 1864 to lay down humanitarian principles in warfare acceptable to all nations.[13] The red, white and blue stitched fabrics of the Red Cross uniform powerfully evoke a sense of calm, purity and impersonal medical aid, with the splash of red implying that the wearer could deal with injury; the enveloping deep-blue cloak and red lining giving a sense of the organisation's strength and seriousness of purpose.

Just to join the JWO required the commitment of both clothing coupons and money, for volunteers had to provide their own uniforms.[14] The female JWO uniform consisted of: three dresses (Red Cross blue; St John grey; Officers black and white stripe) twelve aprons, three belts, six collars, three pairs of cuffs, four caps, two pairs of black shoes, six pairs of stockings; and for outdoors: a greatcoat, hat, gloves, jacket, skirt, blouses, tie, belt, cardigan, and waterproof, plus a suitcase and towels. All of this was a considerable expense, although one could use a 'Uniform Permit' to apply for a grant, and the possession of a Certificate of Service meant that no clothing coupons would be required.

1942   **The Red Cross**

Uniform by
GARROULD

In our **READY TO WEAR SERVICE** will be found **CORRECT UNIFORM** comprising :—
41 STOCK SIZES IN GREATCOATS
19 STOCK SIZES IN DRESSES
72 STOCK SIZES IN APRONS
made from good quality materials with high grade workmanship which ensures smartness and hard wear, guaranteed to fit 90 per cent. of our clients.

B.R.C. REGULATION APRONS

Hand cut from linen-finished apron cloths. Depth of Bibs : 10½, 11, 11½ in.
Lgth. of Skirts : 26, 28, 30, 32 in.
Waists : 26, 28, 30, 32 in. .... 5/3 & 6/3
Without cross 6/-
Depth of Bibs : 11, 11½, 12 in.
Lgth. of Skirts : 28, 30, 32 in.
Waist : 34 in. .... 5/6 & 6/6
Without cross 6/3
Waist 37 in. .... 6/3 & 7/3
Without cros 7/-

B.R.C. REGULATION DRESSES

Hand cut and made from fast dye and fully Sanforized-Shrunk materials.
Commandant, Women's sizes 25/6
Commandant, O.S. 27/9
Lady Superintendent and Trained Nurse Women's sizes 27/6
Quartermaster and Members, Women's sizes ... 16/11
Quartermasters and Members, O.S. 18/11
Quartermasters and Members, X.O.S. 21/-
Stock sizes :
Bust : 32, 32, 34, 34, 34, 36, 36, 38, 40*, 40* in.
Lgth : 44, 46, 44, 46, 48, 46, 48, 48, 48*, 50* in.
* 1/- extra.
O.S.—   X.O.S.—
Bust : 42 in.   44, 46 in.
Lgth : 48 in.   48, 48 in.
Prices of made to measure garments sent on request.

B.R.C. CAPS

Members, 28 x 19 in. 2/8
Without cross 2/6
Storm Cap .... 15/3 including Badge

B.R.C. REGULATION CAPE

Made in good quality Navy Serge, lined with " A " quality all wool red flannel 45/-

B.R.C. REGULATION COAT

Cut and tailored from all wool fully shrunk and shower-proofed materials.
                              O.S.   X.O.S.
*Serge BX7   ... ... £4 17 6 ... £5 1 0 ... £5 7 6
*Serge BX9   ... ... £5 19 6 ... £6 5 0 ... £6 12 6
*Cheviot   ... ... £5 12 6 ... £5 16 6 ... £6 5 0
*Fine Summer Serge £5 7 6 ... £5 12 6 ... £5 19 6
* These materials kept in stock.
Women's Stock Sizes :
Bust : 32, 32, 33, 34, 34, 34, 34, 34, 35, 35, 35, 36 ins.
Lgth : 42, 44, 43, 40, 42, 43, 44, 45, 46, 43, 44, 45, 47, 42 ins.
Bust : 36, 36, 36, 36, 36, 37, 37, 38, 38, 38, 38, 38, 39, 39 ins.
Lgth : 44, 45, 46, 47, 48, 46, 47, 44, 45, 46, 47, 48, 47, 48 ins.
O.S.,   Bust : 40, 40, 40, 40, 42, 42, 42 ins.
        Lgth : 44, 46, 47, 48, 46, 47, 48 ins.
X.O.S., Bust :   44, 44, 44, 46, 46, 48 ins.
        Lgth :   46, 48, 50, 46, 48, 48 ins.

COUPON
EQUIVALENT
AND
PERMIT MUST
BE SENT
WITH
EVERY ORDER.

All prices in this advertisement are liable to advance without notice.

E. & R. GARROULD LTD., 150-162, Edgware Road, LONDON, W.2
457

(Courtesy of British Red Cross Museum and Archives)

The sight of these fresh, clean uniforms was especially needed in the badly lit, cramped, and often unhygienic Second World War air-raid shelters where the JWO organised toilets and set up medical centres similar to doctors' surgeries – an invaluable service as hospitals were tremendously busy – if patients could manage to get to them[15] and JWO volunteers also supervised nightly 'food trains' through the nights of the Blitz for people sheltering on the crowded platforms and escalators of London's Underground. At under-staffed clinics, where care was needed for expectant mothers and children, JWO nurses bravely dealt with the rising incidence of scabies and louse-borne infections. Volunteers were also prepared to staff isolation hospitals in the event of an epidemic.[16]

Children traumatised by bombing came to associate the JWO uniforms with the peaceful security of Day Nurseries where disruptive and disturbed behaviour was gradually calmed by friendly, understanding, cheerful activity, and mothers who were required to work night-shifts could safely leave their children from bed-time until morning.

> The kids used to come very often straight from the shelter … Half of them never saw their homes, they went from the shelter to the nursery and back to the shelters. … We had children from a few weeks old, till five.[17] (Anne Wisla, St John Ambulance, London)
>
> Ghost children who had no idea how to play have become real again and love their games.[18] (Sister in charge of a residential nursery)

In 1940, when injured servicemen and victims of enemy bombing filled hospitals to overflowing, the JWO set up auxiliary hospitals and convalescent homes in the beautiful surroundings of 240 of Britain's large country houses where they were to care for civilians and over 500,000 British and Allied troops throughout the war.[19] Amongst other duties, the volunteers polished floors, made beds, emptied bed-pans, gave blanket baths and provided meals.

Again, after the D-Day landings of 1944, when wounded men poured back to crowded hospitals, JWO volunteers found themselves tending to the wounded anywhere that beds could be found. Twelve thousand exhausted, traumatised and injured BEF troops were landed at Portsmouth Dockyard alone[20] and nurses tried hard to keep smiling as they undressed and washed the men, many of whom had fallen into deep sleep. Scissors were blunted with cutting through khaki and socks to remove uniforms which had survived bombing, strafing and sea; the nurses making sure to preserve the fabric for future use by cutting close to the seams.[21]

JWO nurses as young as sixteen also tended men who were suffering from the physical, mental and emotional effects of the atrocities of POW camps, and the terrible facial disfiguration caused by burns, which was a particular risk for men of the RAF. Pioneering techniques in plastic surgery were also supported by JWO nurses who not only cared for the skin grafts but also the psychological trauma, their smiles sometimes bringing about as much healing as the expert medical care, for 'R & R' (rest and recreation) in the care of JWO nurses could be depended upon to restore confidence, hope and morale. On the wards, they became welfare workers, writing letters for patients, giving out newspapers, magazines, fruit and flowers, shopping and entertaining, escorting wounded servicemen and caring for the relatives of dangerously sick or dying patients.[22]

The JWO also set up a Central Hospital Supply Service (CHSS) to fill the needs of hospitals at home and overseas, hospital ships and trains, and convalescent homes for, using sewing machines, or hand-stitching, volunteers managed to provide a staggering 2,724,000 hospital garments and 720,418 bandages between 1939 and 1943[23] including Dorothy bags, pneumonia jackets, dressing gowns and shirts[24] and in the first fortnight after D-Day, they were able to supply 19,000 handkerchiefs and 29,000 pairs of pyjamas, 5 million cigarettes, 53,500 razor blades and 17,500 packets of stationery to Britain's troops at home and in France.[25]

Volunteers also worked steadfastly in the Red Cross Prisoners of War Department[26] to provide items such as educational and vocational training material, books, games and musical instruments to keep up the morale of thousands of prisoners of war; as did their organisation of correspondence between the prisoners of war and their next-of-kin, including the quarterly allowance of 10lb parcels containing clothing and 'comforts'.[27] Twenty-five JWO food-packing centres around Britain packed some 20 million food parcels for prisoners of war in Europe[28] for: 'German rations were just enough to ensure starvation in its most prolonged and unpleasant form'.[29]

> They were essential food parcels that we were packing and they were packed in a very special way… a production line, because we all were in rows and we did different things. Do you see how hygienic they are? They're all dressed in white overalls with caps … To show you that even in those days we were careful to be completely right. (Julie Draper)[30] (Courtesy of British Red Cross Museum and Archives)

With the war drawing to a close, Germany was forced to retreat from the Channel Islands, and the British Red Cross negotiated to transport relief supplies to its starving civilians and the isolated remnants of German occupation. The British Red Cross was also the first to deal with the unimagineable horrors of the Nazi concentration camp at Belsen after its liberation.[31]

Incredibly, this vast amount of aid depended primarily upon donations and determined fund-raising, but the British public responded magnificently, mainly through the Duke of Gloucester's Red Cross and St John Appeal, which raised an astounding £54 million during the war from an enormous variety of sources,[32] including the auction of a sampler worked by Charlotte Bronte aged twelve and some £8 million raised by the Red Cross Agriculture Fund which included donations by the 20,000 children who received an income from growing onions for the services.[33] Some £7.5 million was also raised by Clementine Churchill specifically for the Aid to Russia Fund.[34]

Once the war had ended, the JWO continued their wartime work as 'searchers', recording the missing and wounded and also tackling the massively complex and important task of establishing 'the whereabouts, health and welfare of relatives separated as a result of armed conflict, natural or other disasters' in order to put them in contact with each other.[35] Volunteers engaged in this work were identified by an embroidered armband: 'WOUNDED MISSING & RELATIVE DEPT Searcher BRITISH RED CROSS AND ORDER OF ST JOHN.'

The repercussions of war continued as aid was needed in Austria and for tens of thousands of Hungarian, Palestinian, Indian and Pakistani refugees but the Joint War Organisation was finally dissolved in 1947, a year of massive flooding in Britain, during which the British Red Cross provided rescue, shelter and aid in thirty counties. As severe rationing dragged on in Britain, parcels of food were generously sent from Canada, which the British Red Cross distributed to those those in most need.[36]

Throughout the war and in the immediate post-war years, the unstinting committment of JWO volunteers had safeguarded the health and well-being of countless servicemen and women, and civilians of many nationalities, both in Britain and overseas. However, their gallant and selfless work had another immense value to the nation, for it relieved the British Government of much of the immense burden of funding such an enormous organisation of community care, thus allowing Britain's scant resources to be stretched to the limit in the pursuit of victory. More fundamentally, while the uniforms of the world's military forces signified upheaval, aggression and death, stitch had also formed the uniforms of the JWO which proclaimed the opposite – the continuance of healing and unprejudiced human care for which cause the volunteers were prepared to give their all.

seventeen

Under Canvas

The word 'canvas' comes from the old French *canevas*. The canvas of the Second World War was woven from hemp fibre which is strong, flexible when woven, reasonably easily stitched and its colours blend well with earth, sand and foliage. Combined with stitch, canvas afforded the possibility of the construction of quite substantial coverings and structures.

Stitched canvas provided the thousands of tents which were used extensively to create sheltered spaces which could be erected and dismantled in rapidly changing situations to accommodate commanding officers, troops, military police, communications and medical specialists, and a supporting organisation of supplies and food.

The stitched canvas fabric of a tent is but a fragile defence in the presence of bombs and bullets, but once within the space of a tent there is an immediate sense of protected shelter, of being withdrawn from the situation outside into a place of safety. Instantly, within a tent, it is possible to set up a constructive atmosphere of rest, friendship and caring support.

Across the world, tents accommodated surgical and dressing stations behind the Front Line and emergency operations were often conducted in close proximity to enemy bombardment. Field surgical and dressing station tents were also rapidly erected by the Parachute Field Ambulance who accompanied the paratroops of the Airborne Divisions.[1]

Three hundred of the children who arrived in Britain on *Kindertransport* trains from German-occupied Europe found temporary sanctuary in tents,[2] as did men of the weary, shell-shocked regiments, who also escaped the Nazi terror in the evacuation of Dunkirk, 1940. A Boy Scout who helped to erect 400 tents in the early hours of the morning for their temporary accommodation was glad to play his part in their return home, for their arrival, uncomplaining and still managing to smile, made a memory to last a lifetime.[3]

The mass of British and American troops who waited to redress this defeat by the invasion of Hitler's 'Fortress Europe' in 1944, were also temporarily housed in encampments of tents which were surrounded by barbed wire in order to maintain the secrecy of the massive operation.[4] Secrecy was also imperative for the occupants of the carefully camouflaged tents of 'Operation Sherwood' in the Forêt de Vendôme, France, and forests in Brittany and northern France which hid troops who were waiting for the Allies to break out from Normandy after the D-Day invasion.[5]

Stitched canvas was also useful as canopies against sun, wind, rain and sand for Second World War vehicles, including the lorries which transported folded tents! Painted stitched canvas could transform tanks into trucks,[6] but it played a much greater part in deception when it was used across the whole of the Allied war campaign to successfully divert enemy bombers over empty fields, lakes, and beaches, where the bombs would be wasted on fake Army and Navy bases.[7] Painted canvas could also be made to appear from the air as streets, bomb craters and partially destroyed buildings, submarines or battleships[8] and in preparation for the Normandy land-

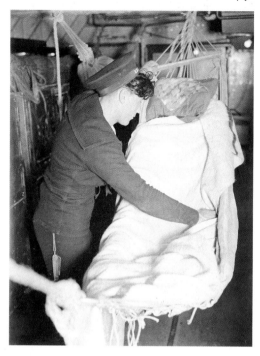

A standard canvas hammock. (Courtesy of the Imperial War Museum, London A 167)

ings, canvas-covered 'landing craft' made of oil drums and scaffolding were used in the massive deception of 'Operation Fortitude' which successfully turned the attention of the Nazis to the Pas de Calais as the probable landing area.[9]

After the evacuation of Dunkirk, factories were set to work to produce an army of dummy soldiers and guns to apparently augment Britain's slender military resources[10] and a similar ruse was employed in the struggle to force the retreat of Axis forces from the Western Desert in their attempt to gain control of the Suez Canal, when the magician Jasper Maskelyne used canvas to create the appearance of a large encampment of British troops until the real reinforcements of the 51st Division gradually arrived to replace them. Reconnaisance photographs taken from enemy low-level spotter planes[11] 'revealed' that more soldiers were arriving daily to occupy the growing rows of tents which were increasingly surrounded by armaments, tracks of trucks and the dust raised by heavy construction vehicles. Campfires burned and smoke rose from cookhouses. Footprints in the sand attested to the presence of thousands of soldiers who could be seen going about their duties but in fact only the tents were real, and it was the task of around just one hundred soldiers to actually live in the camp, make the footprints, keep the fires burning, create the appropriate amount of waste and move the 'dummy' cloth soldiers around.[12]

In addition, Maskelyne carefully conserved materials in the construction of these dummy camps by having them constructed to one-third scale; for in the desert there were no other structures with which the German reconnaisance could make comparison. To add to the illusion, he also created a fake fifty-two-carriage train moving along a fake railway line in the desert south of Cairo.[13]

Again, Maskelyne's tents and cloth dummies played a vital role in the successful Allied penetration of the heavily defended Alamein Line with its 'Devil's Garden' of Axis mines and artillery which, in places, was five miles deep.[14] This time, his task was to convince the enemy that an Allied attack was about to take place to the north of the Line, when, in reality, it was General Montgomery's plan to attack to the south; and also create confusion as to the timing. Inspired use of canvas, stitch and colour allowed the concealment of 150,000 men, 1,000 tanks and 1,000 guns in a desert as exposed and 'flat as a billiard table' whilst under the close surveillance of enemy spotter planes which could easily see every movement and track.[15] Gradually, two camps were established – a real force in the north hidden under an apparently inactive mass of seeming support vehicles which actually concealed 700 tanks and twenty-five pounders; and a fake supply dump in the south where thousands of cloth 'soldiers' inhabited fake 'bivvies', with dummy tanks and weaponry. Then after the occupants and vehicles of the two camps were secretly interchanged on the night of 23 October 1942[16] the attack took place, causing such surprise that many German *Panzerarmee* troops died of shock in the noise and reverberation of Allied artillery.[17] Some three months of bloody fighting ensued before the Axis force finally retreated.

Tents provided British troops with rapidly erected and easily moved shelter. (Courtesy of the Imperial War Museum, London A 13668)

Tents also served the civilian population of Britain. This Lifebuoy Emergency Service bath tent offered a place for victims of enemy bombing to wash away the dust and smoke which pervaded the streets and buildings of blitzed neighbourhoods. (Courtesy of the Imperial War Museum, London ZZZ 89386)

Equipped with tents, RAF pilots who accompanied the British Expeditionary Force into France from 1939–40 could remain close to their aircraft. (Courtesy of the Imperial War Museum, London C 357)

The temporary shelter of tents was also useful to Britain's 'trekkies' who spent their nights out in the countryside to avoid enemy bombing raids. (Courtesy of the Imperial War Museum, London HU 36244)

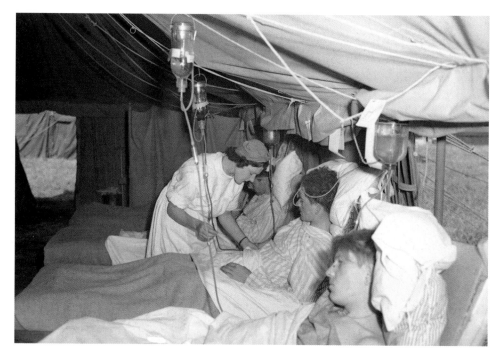

A hospital tent in Normandy. (Courtesy of the Imperial War Museum, London B 9222)

The tents of Army Rest Camps allowed men a short respite from the horrors of the Front Line. Here, men are queuing for the first part of the recuperation process, the luxury of a hot shower and clean clothing. (Courtesy of the Imperial War Museum, London B 9445)

William Clark, Royal Corps of Signals with the Durham Light Infantry. (By kind courtesy of Belinda Ratnayake)

The British canvas tent had its major drawbacks, however, which were discovered when soldiers in Burma captured some of the silk tents of the Japanese:

> We pick it up and it is so light that a couple of men could carry it all day, in addition to their personal gear, without being fatigued…. Our tents are bulky and clumsy to erect and strike, and seem to have innumerable iron-tipped poles. They are so heavy that ox-carts or trucks are needed to transport them, which can be impossible in rough country campaigning. They are made of thick canvas-like material that is quickly saturated by rain, which doubles its already considerable weight. If not dried out before it's folded up, which requires an age of continuous fine weather, it soon becomes stinking and mouldy.[18] (Ian Denys Peek)

If stored damp, the rotting fabric would split and tear when the tent was unfolded.

Under the Japanese, British prisoners of war were forced to use the captured British tents with which they were provided, if any. Branches had to be found to replace missing support poles, but there might not be enough shelter for every man even when inner and outer tent coverings were separated to make two tents, and eight men might have to crowd into tents designed for two. Rain lashed in through open ends, and the chill night made prisoners shiver as they lay naked on the muddy ground trying to sleep.[19]

It was a similarly crowded situation at sea, when liners such as the *Queen Mary* were adapted as troop carriers and temporary stitched canvas and tubular metal 'Standee' bunks allowed the ship to carry up to 16,683 men in accommodation designed for 3,200 passengers and crew, which was 'The greatest number of human beings ever embarked on one vessel.'[20] As the bunks were fitted in tiers of six and used in three separate shifts throughout each twenty-four hours, fifty-four men could sleep in a cabin designed for just one couple.

A stitched canvas pool on the ship's deck was a very welcome place for sailors to bathe. (Courtesy of the Imperial War Museum, London A 30890)

In fact, British sailors were often quartered in cramped accommodation, having to duck their heads to avoid their canvas kit bags suspended from the cabin roof,[21] however stitched canvas also afforded them the chance to practise bayoneting, using cloth dummies suspended from cross bars.

Stitched canvas was also used for the sad ceremonies of Second World War sea burials:

… before they could be given a decent burial at sea they had to be sewn up in canvas with a heavy 'fire-bar' at their feet to make sure they sank. Four of us were given this unenviable job under the guidance of the bo's'n who'd had experience of this task in the past. We didn't waste any time, I can tell you, and where one normal canvas sewing would have about eight stitches to the inch we made do with about one to the inch and soon got the job done. … all normal activity on board was halted. Those of us who'd recovered the bodies from Syracuse harbour and subsequently sewn them up were assembled on the ship's after rails for the burial service. The ship's engines were almost stopped and the chief officer read a simple service. Then one by one the canvas wrapped bodies were placed on a large board which rested on one end of the rail, and committed to the sea. There was no pressure put on anyone to attend this ceremony, and yet the afterdeck was crowded with men paying their respects to four unknown servicemen who'd made the final sacrifice.[22] (Charlie Workman)

It was within a canvas structure formed by stitch, on Monday 7 May 1945, that one of the most historically important events of the Second World War took place: within the tent of General Montgomery in his Tactical Headquarters on Lunenberg Heath in Germany. Peace was restored to Europe as German commanders signed the document of unconditional surrender of German forces in Holland, Denmark and north-west Germany.

Signing the document on Lunenberg Heath. (Courtesy of the Imperial War Museum, London BU 5207)

eighteen

Coupons

"**Modom should not upset herself by watching while her coupons are removed.**"

[*Punch*

(Reproduced with permission of Punch Ltd, www.punch. co.uk)

From 1940 to 1949, the stitching of the British nation's clothing was controlled by the Government in order to supply the needs of the military.

In 1939, uniforms had to be found for 200,000 national servicemen and 270,000 Territorials[1] when just 20 per cent of the pre-war tonnage of wool and cotton was getting through to British ports.[2] The British wool clip was requisitioned, wool was bought from Australia, New Zealand and South Africa,[3] and Wool Control was introduced. In addition, to cope with the shortage of silk for parachutes, factories were adapted for production of the new synthetic fabrics – nylon and rayon[4] – output rose from nothing to 1 million lb a year with rayon proving to be especially suitable for strong, supply-drop parachutes.[5]

By 1941, the majority of military clothing contracts had been fulfilled[6] and production of services' clothing was reduced by 45 per cent,[7] allowing that of civilian clothing to be increased to 35 per cent of pre-war consumption.[8] However, the manufacture of armaments had to take priority in factory space and labour,[9] and the Government was forced to introduce a 'concentration' scheme for textile factories, with the majority of Britain's clothing being made in Manchester, Glasgow, Leeds and London.[10] One hundred and sixty clothing firms were closed down[11] and 680 factories were awarded 'Nuclear' status, by which they were assured of full labour[12] and a supply of 60 per cent of the nation's wool cloth, mainly for the production of Utility garments.[13] 'Non-Nuclear' factories had to cope as best they could.[14] Two hundred of Britain's 520 cotton spinning mills were also closed,[15] which unfortunately led to problems when cotton clothing was urgently needed for tropical warfare and shipment to Russia.[16]

Additionally, from November 1940, secret preparations were in hand for the rationing of 'all cloth made wholly or mainly from any textile (other than jute), wearing apparel including handkerchiefs, footwear and hand-knitting wool' and un-rationed items were: 'Headgear, fur garments, household textiles, second-hand goods, infants' garments (appropriate to children under four) and miscellaneous textile goods not suitable for clothing – e.g. tracing cloth, surgical belts, black-out cloth, mending wools and ribbons'[17] which, however, *were* later turned into clothing by ingenious stitchers.

To work out the suitable amount of clothing needed for wartime use, statisticians took averages from the pre-war consumption of each type of garment, based mainly on the Census of Production figures for 1935–37,[18] which they then reduced by one-third[19] – being relieved to find that this was equivalent to the amount of clothing which the country could now produce.[20] Garments were then allotted coupon values based upon the amount of materials and labour needed in their production, and a system of organisation from manufacturer to shop-keeper was worked out; also such complexities as the number of coupons needed by fast-growing babies, small children and adult-sized children, lost or stolen coupons, coupons destroyed by enemy action, the clothing needs of people in various occupations, and those belonging to the deceased.

By the summer of 1941, it seemed that clothes rationing *must* be introduced: the price of clothing had almost doubled,[21] including Purchase Tax, and civilian consumption was still too high. Yet Churchill objected strongly, saying that it would 'strip the poor people to the buff' and Oliver Lyttleton, President of the Board of Trade, commented that it 'only slipped past him' when he became absorbed in the search for the deadly German battleship, *Bismark*.[22]

Clothes rationing began on 1 June 1941, allowing shop-keepers time to re-label their stock over the Whitsun Bank Holiday and Government leaflets explained that:

> Rationing has been introduced not to deprive you of your real needs, but to make more certain that you get your share of the country's goods – to get fair shares with everybody else. … When the shops re-open you will be able to buy cloth, clothes, footwear and knitting wool only if you bring your food ration book with you. … You can buy where you like and when you like without registering.

Henceforth rationed garments would have to be paid for both in coupons and cash[23] and the public was informed that they could use the spare twenty-six margarine coupons in their food ration books until proper clothing coupons could be issued through the Post Office.[24]

The system was a triumph: 70 per cent of the British public thought it fair[25] and coupon values could be quickly adjusted in response to variations in supplies of raw materials, public or military demands, and the weather – for instance, the hosiery industry was allowed more rayon and cotton for the manufacture of warm underwear during the bitter wartime winters to avoid loss of working hours to illness.[26] Also the number of coupons needed for unpopular austerity garments such as short socks and trousers without turn-ups could be reduced as the war seemed to be coming to an end.[27] However, Mass Observation was to discover that the public placed the need for clothing coupons fourth in their top six main inconveniences of the war[28] and, even though the majority of people kept to the regulations,[29] the scheme would invite theft and deception on a massive scale.

Initially, the allowance for each man, woman and child was calculated to be enough to buy a new outfit annually, although they were strongly encouraged *not* to use their full allowance. A poster shown in the exhibition 'The Use of the Clothing Coupon' stated: 'If everybody took a pair of scissors and cut out and gave to salvage one coupon, it would release 8,000 workers, and 5,000 tons of raw material, which could be used to make 2,000,000 battle dresses or clothe 500,000 soldiers from head to foot, including underwear, boots and greatcoat!'.[30]

When coupons were to be used for clothing, my Dad decided that was where we could really help the war effort (apart from the fact that he was a full time Civil Defence Warden and I did my stint at first aid etc.). So he decided we should not use our coupons at all. ... I had a fairly good wardrobe anyway and his uniform was provided. (Jean Hooper)

The 1941 coupon values were:

Women's clothing: tweed suit 18; coat 18; jacket 11; skirt 7; waistcoat or jumper 5; handkerchief 2; shoes 7; apron 3; corset 5 (girl's corset 2); woollen dress 11; dress in any other fabric 7; unlined mackintosh 9; blouse 5; stockings 2; vest 3; knickers 3; bra 1; suspender belt 1.

Men's clothing: overcoat 16; shirt 5; underpants 4; suit 26; vest 4; socks 3; shoes 7; tie 1; handkerchief 1; pyjamas 8; dressing gown 8; trousers 8; kilt 6.[31]

The immediate public reaction was, of course, to make full use of any unrationed clothing such as bib-and-braces overalls, and to quickly buy up as much clothing as possible just in case coupon allowances were reduced[32] – which they were – from sixty-six for adults in 1941 down to forty in 1943, forty-eight in 1944,[33] and just thirty-six in the eight months from September 1945,[34] although the number of coupons required for each garment was constantly raised or lowered throughout the war.

Unfortunately, home stitchers could not escape the restrictions of rationing, for 36in-wide woollen cloth required three coupons per yard[35] and it was now made from 'shoddy' – the raw materials which had previously been used in the production of furnishing fabrics.[36] When dressmakers began to utilise sheets and furnishing fabrics and consumption rose, these were also rationed[37] resulting in the demand for black market dress-making fabric being met by the cloth-workers of cities such as Leeds and thefts were so widespread that they were impossible to control.[38]

My mother was a dressmaker, working from home, and made mostly dresses for various local ladies. During the war, she was often brought a discarded man's shirt – 'is it possible to make me a blouse out this?' and mother would usually oblige. The customers brought their own materials and my mother always wrapped up the finished garment with the leftovers. Quite often they used to reject these – 'perhaps your daughter would like to make some doll's clothes' – sometimes there would be enough to make a blouse! Then with the advent of clothing coupons it would probably be a question of 'what else can you make for me out of this?' (M.E. Harris)

Business boomed for dealers in unrationed second-hand clothes. Wives reluctantly sold the clothing of men who were expected never to return or those of their children, which had been stored away when outgrown. In saying that the very poorest people in Britain would be even worse off under clothes rationing, Churchill was proved correct,[39] for, although they had the same number of coupons as the most wealthy, they did not have the necessary cash. They *did* find, however, that their coupons could be exchanged for second-hand clothes or sold illegally, either privately or through second-hand clothes dealers or market traders and dealers often made a considerable profit by using these coupons to pay for clothing which they were offered, or to sell on to wealthier customers who had the cash but not the coupons.[40]

Cloth, or clothing, which had been damaged due to enemy action was given a maximum price and could be sold for a reduced number of coupons,[41] however, this was open to abuse despite the steep fines if a trader should happen to be caught.

Shop-keepers were not allowed to accept loose clothing coupons, however a blind eye was turned on family members who contributed their coupons to each other:

My mother made the most of my clothes, but I have a special memory of one particular dress. In about 1943 … my grandmother gave me some of her precious clothing coupons as a present. She, my mother and I travelled to Lichfield specially to use them to buy material for my mother to make me a new dress. It was exciting to have extra coupons and we chose some very pretty cotton material in a pink and blue floral design and bought a paper pattern in my size. But I started to grow very rapidly and unfortunately the dress was too small for me the next year. It was such a disappointment. (Heather Fogg)

I was lucking coming from my mother's family who bought very good clothes and took great care of them to last a very long time. I was always freely given ration coupons or material when I needed them. (Olive Castleton)

My father … had no interest in clothing coupons so gave us his to supplement our own. (Denise Cochrane)

I remember shortly after starting work, selecting a coat in C&As and having it reserved until my next issue of coupons came out. My mother and I used to plan what we would get with my grandmother's coupons – then at the last minute she would decide she wanted a new dress! (M.E. Harris)

In a way, the black market allowed people to cope with situations such as the need for a wedding dress or school uniform and even though the wartime cost of living rose by 50 per cent, incomes had risen by 80 per cent and many people could afford to pay the racketeers' extortionate prices:

Petticoat Lane offered a … sophisticated service for buying suits and overcoats without the need for coupons. A tout would accost a passer-by and say, 'We have got a nice suit to fit you', or 'What about a nice mackintosh or overcoat without coupons?'. When the purchaser asked about the shop, he was told, 'You come with me and if you get fixed up, you give me five shillings … when you come out.'[42]

Even those who wouldn't normally dream of using it felt it necessary to clothe their children with the aid of black market coupons.[43] (David Howell)

Unfortunately, dedicated gangs of black market 'racketeers' found clothing coupons easy to steal or forge, in breathtaking quantities. In July 1944, 600,000 coupons worth around £30,000 were stolen from a City of London employment exchange, to be sold on to wholesalers or retailers, or in pubs, bars, night-clubs and hotel lounges.[44] A group of women clerks and typists in Liverpool were discovered to be carrying on a 'big-scale traffic in clothing coupons' in 1944,[45] and in 1943, there was a theft of 5 million clothing coupons from an Army store near Wandsworth.[46]

Not surprisingly, by July 1944, after five years of coupons and rationing, a shabby and threadbare British public was getting tired of doing without and many felt that it was 'increasingly difficult to keep themselves respectable'.[47] However, the worst was yet to come! When V-1 and V-2 flying bombs caused the deaths of many clothing workers in London at a time of imminent need for thousands of demob suits plus jungle warfare uniforms, skilled clothing workers had to be released from munitions work,[48] yet demand still far outstripped production, particularly when Japan unexpectedly surrendered, resulting in a sudden increase in the number of servicemen being demobbed. The result was a further reduction in the clothing civilian coupon allowance.[49]

Then, as soon as the war ended and the new Labour Government had the task of rectifying Britain's dire financial situation, it was decided that rationing should continue – with greater severity. The thefts and illegal trading of cloth, clothing and clothing coupons continued: in February 1946, forty-eight people were implicated in the theft of thirty rolls of cloth worth £1,600 for not only were the thieves convicted, but also the people who had bought the fabric. The crime had been discovered by a small boy collecting car numbers who had noticed the thieves' car parked outside the warehouse.[50]

By the winter of 1948, governmental control was approaching the Gestapo state which Churchill had been so condemned for predicting. It was clear that the British public could tolerate no more. Finally, the Government began to reduce the number of coupons needed for clothing which was continued, to the utmost relief of all, by the ending of clothes rationing on 15 March 1949.[51]

By this time, Britain's factory-produced and home-stitched clothing had been under the control of the Government for some nine years. However, coupons, rationing and the compulsary reorganisation of the nation's textile factories had indeed successfully underpinned the nation's services and civilian well-being, for if the shortages of materials, labour and factory space, combined with rapid changes in demand, had not been handled correctly, Britain's war effort might well have foundered. The majority of the British public had risen to the years of coupons magnificently, even finding the endurance to cope with coupons and their patched, darned, dyed and renovated clothing for some four more years after the war had ended in order to ensure the recovery of the nation's economy – a double victory!

nineteen

Women's Fashion and the War

'It's your job to spend gallantly (to keep the national economy going), to dress decoratively, to be groomed immaculately – in short, to be a sight for sore eyes.'[1] (*Vogue*, 1939)

Upon the declaration of war with Germany in 1939, the stitching of women's fashion in Britain was thrown into disarray. Thousands of the dressmakers and tailors who had 'run up' the latest fashions to order were taken away into the services; many clothing firms were now classified as 'luxury industries' and had to adapt the production to services' uniforms and equipment, and the staff of wealthy families who took care of extensive wardrobes and helped to dress their mistresses in frequent changes of clothing were also spirited away by the demands of war. Then, after the fall of France to the Nazis in 1940, Britain was cut off from the *haute couture* of Paris, although designers such as Charles Creed, Captain Edward Molyneux, Paquin and Elspeth Champcommunal of Worth had managed to move to London[2] – Molyneux on a coal barge, at the last minute, as the Nazis entered France.

However, the patriotic ladies of Britain were glad to follow the lead of the royal family and adapt to the changes which the war had brought, and very soon the clinging bias-cut voiles, crêpes, silks and satins of the 1930s appeared as frivolous betrayals of the nation's forces who were, maybe, dying at the Front. Propaganda posters featuring the 'Squander Bug' also reminded everyone to conserve the nation's supplies of raw materials by buying clothes only when absolutely necessary.[3]

Suddenly, the streets of Britain were filled with drab-coloured military uniforms, fashionably echoed by the designs of couturiers such as Schiaparelli and Rochas,[4] who had already embraced a masculine influence for some three to four years. The *tailleur*, or expertly tailored suit, rapidly became popular for its businesslike, almost military practicality,[5] for ladies now needed clothes which allowed for ease of movement, and one of the most fashionable of accessories was a custom-stitched gas-mask cover.

Fashions would continue to change through the war, if more slowly, and use colour to relieve the drabness of war: pastels in the spring and summer of 1942 and vivid, bold shades of buttercup yellow, pillar box red and bright green in 1944[6] mixed in contrasting backs and fronts, sleeves and bodices.[7] However, uniforms soon became essential items in the fashionable lady's wardrobe.

Understanding that the morale of the nation depended largely upon its women, who were being forced out of their 'womanly' role of dependency into 'unfeminine' war work, maybe in the services or dirty, noisy factories, the British Government worked with a team of editors from British women's magazines to present images of the patriotic, beautiful, brave, smiling British woman who always managed somehow to 'make enormous sacrifices while appearing as if they had not done so',[8] thus making Beauty as Duty' more important than a fashionable appearance. The aim now was to have an *inner* beauty and be well-groomed, capable and

Above Fashion parade of 'Utility' designs.
(Courtesy of Hulton Archive 2696649 (RM).
Photo by Fox Photos)

Left Fashion student's drawing, 1946. (By
kind courtesy of Pat Salmon)

Below The 'Utility' stamp 'CC41', civilian
clothing 1941.

responsible in both civilian clothes and uniform and femininity in clothing would be conveyed by designs accentuating the waist.[9] Indeed a woman who achieved this ideal experienced a sense of personal triumph – it was a way of showing that Britain could not be beaten.

For the sake of the war effort, even the most fashionable of Britain's women tried wearing trousers, or 'slacks' for the first time and found that not only were they warm, but could be worn with socks, thus conserving precious hoards of silk stockings. They also followed the example of Clementine Churchill by wearing a turban, or a headscarf as worn by the Princesses Elizabeth and Margaret Rose. Clementine, or 'Clemmy' Churchill, the wife of the Prime Minister, had even adopted the 'turban-bandanna' as her 'trademark', in 'silk, cotton, crêpe, tulle and chiffon' to pay 'a graceful compliment to all the thousands of women factory workers throughout the country' who were wearing the turban out of necessity.[10]

When head-scarves and dress material became a valuable source of export revenue, the Government allowed Jacqmar a special quota of silk in order to fulfill an order of 10,000 yards of fabric from the USA[11] and in 1942, Jacqmar commissioned artists such as Arnold Lever to design prints using slogans such as 'Careless Talk Costs Lives', 'Dig for Victory' or 'The Navy's Here'. Much prized for their witty and patriotic messages, they were a popular, if expensive 'sweetheart gift'. Arnold Lever's fabrics for Jacqmar also included prints such as '66 Coupons', which used small repeats in order to save wastage when matching at the seams. Made up into garments by Bianca Mosca, they were photographed on ladies chosen from the aristocracy, or actresses such as Vivien Leigh.[12]

Sadly, the creations of Britain's own couturiers were largely out of reach of the fashionable ladies of Britain, as maximum sales were needed in the export market to bring in urgently needed revenue for the British Government and to this end, Captain Edward Molyneaux formed what would become the Incorporated Society of London Fashion Designers (Inc. Soc.) in 1942, which would eventually include: Digby Morton, Victor Stiebel, Bianca Mosca, Peter Russell, Angele Delange, Lachasse, John Cavanagh, Mattli, Michael Sherard, Charles Creed, Ronald Paterson and Champcommunal at Worth.[13] Nine models were sent to America to support the 'Buy British' shops which had been opened in New York[14] and orders flowed in from mainland Europe, America and the British Colonies, particularly to the house of Molyneux, and to avoid the possibility of 'pirate' copies being sold before the originals had made their uncertain crossing of the wartime oceans, he organised secret fashion shows – with great success – as valuable sales were generated with Canada, Egypt, Australia, Sweden, Switzerland and Iran[15] and he was able to generously donate some $3 million to the British Government for the production of munitions.[16]

In 1941, a Government Utility Scheme was introduced to reduce the civilian consumption of raw materials and also release some 367,000 garment industry workers for armament production and Utility fabrics had to be manufactured to conform with their detailed specifications regarding weight and fibre content per square yard.[17] Manufacturers who decided to join the Scheme were obliged to abide by Utility regulations for the first 85 per cent of production but were then free to make non-Utility garments using non-Utility fabrics. They could see 2,000 samples of 160 Utility-approved fabrics at the Cotton Board's Colour, Design and Style Centre in Manchester, ranging from 1s 4d to 3s a yard for cottons and 2s to 6s a yard for rayons[18] and fabrics included cotton, wool, moygashel and artificial silk in a range of colours including Flag Red, Victory Blue, purple, green, yellow, black and white, in spots, stripes and florals.[19] Utility clothing was eventually to comprise 90 per cent of Britain's garment industry output,[20] both the fabrics and garments being stamped with the approval mark of the Board of Trade – the 'two cheeses' – 'CC41'.

To ensure that the public, especially women, would find Utility clothes attractive, the Board of Trade invited couturiers including Hardy Amies, Digby Morton, Bianca Mosca, Elspeth Champcommunal at Worth (London) Ltd, Peter Russell, Victor Stiebel, Charles Creed and Edward Molyneux of Inc. Soc.[21] to each submit designs for four basic outfits – a suit including a shirt or blouse, an afternoon dress, a coat and a cotton overall dress suitable for office work.

Queuing at Portsmouth Guildhall to apply for an air-raid shelter. (By kind courtesy of *The News*, Portsmouth 923)

As a further incentive, Utility clothing was made exempt from Purchase Tax[22] and a maximum retail price was set for each type of garment – which, unfortunately, allowed no profit margin for professional dressmakers.

Thirty-two of the designs were chosen by the Board of Trade with representatives of the clothing industry,[23] to offer an enormous variety in combinations of basic elements and manufacturers were offered size-graded templates[24] at 7s 6d for blouses and 10s 6d for costumes (suits), overcoats and dresses.[25] This new standardisation of sizing by the British Standards Institution encouraged streamlined production and manufacturers were requested to set up long runs only, and also limit the annual number of basic designs used.[26] The careful consideration of costing and sizing was, in fact, to prove a long-term benefit to British ready-to-wear industry.[27]

For the first time in British history, all levels of society could afford well-designed, good-quality clothing and the Utility Scheme would change the face of the ready-to-wear industry for now people were not satisfied with lower quality. Magazines patriotically praised the prestigious couture designs; the collection was shown to the press in 1942,[28] could be bought in the shops in the spring of 1943,[29] and even Princess Elizabeth and the fashion icon the Duchess of Kent were amongst those seen wearing the elegantly simple 'tailored look'.[30]

Utility garments varied in price and could be bought at Marks & Spencer's for below the maximum ceiling price, or at the top price from Norman Hartnell at Berketex, Dereta and Austin Reed[31] in the West End of London. One could even buy a Utility corset or an adaptable Utility blouse constructed in two separate halves which buttoned at the shoulders and sides, allowing different fronts to be worn with just one back.[32] Using Utility patterns, home stitchers had the advantage of being able to add the luxury of details such as appliqué, open work, bows, tucks, lace, trimmings and interesting contrasts in fabrics.[33]

The couture designs for the Utility Scheme had also to comply with the Government's 'Making-up of Clothes (Restrictions) Order' 1942, which further limited the use of fabric and labour by dressmakers, tailors and factories alike in the production of Utility and non-Utility clothing.[34] Trimmings and decorations such as fur, leather, embroidery, applique,[35] lace, frills[36] and sequins were banned; the maximum amount of fabric to be used in each garment was stipulated, also the length and width of skirts, number of pleats, pockets, button-holes and number of seams in the skirt. The use of tucks was limited and pleats were required to be standard rather than inverted. Maximum dimensions were also set for tuck-ins of blouses, widths of hems, seams, collars, belts[37] and sleeves. In 1943, the 'Making of Uniforms (Restrictions) Order' also enforced these austerity regulations in Army officers' service dress; and in December 1943, the 'Civilian Clothing (Nurses' indoor uniforms) Order' banned trimmings and uneconomic styles.[38]

In fact, the pared-down austerity designs were elegant in their simplicity, even though the luxury of padded shoulders was retained. The economical cut had produced a narrow silhouette, with long, slim jackets and straight skirts ending just below the knee, featuring, for practicality, a flared panel, kick pleats or inverted pleats. Interest was introduced in a variety of ways including buttons, fashionable military-style breast pockets, belts, small collars and high-cut necks, or slanting patch pockets and draped panels and the overall frugality was disguised by bright colours and colour contrasts.[39] British women found themselves appearing 'neater, often smarter, usually altogether more chic.'[40]

If the fashion-conscious wartime woman could not buy new clothing, she could have her existing garments 'reconfectioned' or re-modelled by the big department stores such as Bourne & Hollingsworth, Peter Jones or John Lewis where skilled stitchers could transform evening gowns or men's trousers into day dresses; change men's suits into women's suits; or turn shirts into blouses.[41] Clothes could also be made to look 'new' when expertly dyed. Perhaps for the first time, many ladies considered second-hand clothing, for it was coupon-free and often of high quality.

The shortages of the Second World War inevitably caused great difficulties for students of fashion, and studies had to include renovation and the inventive use of any materials which were available:

> The girls had no privileges in obtaining coupons or materials and many of the garments were transformed from men's suits, discarded evening dresses and even bedspreads and curtains. (Margaret Blow)

For the majority of British women, however, the daily struggle of war work, queueing for anything and everything, the nagging anxiety for the safety of men in the services, sleepless nights in air-raid shelters, the dust and dirt, interrupted water, gas and electricity supplies and Make Do and Mend left little time and energy for fashion, especially the pre-war ideal of matching hat, shoes, bag and gloves, rolled umbrella and 'smart' appearance. However, a close sense of companionship, even humour, was felt, for everyone was 'in the same boat' and only one item of clothing retained its unique importance throughout the war – the coat – essential to the 1940s woman as a declaration of respectability, and also absolutely invaluable through the months of exceptional cold in the severe winters of 1939, 1940 and 1946. To be seen wearing a patched and worn coat would cast shame on a woman's entire family and she might even feel that it was better to stay indoors despite the many difficulties which this would obviously entail.[42]

Most of the wartime regulations regarding women's clothing were removed in 1946,[43] Utility regulations for women's clothing ended in 1948,[44] and there was the post-war excitement of Dior's 'New Look', but it would not be until 1949, when clothes rationing finally ended – after nine long years – that most women could, once more, enjoy dressing themselves fashionably.

twenty

Mrs Sew-and-Sew

A sewing machine can be almost as much a weapon as a spade. (Harrods' advertisement)[1]

> If it could be made with a needle of any description, we made it. (Barbara Parsons)

Hitler's strategy of destroying Britain's merchant ships and imports of raw materials was very successful in the early years of the Second World War; however the 'greatest Field Commander of all time' had not bargained for 'Mrs Sew-and-Sew'. Invented by the Ministry of Information to inspire a habit of 'Make Do and Mend', she appeared everywhere – in magazines and newspapers, on posters and leaflets, explaining how to patch, darn, re-model, alter and transform clothing and cope with almost every household problem to do with textiles; which, for many was actually just a continuation of pre-war necessity. The booklet *Make Do and Mend*, published by the Board of Trade in 1943, had sold over 1.4 million copies by 1944.[2]

Fortunately, wartime Britain was a nation of stitchers, both professional and skilled amateurs, male and female, for sewing was regarded as a feminine skill in the 1930s. Girls were taught at home and in school in preparation for home-dressmaking or employment as a tailoress, dressmaker or upholsterer. Dress patterns and fabrics were inexpensive and widely available and it was usual to 'run up' garments at home or employ a professional dressmaker or tailor. Stitchers revelled in design details such as fabric-covered buttons and belts, embroidery, smocking, pleats and tucks and there was generally a 'feel', or affectionate appreciation, for all kinds of fabrics. Men and women expected to get 'the wear' out of their clothes and a new garment was like a new friend, for it would be part of one's life for years to come.

Upon the outbreak of war, if sewing was not one of your skills you had to learn quickly. Classes and demonstrations were rapidly organised by the Board of Education, the WI, WVS or groups of friends, where one could seek advice, or share skills, equipment and laughter whilst turning something old and worn into something 'new' and useful and neighbours would often contribute materials:

> If one was a stitcher, friends often gave threads or spare wool, so I was lucky in that I did get given quite a lot. (Virginia Leonard-Williams)
>
> Mum always seemed to have a vast store of bits and pieces and friends, neighbours and family would come in with various 'finds' or cast offs either worn out or too small as children grew. Unpicking and re-modelling went on all the time. (Stroma Hammond)

Mrs Sew-and-Sew.
(Courtesy of the National
Archives INF 13/144)

Mother would accept any good clothes from neighbours for making things, or using the buttons etc. (Sheila Westall)

Nothing was thrown away. Buttons were cut off old clothes, and carefully kept, so were zips.' (Virginia Leonard-Williams)

As a small child I used to watch my mother make tacking marks on the fabric and pull the length of tacking cotton out again carefully and re-use it. (Tacking was the British word for what is now called 'basting'.) (Wilma Ramauti)

Many home-dressmakers still stitched by hand, although quite a few owned a hand, treadle, or even an electric sewing machine. When the Singer sewing-machine factories in Elizabeth, New Jersey and Scotland had to be turned over to the production of military equipment, sewing machines became expensive and hard to obtain, so they were taken along to be shared in 'Equipment Pools'.

I borrowed £30 from my father to go on the waiting list for a Singer sewing machine. £15 for the plug in, electric 'foot', and I made clothes for people [to pay my father back for the loan] including two uniform dresses for our ten Sisters in Charge.... I just like sewing – a family thing. (Denise Cochrane)

Patterns for home-made garments could be bought, or copied from women's magazines, especially *Home Chat*, which featured the useful patterns by 'Bestway'. Experienced stitchers also improvised, sometimes adapting their existing patterns for both summer and winter-wear:

Above, left 'Keith and myself on one of his few leaves before going overseas. The dress was the first dress I made for myself. It was a "Miss Muffet" print in green and white.' (By kind courtesy of Peggy)

Above, right 'Me in the scarlet crêpe dress which my mother had made for me. It looks a bit crumpled because the original was carried by my husband all through his RAF service.' (By kind courtesy of Peggy)

Any clothing, from coats to vests, had to be made to last as long as possible, and 'Mrs Sew-and-Sew' recommended: 'Always carry a needle and cotton and mending silk with you – this will save many a ladder in stockings or prevent the loss of buttons; your friends will thank you, too. How many times have you heard someone say, "Has anyone got a needle and cotton?"'[3]

A home-made dress. (By kind courtesy of Peggy)

Using a sewing-machine in an Equipment Pool. (Courtesy of the Imperial War Museum, London D 12887)

She had one or two paper patterns, but mostly she copied existing clothes. (Sheila Westall)

Mum used to adapt patterns by making folds in them if they were too big and adding, with chalk lines, extra edges around the seam lines if they were too small. We were lucky living in Salisbury as chalk could always be found in the garden if we ran out. With favourite garments that had worn out, Mum would carefully take them apart and use them for a pattern to repeat the garment in a fresh material. She would lay everything out on the floor and then crawl around on her hands and knees doing the cutting out with a giant pair of very sharp scissors I was never allowed to touch! (Stroma Hammond)

My patterns may have been made of newspaper after a great deal of measuring. (Gwen Jones)

With such a shortage of materials, stitchers had to exercise great ingenuity to make the most of even the badly worn garments which they already possessed and *Home Chat* featured a weekly 'Ten Shilling Transformation' series in which readers could win 10s for their clever ideas. Combining two or more worn-out garments to make something 'new' was common practise.

'Mrs Sew-and-Sew' also warned, in 'Hints on Renovating and Recutting!': 'THINK BEFORE YOU CUT – Never be hasty about cutting up clothes. Freshened and brought up-to-date, a "good" coat, suit or dress will be a far better coupon-saver than if you tried to turn it into something else'[4] and, in 1949, Agnes M. Miall, in *Pearson's Complete Needlecraft*, also pointed out the obvious problems:

Airy articles are often published suggesting that it is the easiest job in the world to take two old dresses and combine them into one smart new one, however garments will almost always have been worn in the same places and it would be a happy co-incidence if the colours and fabrics of available garments would actually blend ... always make a smaller garment that will absorb only the good portion of the original one. ...[5]

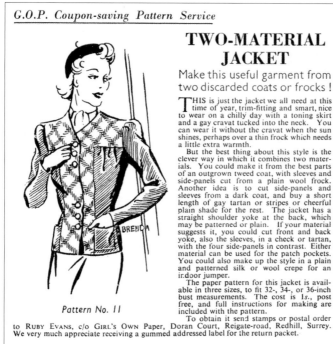

TWO-MATERIAL JACKET

Make this useful garment from two discarded coats or frocks !

THIS is just the jacket we all need at this time of year, trim-fitting and smart, nice to wear on a chilly day with a toning skirt and a gay cravat tucked into the neck. You can wear it without the cravat when the sun shines, perhaps over a thin frock which needs a little extra warmth.

But the best thing about this style is the clever way in which it combines two materials. You could make it from the best parts of an outgrown tweed coat, with sleeves and side-panels cut from a plain wool frock. Another idea is to cut side-panels and sleeves from a dark coat, and buy a short length of gay tartan or stripes or cheerful plain shade for the rest. The jacket has a straight shoulder yoke at the back, which may be patterned or plain. If your material suggests it, you could cut front and back yoke, also the sleeves, in a check or tartan, with the four side-panels in contrast. Either material can be used for the patch pockets. You could also make up the style in a plain and patterned silk or wool crepe for an indoor jumper.

The paper pattern for this jacket is available in three sizes, to fit 32-, 34-, or 36-inch bust measurements. The cost is 1s., post free, and full instructions for making are included with the pattern.

To obtain it send stamps or postal order to RUBY EVANS, c/o GIRL'S OWN PAPER, Doran Court, Reigate-road, Redhill, Surrey. We very much appreciate receiving a gummed addressed label for the return packet.

BRENDA

Pattern No. II

"'Two old dresses into a Coat-Frock." Here is an idea for a dark woollen dress that is worn in front and is too tight for you. Open it from neck to hem. Then use the best part of the silk from an old printed dress or any other material you may have, in a contrasting colour, and gather it in a panel down the front – the effect of a Redingote worn over a dress.'[6] *Girls Own Paper* (Courtesy of Lutterworth Press)

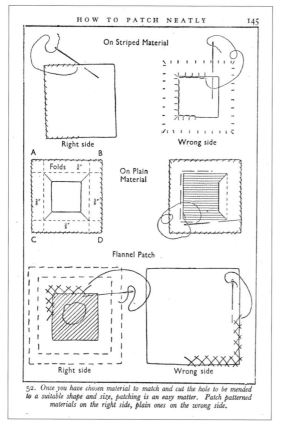

On Striped Material

Right side

A   B

Folds ⅜"

⅜"

⅜"

⅜"

C   D

Wrong side

On Plain Material

Flannel Patch

Right side   Wrong side

52. *Once you have chosen material to match and cut the hole to be mended to a suitable shape and size, patching is an easy matter. Patch patterned materials on the right side, plain ones on the wrong side.*

Patches which had to be applied over worn-through elbows soon became a fashionable emblem of patriotic pride and there was always advice from 'Mrs Sew-and-Sew':

When you can't get a patch to match the cloth, make your mend as decorative as possible … sharp colour-contrast to the original material. Give it a fancy shape; for instance, you can hide a worn elbow with a diamond or heart-shaped patch, and add a pocket of the same material on the bodice or the skirt, to make it look intentional.[7]

In places that don't show, never mind what colour it is as long as it is mended. Reinforce a thin spot with a light patch on the inside.[8]

1947 Elizabeth Craig. (By kind permission of HarperCollins Publishers Ltd)

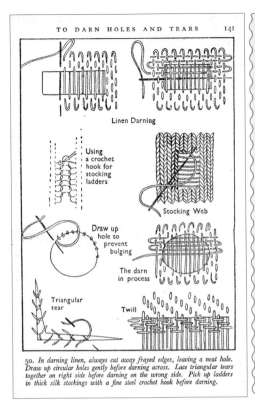

Linen Darning

Using a crochet hook for stocking ladders

Stocking Web

Draw up hole to prevent bulging

The darn in process

Triangular tear

Twill

50. *In darning linen, always cut away frayed edges, leaving a neat hole. Draw up circular holes gently before darning across. Lace triangular tears together on right side before darning on the wrong side. Pick up ladders in thick silk stockings with a fine steel crochet hook before darning.*

A woman's woolly jumper, or silk blouse or frock that has a lot of small holes while collar, cuffs and underarms are still in good condition can be repaired decoratively by embroidering small flowers or other designs in wool or silk over the holes.[9] (*Elizabeth Craig's Needlecraft*)

Of course mothers were always darning socks … My father could also darn. He would darn the holes in my teddy beautifully. (Sheila Coatsworth Brown)

I think mending/darning wool was not rationed. The colour range was huge. I can remember seeing them all hanging in rows in Woolworths. I remember wondering who darned in red. (Elizabeth Wade)

Dad's socks became 'decorated' with various darning wools! My darning was nearly a work of art on his socks and shirts. (Jean Hooper)

Garments could also be un-picked – being careful to save the thread – washed, and then turned so that the fresher inside was now on the outside.

Versatile, multi-purpose garments were a useful wartime stand-by and the pinafore became particularly popular, especially as it was quick and easy to make from existing garments:

Fused to make Pinafore Frocks from old winter coats. I used to go and stay with a friend for the weekend and make one and incidentally eat some of their rations. I used the lower part of the coat to make the skirt, join down the back and cut into a sort of 'A' line. The top part of the back made the front. The sleeves made wide back straps. If they wanted a belt and had not got a buckle I used to buy a leather wrist support and cut it in half so having straps one side and buckles the other. These made a very warm garment. Underneath you could wear any old garment (because not much showed) blouse, shirt or jumper. (Pat Salmon)

The useful pinafore dress. (By kind courtesy of Pat Salmon)

OUR HELPFUL TWELVE-PAGE SUPPLEMENT—A PRACTICAL GUIDE TO

Sewing for the HOSPITALS

IN these days of war-time every woman longs, with all her heart, to do her bit for her country. And—though not every woman can take a War-time job, there is one form of National Service open to all, but especially to the stay-at-homes . . . sewing for the hospitals which care for our gallant sick and wounded soldiers.

There is a tremendous need for hospital garments of every kind, things that any woman can make—in single numbers—at home, or—in bulk—at a working party. In giving up a few hours of your time to making the garments the hospitals so urgently require you will be playing a great and wonderful part in National Service . . . doing something truly worth while.

Because it is so necessary to have some guide as to the garments you should make, we of HOME CHAT bring you, this week, this SPECIAL SUPPLEMENT and our FREE PATTERN for Hospital Sewing.

The hospitals are wanting Bed-jackets . . . Hospital Shirts . . . Helpless Case Shirts . . . Vests . . . Short Drawers . . . Pyjamas . . . Day Shirts . . . Dressing-gowns . . . Bandages and Swabs . . . Surgeons' Masks and Coats . . . Dressing Aprons . . . Abdominal Towels—and, in planning this Supplement, we have included all these, as well as suggestions for convalescent wear for overalls and lingerie for those actually engaged in hospital work.

We have also incorporated in this Supplement designs which kind-hearted readers may like to make for the evacuated children, for whom the "Save the Children Fund" is doing such magnificent work.

Even if you can only make an occasional garment, the Hospitals will be grateful. But if you can interest a circle of your friends in Hospital Sewing, what a wonderful collection of garments could be gathered together.

By the way, on page 480 we give you addresses of where to send your contributions.

Central Press Photos Ltd.

ALWAYS an inspiration to the women of Britain, our beloved Queen holds weekly Sewing Parties for the wives of the staff of the Royal household.

OUR BARGAIN PATTERN

Bestway Bargain Pattern No. 17,399.

Price 4½d. Overseas, 9d. With coupon on page 506. Allow 3¾ yards of 31 to 36-inch material for " helpless case " shirt, and 1¼ to 1⅜ yards of 31 to 36 inch material for the short drawers. Cut in small, medium, and large sizes.

FOR the badly wounded cases the hospitals ask for specially designed shirts, fastening with ties down the front, to facilitate easy dressing. Our Bargain Pattern includes this shirt design—an authentic hospital "model"—and a pattern for the short drawers that will be worn under hospital suits when the patients are able to get about again. Both these you'll make in flannelette or winceyette, preferably in pale blue.

The 2 December 1939 issue of *Home Chat* patriotically featured a special twelve-page supplement appealing to its readers for their help in making 'Garments for our wounded and badly wounded on the Wards and off' including diagrams for making various bandages and a dressing apron for surgeons, plus the offer of a 'Bargain Pattern' of garments for the badly wounded. Illustrations of other 'Bestway' patterns included night-dresses and pyjamas for convalescents of all ages, an operating gown, nurses' coat-overalls and a doctor's coat-overall. Readers were told: 'Any number of bed-jackets, undervests and night shirts will be welcomed by the hospitals, for the use of the sick and wounded. These garments are simple enough for anyone to make who can do plain sewing …'. To give maximum encouragement to home stitchers, the supplement also showed the her Majesty the Queen, the President of the Red Cross, with a group of stitchers working on hospital clothing at Buckingham Palace. (Courtesy of © IPC + Syndication)

Then there was always the option of 'Refreshing':

> When a dress is not shabby, but you are merely tired of it, much smaller alterations using only oddments of material can be made. A contrasting yoke inserted into a plain bodice, a new collar of a different type and colour, fresh buttons or other trimming, long sleeves cut short above the elbow, with contrasting bishop sleeves added from there to the wrist – something of this sort, according to what is being worn, gives a fresh and up-to-date not with very little trouble or new stuff.[10]

At the beginning of the war there were still small quantities of pre-war furnishing fabic available, second-hand clothing could be obtained coupon-free at fund-raising bazaars or the few jumble sales, and market stalls sold – or claimed to sell – the damaged stock of bombed-out shops and warehouses. However, it was usually the case of making the most of whatever came one's way.

> I can still recall the smell of this wet, singed cotton that was sold on the market stalls at Market Drayton, and I remember my mother washing the long pieces and hanging them out to dry in the garden. (By kind courtesy of Marjorie Williamson 'From Inside the Wardrobe')
>
> I had some old material pattern books and made myself a patchwork jacket, feather stitched all round the pieces. (Kathleen Lever)
>
> We had plenty of lace, as my father's factory had to close down, as he made non-essential maids' aprons and caps, but also nurses' aprons and caps. (Frances Wilson)
>
> I was evacuated and working in Shropshire where we found a draper's shop which sold 'cheesecloth' and 'dusters'. … [the cheesecloth] was more like a thin winceyette. Several of the girls made nightdresses trimmed with bias binding and very serviceable they were. The dusters were at least 18in square and made of thick check cotton. I used some to make a yoke and sleeves of a dress with a small remnant. This eked out the clothing coupons. (Anon)

Sale of remnants and oddments. (Courtesy of the Imperial War Museum, London HU 36215)

A friend also made my mother a cotton dress made from 1 yard of material. I would love to know how!' It was short-sleeved and round-necked with no collar and a panel was let into the side bodice. The neck edge was probably bound instead of faced. 'I can remember my mother being so excited that this dress was being made for her.' (Angela Cole)

Flour bags became a most sought-after commodity and smuggling them out of the Docks unnoticed by the policemen on the Dock gates was a problem solved by fair means or foul (even beneath ladies' 'unmentionables' we were led to believe). After being washed, boiled and dyed, flour bags were made into curtains, pyjamas and even a smart 'linen' two-piece dress. (June Simper)

I loved my 'flour-bag' handkerchiefs, much softer for a sore nose now and then. (Barbara Parsons)

Cloth (cotton) sugar bags – my mother unpicked them for handkerchiefs. They were like muslin, soft on sore noses with a cold. Men's hankies were made from flour bags. Ladies' and children's hankies (were) made from sugar bags. (Betty M. Whenray)

My father sometimes brought home from his office (he was in the Royal Navy) rolls of a blue substance that was like modern plastic. She [mother] would wash it over and over again until all the blue and stiffness disappeared leaving a soft white fabric like cotton. We made blouses and handkerchiefs from it. (Delcia Miles)

Used sugar sacks made overalls for boys. (Barbara Adams)

I remember sending for parachute silk maps of East Asia, after reading an advert in the *Daily Telegraph*. They were a good size and I was able to make two pairs of pyjamas … I think the silks cost 3s 6d each and I bought four. They washed well and so lasted well too. (Joan Trethewy)

We could get a Viyella-type material and nuns' veiling without coupons, first used for night wear (the nuns' veiling must have been pure wool, it was very uncomfortable to put on – stopped prickling as you warmed up in bed). (Doreen Newson)

We had a lodger who was the manager of the local cinema, apart from the free seats at the pictures we had the added perk of the banners which advertised the films. I don't know how they were painted as I don't think the advertising ran, but we used to soak them – I think it must have been in soda water – it would have been cold water as we didn't have any hot to spare. These banners were made of cotton of various qualities. These were then made into sheets – run and fell seams to join them together. Coarser ones – tea towels and floor cloths. I had my dresses made from the fabric dyed in the copper and RicRack over the seams. (Susan Reynolds) (See photograph page 167.)

Also un-rationed were curtain net, cheesecloth and the butter muslin in which carcasses were wrapped, and, if one had a friendly butcher, it was possible to make nightdresses, dish-cloths, blouses and dusters. With a little ingenuity tablecloths, curtains, bed-valances and even rolls of cleaning rag, undertakers' white muslin for lining coffins ready for cremation and surgical lint could all be used."

'Mrs Sew-and-Sew' also tackled the 'Make Do and Mend' problems of men's clothing. 'SOME USEFUL HINTS FOR REPAIRING MEN'S AND BOYS' CLOTHES Smarten up your men!'[12] showed stitchers how to deal with worn pockets, 'trouser ends', shirts, trouser seats, vests, pants and pyjamas. Shirt collars could be repaired with material taken from the tails, which were replaced by oddments.[13]

My grandmother spent her evenings turning collars and facing worn cuffs. When shirts were no longer 'tidy' enough for the menfolk to wear, the best parts were made into blouses or pet-ticoats for me. (Audrey Hussey)

Collars and cuffs of men's shirts were repaired with material from the shirt's tail, which in turn would be replaced by material from the useful drawer. (Rosetta Price)

There was always the temptation, if one's husband or son was away, to transform his trousers, plus-fours, coats, jackets, pyjamas, shirts, cricket whites, sailors' whites and navy-blue bell-bottoms into clothing for the family – or oneself – for a man's suit could make a very smart new woman's suit. A wife was lucky if her husband was tall or heavily built – there was more fabric to use. Underpants could also be transformed into knickers with the addition of unrationed lace; shirts could be worn as blouses and even a pyjama jackets could be used as a blazer.[14]

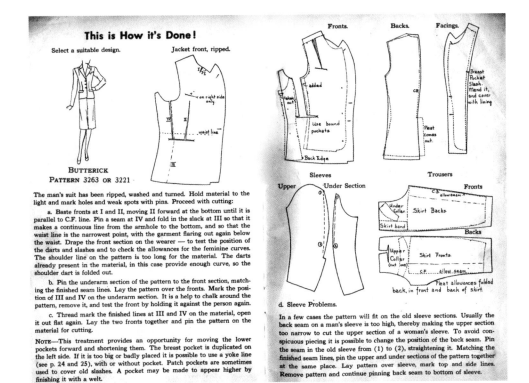

This is How it's Done!

Select a suitable design.   Jacket front, ripped.

BUTTERICK PATTERN 3263 OR 3221

The man's suit has been ripped, washed and turned. Hold material to the light and mark holes and weak spots with pins. Proceed with cutting:

a. Baste fronts at I and II, moving II forward at the bottom until it is parallel to C.F. line. Pin a seam at IV and fold in the slack at III so that it makes a continuous line from the armhole to the bottom, and so that the waist line is the narrowest point, with the garment flaring out again below the waist. Drape the front section on the wearer — to test the position of the darts and slashes and to check the allowances for the feminine curves. The shoulder line on the pattern is too long for the material. The darts already present in the material, in this case provide enough curve, so the shoulder dart is folded out.

b. Pin the underarm section of the pattern to the front section, matching the finished seam lines. Lay the pattern over the fronts. Mark the position of III and IV on the underarm section. It is a help to chalk around the pattern, remove it, and test the front by holding it against the person again.

c. Thread mark the finished lines at III and IV on the material, open it out flat again. Lay the two fronts together and pin the pattern on the material for cutting.

NOTE—This treatment provides an opportunity for moving the lower pockets forward and shortening them. The breast pocket is duplicated on the left side. If it is too big or badly placed it is possible to use a yoke line (see p. 24 and 25), with or without pocket. Patch pockets are sometimes used to cover old slashes. A pocket may be made to appear higher by finishing it with a welt.

d. Sleeve Problems.

In a few cases the pattern will fit on the old sleeve sections. Usually the back seam on a man's sleeve is too high, thereby making the upper section too narrow to cut the upper section of a woman's sleeve. To avoid conspicuous piecing it is possible to change the position of the back seam. Pin the seam in the old sleeve from (1) to (2), straightening it. Matching the finished seam lines, pin the upper and under sections of the pattern together at the same place. Lay pattern over sleeve, mark top and side lines. Remove pattern and continue pinning back seam to bottom of sleeve.

Transforming a man's suit. Instructions from the Ministry of Information: *MIRACLES OF MAKE-DO A REVISION OF RE-MAKE WRINKLES.* (Courtesy of The National Archives)

Everyone made skirts out of men's discarded trousers. (Frances Wilson)

… when my husband was away on a foreign commission (he was in the Royal Navy) I found his cricket flannels and cut them up to make a very nice cream wool coat. I was not a very popular wife when he came home and found out what I'd done. (Barbara Adams)

A pattern was produced for a woman's blouse that could be cut out from the unworn parts of a man's shirt (they had tails then). It's a family joke that my Dad said that his shirts used to disappear before they were worn out. (Barbara Saunders)

One lady made herself a skirt out of her son's trousers. 'Takes two pairs of they to go around I.' (Anne Honeybone)

Sadly, some attempts at 'Make Do and Mend' weren't entirely successful for various reasons:

The dress I hated most was made with parachute 'silk' – more like taffeta – maybe this was after the war – it was a dreadful shade of pink/orange and would never lie flat. (Sheila Coatsworth Brown)

My mother would use men's old trousers which were really worn at the rear and knees, and she would wash them, cut off the legs below the knees, open the seams, reverse the fabric inside out and turn it upside down. The seams were re-stitched in four panels and made up into skirts for me (which I hated!). (Valerie Watson)

I tried once to make a skirt out of a pair of short trousers for a friend's daughter – it really did not work because of the shape of the upper legs! (Delcia Miles)

[Mother's] most disastrous idea happened when she managed to get hold of some parachute silk. She made us each a pair of knickers out of this. They were comfortable and it would have been alright if the fabric had been white – but it was not. The silk was a lurid shade of bright yellow. My sister refused to wear them. I felt sorry for my mother after all that work and wore them to school. Of course the other children discovered that I was wearing these and I was known as 'parachute pants' for a while after. (Margaret Gibson)

Another little girl managed to rip, within the first hour of wearing, her 'beautiful cream silk crêpe dress piped with red' newly made by her mother from a tennis dress. (Angela Cole)

Parachute knickers and petticoats – my mother would make little rosebuds with ribbon to decorate all this sort of thing. My first bra was made of this same fabric, beautifully finished, but it still caused me great shame because all my classmates had bought ones! The elastic on my bra was knicker elastic, two lengths stitched to one corner of each triangle, crossing at the back and brought round to fasten at the front with a little loop over a button. (Sheila Westall)

I also made a pinafore dress out of [blackout material], but when I washed it, the weft was grey, while the warp was black. I remember seeing the scorn of my 'friend's' face… (Frances Wilson)

Left 1 This cross-stitch tablecloth (39½ x 40½in) catches Germany at a time of change, when new machines of the future upset the quiet of settled rural life. The children are waving their flags. (By kind courtesy of Liesl Munden)

Below 2 The *Ausieschaner*, 'a present peeking out of a pocket'.(Courtesy of the Imperial War Museum, London EPH 3872)

3 (By kind courtesy of Ester Friedman)

Clockwise, from top 4 This nightdress case was embroidered during the Second World War by a six-year-old girl, in her school air-raid shelter. As Needlework Monitor she found a school transfer for a crinoline lady and persuaded her teacher to let her embroider it. (A transfer was a mass-produced design drawn in thick ink on tissue paper. When ironed, ink side down onto fabric, the ink lines were transferred onto the fabric's surface. The usual source of embroidery designs, they were easily bought and often received free with magazines.) The school was able to supply the linen and threads. (By kind courtesy of Mary Harman. Photograph by David Pearce) (See page 18.)

5 Winston Churchill's siren suits were made in various materials and colours.[1] This siren suit is held by the National Trust at Chartwell, Kent. A similar green version is displayed by its makers, in the Churchill Room of Turnbull & Asser, London, having been one of a collection commissioned by Churchill's wife Clementine. (By kind courtesy of the National Trust. Photograph by Fiona Watson) (See page 21.)

6 Typical hand-embroidered wartime tablecloth which was embroidered while sheltering during air raids under the stairs. (By kind courtesy of Sheila Brown. Photograph by David Pearce) (See page 39.)

Note
1 Best, p.165

Clockwise, from above 7 Needlecases embroidered at junior school.(By kind courtesy of Jean Brown) (See page 68.)

8 Shoe-bag stitched at school by a girl aged eight.(By kind courtesy of Sheila Brown. Photograph by David Pearce) (See page 68.)

9 'Peggy and Golly.' (By kind courtesy of Janet White. Photograph by Pete Greenhalf) (See page 78.)

10 Rap doll stitched by a girl aged seven. (By kind courtesy of Gloria Barker. Photograph by David Pearce) (See page 79.)

11 Dolls' house pram and bedding. (By kind courtesy of Jean Brown) (See page 79.)

Left 12 'Suzy' was rescued from enemy bombing. (By kind courtesy of Gill Garratt) (See page 79.)

Below 13 Lucile Paray's gown for Marianne was decorated by fine, intricately twisted fine stems of golden corn delicately couched onto a ground of ivory silk organza and France's white organdie garden-party dress was embroidered with posies of the French wild flowers – poppies, marguerites and cornflowers, which were traditionally given to visitors in the French countryside.[2] (Courtesy of Collection 2007 Her Majesty Queen Elizabeth II) (See page 80.)

Note
2 Eaton, Faith, *Dolls For the Princesses*, Royal Collection Enterprises, pp.63-64

Clockwise, from above 14 The Japanese 'Changi Quilt'. (Courtesy of the Australian War Memorial, Canberra RELAWM 32526) (See page 184.)

15 Sheila Alan (left), internee of Changi Prison, with the 'Girl Guide Quilt'. (By kind courtesy of Betty Hall) (See page 184.)

16 'Kiri', from the Hilda Lacey Sheet. (Imperial War Museum, London EPH 4566) (See also pages 185–86.)

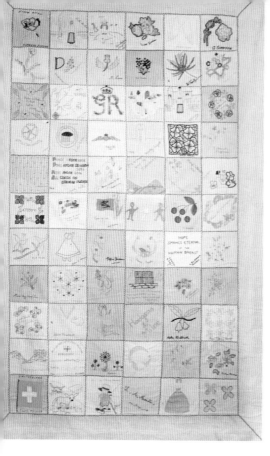

17 The British 'Changi Quilt'. (Courtesy of
the British Red Cross Museum and Archive)
(See page 184.)

18 The Australian 'Changi Quilt'. (Courtesy
of the Australian War Memorial, Canberra
REL/14235) (See page 184.)

Top and above 19 and 20 Details from the 8ft x 7ft 'Sheet' of Day Joyce. (Imperial War Museum, London 96/75) (See page 186.)

21 'Parable 1' by Lilian Dring. (Courtesy of the National Museum of Scotland a. 1962 1059) (See page 196.)

Left 22 Uniform of a captain in the 'Buffs'. (By kind courtesy of Kate Farrer)

Right 23 and 24 (By kind courtesy of Maureen Spencely. Photograph by David Pearce) (See page 188.)

25 A 'Penelope' kit of the badge of the Royal Army Medical Corps. One of the badges designed by the Royal School of Needlework for *Badges of H.M. Services*. (Held by the Imperial War Museum) (See page 188.)

26 'Covering Blanket.' (Courtesy of the Imperial War Museum, London EPH 2519) (See pages 191–92.)

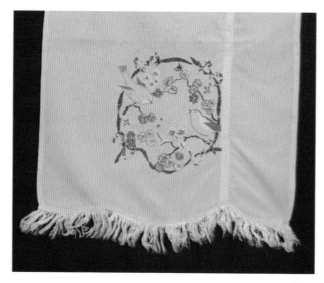

Clockwise from above 27 One of a pair of 'Bluebird' chairbacks embroidered on pieces of parachute.(By kind courtesy of Jo Humphries. Photograph by David Pearce) (See page 189.)

28 A 'Penelope' tablecloth kit used for forces' occupational therapy. (By kind courtesy of Delcia Miles. Photograph by David Pearce) (See page 192.)

29 Sampler. (By kind courtesy of Virginia Leonard-Williams. Photograph by David Pearce) (See page 191.)

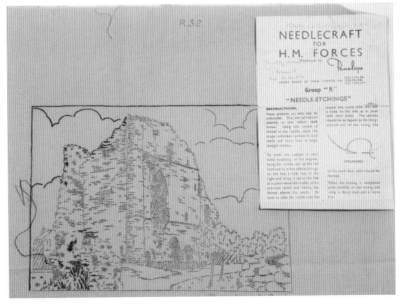

30 'Three Leaf Screen' embroidered by Her Majesty Queen Mary. (Courtesy of The Royal Collection © 2008, Her Majesty Queen Elizabeth II) (See page 193.)

31 'Penelope' kit bag and 'needle etching' kit of Knaresborough Castle. (By kind courtesy of Vera Goode. Photograph by David Pearce)

32, 33 and 34 A wedding gown made from a parachute. The maker solved the problems of radiating seams and bias cut by forming the complete circumference into a softly draped skirt and using the rigging cord to create a luxuriously ruched bodice. The hemline has been altered three times, for three different weddings. (By kind courtesy of Flambards Experience, Helston, Cornwall. Wedding Dress collection) (See page 198.)

35 Detail of Princess Elizabeth's wedding gown (20 November 1947) designed by Norman Hartnell. The Queen, Her Majesty Queen Mary and the eight bridesmaids were also dressed by Hartnell. (Courtesy of The Royal Collection © 2008, Her Majesty Queen Elizabeth II) (See page 212.)

36 *Finis*, from the sampler book of St Osyth Mahala Eustace Wood. (By kind courtesy of the family of St Osyth Mahala Eustace Wood and the Embroiderers' Guild) (See pages 210-14.)

37 'Queen Mary's Carpet.' (By kind courtesy of the National Gallery of Canada, Ottawa. Gift of the Imperial Order of Daughters of the Empire (Canada), 1950. 6081) (See page 216.)

38 'The Country Wife' depicts some of the activities of the members of the WI in 1951. (Copyright of The National Needlework Archive) (See page 225.)

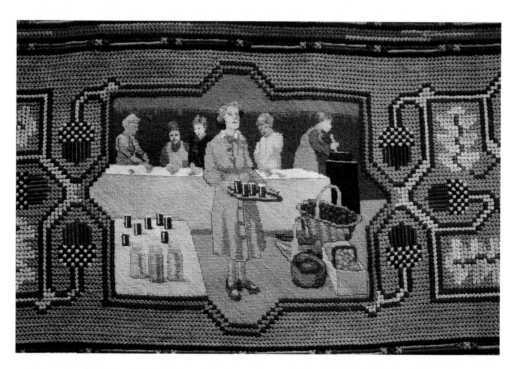

39 Preserving fruit. Detail of the Women's Institute tapestry 'Women's Work in Wartime'. Started in 1947, it took almost four years to complete. (By kind courtesy of the National Federation of Women's Institutes) (See page 223.)

I was about two and a half – my brother five and a half. I am wearing a white satin dress with smocking I believe it was made from a petticoat… I later remember visiting my dad when he was working on a big job on the River Thames building barges (later used in the D-Day landing I understand). He told me not to sit on the seats as he had just painted them, I of course did not do as I was told and ended up ruining my lovely white satin dress by getting green paint all over the back. (By kind courtesy of Irene Hearl)

I was less than thrilled with a navy coat given by an elderly neighbour to be remodelled for me to start at grammar school. Made of corded material the top half of the sleeve protruded into the bottom half with a point and definitely not uniform. The garment hung straight on my lanky frame with one larged covered button at the neck and a large popper at the waist. As an eleven year old I thought it had an obvious geriatric image. I suffered pangs of guilt at feeling so pleased when I outgrew it thinking of the effort my mother had put into making it thus sparing clothing coupons for use elsewhere. (Valerie Green)

I had an enterprising grandmother who discovered that dusters – the blue and white check kind – did not require coupons, so she bought several and sewed them together to make me a new dress and matching voluminous knickers. I was delighted to put on this quite attractive but rather flimsy dress and went out in the garden to play in it with my sister. I climbed our old apple tree to sit among the branches and contemplate my good fortune, when, horror of horrors! I got caught up on a branch and my lovely new dress was torn from top to bottom!! I was mortified … the material the dusters were made from was very thin. (Gloria Barker)

Wartime stitchers also had to make their own underwear, and that essential item of 1940s clothing, the corset, was perhaps the greatest challenge, and the workrooms of department stores and dressmakers enjoyed a brisk trade in re-boning and re-modelling. Worn-out corsets had to have their 'bones' and fastenings removed for re-use, for steel was urgently needed in military production and also elastic, when the Japanese captured the rubber plantations of Malaya and in 1943 the Government brought in the Elastic (Control of Use) Order (1943 No.90). A Government leaflet advised: 'When your suspenders wear out, cut away the worn part and replace with an inch or two of strong tape or braid.' Lux soapflakes also recommended the use of net curtains to make delicate and feminine brassieres. Petticoats had to be cut up to make knickers, which had to be darned and patched, the gussets maybe replaced with fabric such as worn-out tea-towels, and the elastic replaced with buttons. After this, lace was stitched over the patches and the whole garment dyed, maybe more than once.[15]

G.O.P. *Coupon-saving Pattern Service*

"SHORT LENGTH" SLIP AND KNICKERS

WE all know that home-made undies last much longer than those we buy, and we have designed this special set with present difficulties in mind. Without looking bitty, it combines several short lengths of material in a most attractive way. You may be able to cut the main sections from the best parts of a discarded nightdress or thin frock, and the family piece-bag is sure to provide scraps for the contrasting bands. Or this pattern may give you ideas for renovating your existing undies which are worn at the hems.

You will find undie-making an easy and fascinating job, too. By joining the bands with faggotting you get a luxurious hand-made set, and you can work out all sorts of interesting colour-schemes by varying the stitchery and the added bands. If you are pressed for time, the seams and bands can be stitched on the sewing-machine.

Both garments are cut on slim-fitting lines. The slip has a cleverly planned brassiere bodice, and the skirt fits into the shaped waistline, moulding the hips smoothly and flaring slightly at the hem-line. The knickers are cut in the popular wide-leg style, mounted on a narrow self-material band with a side fastening, so that you won't need that difficult-to-get elastic.

PATTERN No. 9

The patterns are cut to full length, so that you can make them up all in one material if preferred, or vary the arrangement of coloured bands according to taste. The pattern set (both garments) is available in three sizes, to fit 32-, 34- or 36-inch bust measurements. It costs 1*s*. post free, including diagram and directions for making. Send stamps or postal order to RUBY EVANS, c/o GIRL'S OWN PAPER, Doran Court, Reigate-road, Redhill, Surrey. We very much appreciate a gummed addressed label, ready to stick on your return packet.

Ruby Evans is now unable to supply soft toy materials. The paper patterns of all her offers during the past two years are, however, still available.

'New' underwear could be made from the best parts of badly worn garments. (*Girls Own Paper.* Courtesy of Lutterworth Press)

I joined the WAAF in January 1941 and was selected for 'Special Duties' which involved plotting eighty feet underground at Fighter Command HQ at Bentley Priory. To say the least life became hectic during watch with hardly enough time to blow our noses! But when the weather was inclement and flying was not possible we were allowed to take out our sewing – or maybe knitting and embroidery … We mainly loved to sew pretty lingerie – so out would come a positive rainbow of delicious coloured satins, crêpe de chine and oodles of *real* lace! In order to gather it, one just had to pull one of the fine threads at the top. We French seamed everything and the lovely laces had to be oversewn with very fine stitches and the end results were gorgeous. What effect it had on the controllers on a balcony above us, I can only guess. If the air battles above us suddenly started up, then we frantically had to stuff our sewing away out of sight (Muriel Pushman) (By kind courtesy of *The News*, Portsmouth 32/3A)

WAAF plotters. (By kind courtesy of *The News*, Portsmouth 32/3A)

Most prized of all were the clothes and household furnishings which would keep a family warm in the severe 1940s winters. To be cold was to risk illness and the nation urgently needed its workers. Candlewick bedspreads and blankets were turned into coats and dressing gowns – or people resorted to wearing coats at bedtime. It was in the Arctic temperatures of the '40s' winters that the wartime rabbit played its part – for rabbit skins were turned into mittens and coat trims, and also, under the instruction of the WI, they were used to line coats to be sent to Russia.

Early in the war she [mother] started rearing rabbits. Not only useful to augment food rations but after her father had killed them, she would skin them and cure the skins. From these she made numerous pairs of fur gloves and mittens. She made fur gloves for other people too. I think she was commissioned to make a fur coat. I do remember how difficult she said it was. The chief problem was getting the grain of the fur all to run in the same direction. (Mary Howse)

We kept rabbits after we were married for both their meat and skins. Mother began leather-work during the war and made fur-backed gauntlet gloves. (Doreen Newson)

I remember we even made the uppers of slippers from old felt hats. String soles were sold in the shops. It was a very tough job sewing them on! (Frances Wilson)

Before the war my parents had sold woollen rugs and consequently we had bundles of sample patterns so that people could choose the colours and pattern they wanted. Some of the samples were duplicated and were large enough to make slipper uppers. The soles were crocheted with string or binder twine. Pieces of old blanket or an odd sample were covered with material from an old pinafore or shirt and attached to the soles and finally the upper, bound with whatever was available, was sewn on. (Penny Hodgson)

G.O.P. *Coupon-saving Pattern Service*

COSY SLIPPERS

They are warm, gay and easy-to-make—and they will cost you next-to-nothing !

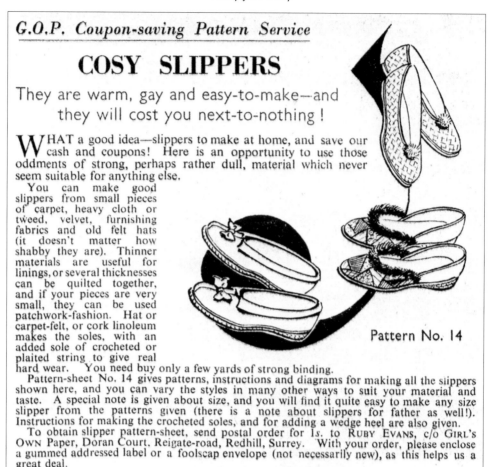

W HAT a good idea—slippers to make at home, and save our cash and coupons! Here is an opportunity to use those oddments of strong, perhaps rather dull, material which never seem suitable for anything else.

You can make good slippers from small pieces of carpet, heavy cloth or tweed, velvet, furnishing fabrics and old felt hats (it doesn't matter how shabby they are). Thinner materials are useful for linings, or several thicknesses can be quilted together, and if your pieces are very small, they can be used patchwork-fashion. Hat or carpet-felt, or cork linoleum makes the soles, with an added sole of crocheted or plaited string to give real hard wear. You need buy only a few yards of strong binding.

Pattern No. 14

Pattern-sheet No. 14 gives patterns, instructions and diagrams for making all the slippers shown here, and you can vary the styles in many other ways to suit your material and taste. A special note is given about size, and you will find it quite easy to make any size slipper from the patterns given (there is a note about slippers for father as well!). Instructions for making the crocheted soles, and for adding a wedge heel are also given.

To obtain slipper pattern-sheet, send postal order for 1s. to RUBY EVANS, c/o GIRL'S OWN PAPER, Doran Court, Reigate-road, Redhill, Surrey. With your order, please enclose a gummed addressed label or a foolscap envelope (not necessarily new), as this helps us a great deal.

Stitchers with strong fingers made cosy slippers to keep feet warm on the icy-cold surface of linoleum flooring. (*Girls Own Paper*, courtesy of Lutterworth Press)

Home stitchers could also earn an income as toy-makers, outworkers for military suppliers, makers of accessories such as rosettes and corsages, or from their patching and darning skills:

My mother had 27/6 a week to live on, from the Army. She decided to take in the mending for the evacuees. The school children evacuated in the village were from a very poor part of Newcastle. She did receive £1 per week for this work. She spent hour after hour trying to repair all these very worn clothes and my memory of that time was of her sitting mending and mending. She often used to say that there was often more holes in the garments than material! (Ann Walker)

An aunt made 'flower brooches' from scraps of felt to be sold at 'Bring and Buys'. (Anon)

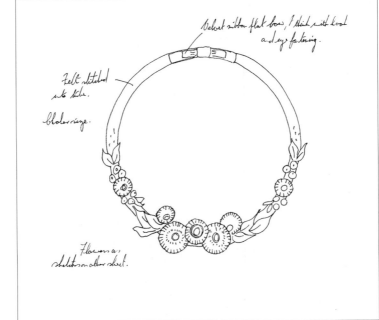

When one was thoroughly tired of wearing the same clothes, a bright felt choker could give it a new look. (By kind courtesy of Wendy Connor)

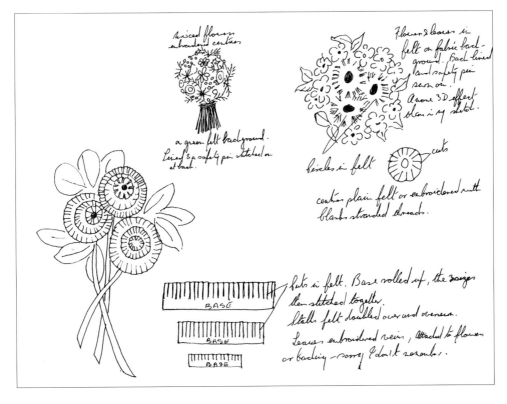

Ideas and patterns for home-stitched brooches could be found in most magazines, particularly *Woman and Beauty*. (By kind courtesy of Wendy Connor)

'One winter we did "Hats" … we were shown how to make our own "blocks" out of calico or old sheeting to measure about 21½in round the circumference. This was put, upside down, in a basin and the gooey stuff poured in and left to set. We used that block for years and years to make all our hats.' (By kind courtesy of Enid Mason)

That symbol of 1940s respectability, the hat, was also tackled with determination by stitchers at home, for hats and hat trimmings were not rationed and, as a consequence, the cost rose by a prohibitive 400 per cent. Professional milliners could re-model an old hat or even transform a man's top hat. Pointed pixie-hoods were quickly slipped on by both women and children, and there was always the turban to be made from a simple rectangle of cloth.[16]

The only thing I remember … [mother] making for other people were berets. From a coat and using a dinner plate as a pattern she would cut rounds of fabric. With a smaller plate to guide her she would cut a circle from the middle of one piece. The two pieces were stitched together on the wrong side, the edge of the inner circle was hemmed or bound and the result was a perfectly serviceable beret. (Sheila Westall)

If stitchers looked forward to the end of the war as a release from the drudgery of darning, patching and Make Do and Mend, they were to be disappointed; the Board of Trade's *MIRACLES OF MAKE-DO A REVISION OF RE-MAKE WRINKLES* informed them:

We are likely to face shortages of textiles for some time yet. While military demands are being rapidly curtailed, relief needs will make heavy inroads on world textile supplies. … Canadians are buying more clothing than ever before and the drain on our supplies is being further increased by the purchases of men and women discharged from the services.[17]

'...my mother did not have any new clothes during the war, owing to the lack of clothing coupons, but she went to a local Auction Sale (raising funds for "War Weapons Week" or some such) and bought some very attractive old pre-war curtains, which a local dressmaker made up for her into very attractive summer dresses. They were made of Cretonne ... and were very pretty with a large floral pattern on them. As my mother was a keen gardener, she loved these dresses and wore them for many years, even after clothes rationing came to an end.' (By kind courtesy of Gloria Barker)

But for anyone who cannot go back that far, it is really hard to imagine the total lack of most of the things which we now take for granted. (Virginia Leonard-Williams)

Because Britain was a nation of skilled and ingenious stitchers, the 'Make Do and Mend' campaign was one of the most successful on the Home Front. Indeed, the 'frivolous' and 'trivial' feminine pastime of sewing became one of the nation's most vital resources. Britain's stalwart band of home-stitchers refused to be beaten in their efforts to keep the nation properly clothed and in good morale despite the extreme shortage of materials. Yet 'Make Do and Mend' went deeper than this: every patch, darn and inventive solution to a clothing need was a statement – an individual's contribution – to Britain's proud boast: 'We can take it!'

Susan Reynolds in her cinema banner dress.

twenty-one

Women in Uniform

'… we were feminine creatures putting our normal lives
on one side to help with the war effort.'[1]

Private Kay Shirley. (By kind courtesy of
Meriel Pardoe)

A survey taken by the *Daily Mail* discovered that the
'wartime hardship' which troubled Britain's population the most was 'Women in Uniform'.[2] However,
taken out of the dependency and isolation of their
male-dominated homes and clad in the stitched
uniforms which declared them to be part of the war
effort, women would prove to be responsible, independent and courageous. Unfortunately in uniform
they would have deeply entrenched male attitudes
and opinions to deal with as well as the war.

Our clothing defines us in the eyes of others
and at the outbreak of the Second World War civilian clothing clearly identified the sexes, also one's
place in society. Men – who wore trousers – fulfilled
the 'masculine' role – going out to work, discussing world events, and maintaining leadership within
the family and community. Women and girls – who
wore skirts – were expected to be the home-makers, busy with their 'trivial' 'little woman' activities
and attention to their feminine appearance. Females
were usually considered to be irresponsible, mentally and physically weak, and of inferior intellect.[3]

When the British Government asked for women to take over the work of men who had
joined the armed forces, many fathers – whose word had to be obeyed – forbade their womenfolk to volunteer on the grounds that they could not be trusted to 'behave themselves' in the
company of so many servicemen, or would certainly be 'coarsened' while doing factory work.
In addition, men in the Trades Unions who had struggled to find work in the Depression of the
'30s, were also naturally loath to see women in the workplace.[4]

However, by March 1941 there was no choice, for Britain became the only nation to introduce female conscription. Nurses up to the age of sixty and women between the ages of
eighteen and fifty who were not already engaged in war work were obliged to register for
work in the services or factories.[5] Women who had serious home commitments were classified
as 'Immobile', and those who could be transferred to where they were needed most, within
Britain or overseas, were listed as 'Mobile'. Then in December 1941, it became compulsory

for women to enlist in one of the Auxiliary Services,[6] but by 1943, even this was insufficient, and the 'Immobile' female population was also called upon for war service within their locality.[7]

By 1944, there were some 7,120,000 women engaged full-time in the war effort[8] including the 160,000 who had replaced conscripted male bus drivers, conductors, and railway staff in the British transport system.[9]

Women's position in society had changed dramatically, and it was a shock to see females in the uniforms which had always been accepted as an expression of male power, however from the women's point of view it was a new, if challenging, experience of freedom, self-reliance and even power, which many eagerly seized, exploited and enjoyed despite the initial male conviction that they were capable only of cooking and cleaning, or maybe nursing. There were also grave doubts that women would have the courage and endurance to stay at their posts under enemy bombing. In time, all this was to be proved wrong:

Mrs E.V. Hunt and Mrs K.E. Devine of Portsmouth were the first two women in England to qualify as double-decker bus drivers. (By kind courtesy of *The News*, Portsmouth)

The men who ran the RAF had been very worried about how the WAAFs would behave once the bombing started. Now those who had been sceptical had to eat their words. The women were frightened. Who wasn't? But nearly all of them got on with the job, just like the men were doing. Some couldn't take it, but neither could a few of the men. They were no different really, all equally brave, all equally scared, all equally determined to keep their base and their pilots in the war.[10]

In 1940, WAAF Daphne Pearson GC was the first woman to be awarded the Empire Gallantry Medal (which was converted into the George Cross in 1941) for pulling a seriously injured pilot from his burning bomber and protecting him as the petrol tanks and load of 120lb bombs exploded.

Every woman who joined one of the forces forfeited her clothing coupon allowance and instead received a full uniform, including underwear: hence, by 1944, the Government was dictating what thousands of the nation's women were wearing at all times, except on leave. Strict regulations defined exactly how the uniforms should be worn: jackets, but not ties, could be taken off in hot weather or at social events such as dances, and the 'short sleeve order' permitted servicewomen to fold – not roll – their shirt sleeves to exactly 2in above the elbow.[11] It was possible, however, to make alterations such as using sanitary towels or folded fabric as shoulder padding, or taking in skirts at the waist.[12]

The alleged pre-occupation of the 1940s woman with her appearance was indeed often a factor in her choice of service, for the khaki of the ATS (Auxiliary Territorial Service) (which had originally been designed in blue, and in a similar style to that of the WRNS) was not as flattering to the complexion as the slate-grey of the WAAF (Women's Auxiliary Air Force), or the navy-blue of the WRNS (Women's Royal Naval Service).

WRNS River Pilots. (Courtesy of the Imperial War Museum, London A 24928)

… the women were tickled by the information that everything she wore was khaki, from panties to bra to greatcoat.[13]

I have to admit that my choice of Service was partly influenced by the fact that khaki would have done very little for my mousy hair and a sallow complexion…[14]

I didn't want to join because I didn't like the colour of the [ATS] stockings. They were a horrible green colour.[15]

I'll never forget the loathing on seeing my legs clad in khaki lisle stockings. I felt like my Gran. (Iris Bryce)[16]

Alas, the uniform did not suit me. For other ranks there were two sizes – too large or too small. … It barred promotion if one's appearance was not up to scratch. So I remained a glorious private.[17]

The Women's Auxiliary Territorial Service did its best to entice women to join – and wear the khaki uniform: they provided a 'specially tailored ATS battledress' to be worn whilst operating gunsites and in 1943 even issued an ATS handbag to accompany the two sets of uniform, four pairs of khaki lisle stockings, three pairs of khaki knickers, two pairs of men's blue and white striped pyjamas, shirts, collars and collar studs, three bras and two corsets. Posters attempting to portray the uniform as glamorous were 'banned for overdoing it'.[18] Nevertheless, the colour was just not appealing.

Maybe as her contribution to the morale of the khaki-clad ATS, Princess Elizabeth was reported to have been pleased with *her* uniform in 1945, when she insisted on enlisting as a Second Subaltern and the ATS uniform was also deemed suitable to appear at the Prime Minister's country house, Chequers, when, in the absence of the regular domestic staff who had been conscripted, ATS and WAAF volunteers took over the running of the house, including catering for continual working-weekend house-parties attended by top-level military, governmental and overseas guests.[19]

The navy-blue WRNS uniform was often regarded as the 'smartest'; however, when the garments became worn, Wrens had to buy their own replacements.[20] It included two uniforms, one for 'best' nicknamed a 'tiddy suit', a greatcoat by Hector Powe, a gabardine mackintosh,[21] white shirts and collars which had to be washed and shrunk before they would fit, and be rubbed with candle-wax to prevent them chafing the neck; navy-blue woollen knickers, bell-bottoms, a seaman's jersey, gloves, shoes, socks[22] and lisle stockings, plus a white jersey, turban and overalls when needed, although eight WRNS might be expected to share just two duffle coats.[23] With few exceptions, for their safety WRNS had to obey their motto 'Never At Sea'[24] even though one of their jobs was to train sailors![25] Any changes in uniform during the war were first considered by the Commandant of the WRNS, the Duchess of Kent.

The WAAF uniform was also worn with pride – sometimes after subtle alterations:

> She quite liked her blue uniform, after she'd shortened the skirt hem from the regulation 12in off the floor, taken it in to stop it looking baggy, adjusted her jacket, narrowed the waist and otherwise done a complete make-over on it. She thought her helmet particularly useful: 'The steel helmets served a very good purpose as far as the WAAF were concerned. Our uniform hats had voluminous tops, so we steamed them, up-ended them and placed our tin hat on top to flatten the crown.'[26]

With very few exceptions, all servicewomen were non-combatant: ATS operating anti-aircraft batteries were not allowed to fire the guns[27] and despite the white wool lining of the WAAF greatcoat, designed to be spread out on the ground to attract the attention of rescuers if one had to bale out, the WAAF were not allowed to fly the planes which they repaired and serviced.[28] It was usually a woman's function to underpin the male war machine – in the background. Only four servicewomen were promoted to the rank of General.[29]

Sometimes there would be men who'd been promoted that day, and we'd end up sewing the new badges of rank on their uniforms.[30]

Just leave it all to the Austin Reed Service

A.T.S. Jacket and Skirt	£11 . 5 . 0
Greatcoat . .	£10 . 13 . 3
Shirt and 2 Collars from	14 . 6
Cap and Badge from	£1 . 3 . 9
Stockings from	3 . 10
Tie	3 . 6
Shoes . . .	£2 . 1 . 0
Gloves . . .	10 . 6
Sam Browne Belt	£1 . 8 . 6

AUSTIN REED
of Regent Street and Principal Cities

London Telephone: Regent 6789

Advertisement for the Auxiliary territorial Service (ATS) uniform. (Courtesy of © IPC+ Syndication)

ATS on duty at an 'ack-ack' gun site, although women were not allowed to actually fire the guns. (By kind courtesy of *The News*, Portsmouth)

Even so, the work of the servicewomen of the Second World War was absolutely essential and some made outstanding contributions: it was WAAF Flight Officer Constance Babington Smith who, after closely studying air-reconnaisance photographs, alerted the RAF to the German V-1 flying-bomb development headquarters at Peenemund in Norway. Target bombing of the site resulted in the failure of Hitler's horrific plan to devastate Britain by sending 200 of the hugely destructive V-1 bombs an hour. This was reduced to 200 bombs a day.

The first task of the British servicewoman was to somehow establish herself in the eyes of male colleagues as reliable, competent and intelligent, whilst at the same time fulfilling the Government's 'Beauty as Duty' campaign which demanded that she continue to appear as attractive as if she were still the pre-war 'little woman'. *Vogue* described her task: 'The woman who could change instantly into uniform, or munitions overall and look charming, soignée and right, is the smart woman of today'[31] and the advice of women's magazines was that she should cultivate a fresh, healthy, natural, smiling face which '… must never reflect personal troubles'.[32] Indeed, when this was achieved, it was deeply appreciated:

> Another outstanding memory was a WAAF we called 'Smiling Morn'. As she served our flying meals she always had a smile for us and brightened up that Sergeants' Mess at Binbrook.[33]

Worrying that if Britain's women lost their feminine appearance there would be a sharp drop in the nation's morale,[34] the War Office commissioned Frederick R. Berlei to design a corset 'to safeguard women's femininity for the duration', in which they could be 'corseted, and corseted correctly'. Thoughtfully, a pocket was incorporated into the waist of this 'military corset', to be used instead of a handbag.[35]

However, no concession was made to the 1940s female desire for luxurious underwear and their uniform-issue knickers were not well received. The WAAF called their practical fleecy-lined military knickers 'passion-killers'[36] and the WRNS referred to their black woollen naval version as 'blackouts'.[37] These were so obviously designed primarily for warmth that they were presented to friends and relatives after the gussets had been removed, the legs joined and armholes cut to transform them into jumpers. Their value as knickers was realised later when on duty in cold and windy places such as the Scottish Hebrides.[38]

As the months passed and it became clear that Britain's women in uniform would not, after all, be a liability, they would actually be an asset, male preconceptions had to be revised and women were pleased to find that there were definite advantages to being in uniform:

> The first surprise was the difference my uniform made. It was quite amazing: I had walked into a world of friendly acceptance. In the train everyone talked to me, not only civilians

who wanted to know where I was off to
… But every one in every sort of uniform
took me for a mate. We were fellow sufferers,
we all had shoes that pinched, our uniforms
were hot, we were in a bloody awful situation taking orders from everybody, but we all
shared in this predicament, thanks to bloody
Hitler. It was suddenly tremendously exhila-
rating.[39]

Forty-three women in uniform were even
admitted into the world of British Resistance
when they were chosen to become members of the top-secret 'Special Duties Section'
operating under cover of the ATS uniform,
which worked in co-ordination with the
secret 'Home Guard' 'Auxiliary Units'.
Initially told that the work would be interesting and possibly dangerous, and after signing
the Official Secrets Act, the 'secret sweeties'
were shown the high-security underground
rooms of control centres where they would
pass on Intelligence gleaned by carefully
trained civilian spies along the south coast.
These 'ATS officers' were fully prepared
to continue broadcasting until invading
Germans were breaking down the doors into

Female pilots of the Air Transport Auxiliary (ATA).
(Courtesy of the Imperial War Museum, London
C 385)

their control rooms. They would only admit to being involved with 'signals'.[40]

But the most prestigious women's uniform of the war was undoubtedly that of the ATA[41]
(Air Transport Auxiliary), which ferried the Second World War aeroplanes to their RAF base
destinations; or, if damaged beyond repair, to the breakers' yards. 'The ATA girls looked sharp.
Their gold-trimmed navy uniform turned heads and secured the best rooms in hotels and good
tables in restaurants. …the uniform represented daring and dynamism to the general public.'[42]

However, it had only been after a determined fight that the first eight qualified women pilots
were allowed to join the ranks of the 'Ancient and Tattered Airmen',[43] being considered 'unworthy physically or temperamentally' for the job by 'the RAF's top brass' and initially, they were only
allowed to fly the open-cockpit de Havilland Tiger Moth and Miles Magister training planes.[44]

As the founder of the ATA, Gerard D'Erlanger, Director of British Airways, 'simply disliked
the sight of women in trousers' he decreed that they should at all times wear their Austin Reed
tailored uniform[45] of skirt, jacket and silk stockings in the freezing temperatures of the planes'
open cockpits from which pilots sometimes had to be lifted rigid with cold. Fortunately, he was
eventually persuaded to allow the women to wear trousers and the Sidcot flying suit, on the pro-
viso that they changed into skirts immediately upon landing, and this rule was later changed to
skirts being obligatory only in London or on leave.[46] Which meant that the female pilots could
'bale out' knowing that their skirts would not ride up embarrassingly during their descent!

Women members of the ATA, including twenty-five volunteers from America and four
Polish exiles, were eventually allowed to fly all of the 200 fighter planes and even heavy bombers which were used in the Second World War and like their male colleagues, they flew up to
four different planes each day, coping with the British weather and balloon barrages without
radio contact or training in the use of navigational instruments, being instructed to fly through,
rather than over, cloud. Just a page of information was issued on the operation of each type of
aircraft, to be read quickly and added to their ring-bound A6 'Ferry Pilot's Notes' kept in the

Three Land Girls of the Women's Land Army (WLA). (By kind courtesy of Dorothea Abbot)

breast pocket of their ATA uniform. 'It was a sustained aerial stunt that one seasoned British Airways instructor long after the war called, simply, "mind-boggling".'[47]

One of the initial problems of the female ATA pilot was obtaining a correctly fitting uniform, as pilots Margot Gore and Philippa Bennet discovered on their visit to the ATA's tailor whose assistants had not measured women for uniform before and were extremely embarrassed, for these were the days of 'respectability' based upon the clear separation of the clothing of the sexes.

> Length of sleeve, both from shoulder to elbow and elbow to wrist, had gone swimmingly, but his approach to the bust had, they thought, been unusual. He would take a few quick steps, throw the tape measure round the back, catch it in mid-air and, turning his head away as if he couldn't bear to look, wait until the two ends met before giving a fleeting glance to the number of inches it recorded.

Inevitably, when the measurements from crutch to ankle were achieved with a 'delicacy' that resulted in an excess of 4in to the trouser seats, they had to be returned for alteration.[48]

A far less glamorous uniform was that of the WVS (Women's Voluntary Service for Civil Defence) despite its designer being the couturier Digby Morton.[49] Originally green, which might have been seen as unlucky, a little grey was added and it was always greeted with gratitude and relief.[50] The WVS had been founded to co-ordinate women's voluntary groups and aid local authorities in welfare work and, in September 1939, it was given the massive task of aiding the evacuation of 1,473,000[51] disabled people, mothers and children; then, in January 1940,[52] the distribution of 45 million food rationing books. By the end of the war, there were 41 million women in WVS uniform.

> The W.V.S, tireless, superbly efficient, infinitely adaptable … distributed hot meals, tea, chewing gum from America, gallons of chocolate. It helped to evacuate from the city 307,768 mothers in 500 special trains. It sent 3,000 of its members with them, and with the members 7,000 urns of tea. … It provided 200,000 garments for people who had lost everything but the things they stood up in … la-di-da milady worked side by side with the cockney street warden, was everywhere, at all times, night and day, wherever bombs were coming down.[53]

Yet another uniformed female force of the Second World War, which was at first distrusted by men, was that of the WLA (Women's Land Army), or 'Land Girls', partly because farmers could not believe that women of smaller stature would be strong enough for the heavy work. Yet by the end of the war there were some 117,000 Land Girls[54] including ex-librarians, shop assistants and domestic servants working on farms and market gardens, draining and reclaiming land, thatching,[55] keeping down vermin, or in the Timber Corps (nicknamed the 'Lumberjills', or 'Pole Cats').[56] Due mainly to their efforts, British timber production quadrupled[57] and the acreage of arable land increased by 43 per cent.[58]

The work was hard for women who were unused to outdoor manual labour, for at the outbreak of war agricultural work in Britain was physically demanding and mainly done by hand, or with horses.[59] However, the 'Girls' of the WLA coped determinedly with the weather, farm animals and farm machinery, and also having to live away from home at an isolated farm or in a WLA hostel. After a hard day's labour many were comfortably accommodated and well fed, but others led a spartan existence, sleeping in unheated rooms on straw mattresses, with no available hot water or flushing toilet.[60] However, many of the women enjoyed greater health and happiness in the WLA way of life. As Doris Benson said: 'I was just given an axe and got on with it. It was as simple as that. But I found it came very naturally to me and I loved the rhythm of it and the sound the axe made. I think most of the girls really loved the life….'[61] and, despite some women disliking having to wear their trousers, their WLA-issue clothing was the best wardrobe some had ever possessed.[62] The 'Land Girls' of the WLA were rather proud of their uniform despite the general public prejudice against women farm-workers.

> There were 'corduroy jodphur-type trousers, knee-length woollen stockings pulled right up to your knee and then turned over – you needed a garter to hold them up. Lace-up brown shoes, green jersey – 'V' necked, with a long-sleeved shirt and tie, and we also had arm bands on our arm – they were green. Top coat and hat … a heavy top-coat with a slit in the back. It came down to your knees, double breasted. And we wore a felt hat and we all wore them in a different way. There was a fawn drill milking coat and dungarees, two aertex shirts, six pairs of woollen socks, canvas gaiters as a substitute for gumboots … I was disappointed to find the greatcoat missing… (Dorothea Abbott)[63]
>
> It was now the end of November [1942] and none of the new girls had yet been issued with greatcoats. The mornings were often frosty or foggy and our drill milking coats were too thin to keep out the cold, even when we wore them with corduroy breeches and green jerseys underneath. Cycling to work became an endurance test. (Dorothea Abbott)[64]

Like factory girls, the WLA found that a headscarf worn turban-style would protect their hair from wind, rain and the fine chaff and cavings thrown out by threshing machines,[65] but they had a constant struggle with their socks:

> Darning was a hated chore, and many were the devices to avoid it. A hardy Suffolk volunteer didn't wear socks at all, having found her boots so comfortable. Many others knitted their own from oiled sea-boot wool. Re-footing and patching were relatively simple solutions, not favoured by the girl from Kent who sewed little wash leather shields into the toes and heels of hers. (Dorothea Abbott)[66]

'Land Girls' even kept up their work on the exposed fields of 'Hellfire Corner', Kent, and as the years passed farmers came to appreciate and value their presence.[67] However, the British women in uniform who were sent overseas possibly experienced the most difficult conditions – but also the greatest appreciation. The Women's Auxiliary Service (WAS) was a band of encoders who 'turned feral' when the Japanese overran Burma, equipping themselves with slacks, bush shirts, gum boots and a mobile canteen with which 'they popped up relentlessly' for three and a half years wherever men were fighting the Japanese in the humid, disease- and insect-ridden jungles across south-east Asia, and even in Japan itself. 'They offered tea to prisoners of war who'd survived forced labour on the infamous Burma Railway, the emaciated men often crying at the sight of the first women they'd seen for years.'[68]

The women of the Queen Alexandra's Imperial Military Nursing Service also served overseas in the midst of enemy action:

> In slacks and battle blouses eight nursing sisters on No.1 Mobile Military Hospital slogged through sandstorms and battlefield debris as part of the expeditionary force, covering well over a thousand miles in seven weeks. Time and again it wasn't their nursing skills which impressed the patients – just the mere fact of being female and being there. No one expected women to submit to such conditions, and to be just on the heels of advancing troops.[69]

Despite being in uniform for up to six years, women did not lose their feminine independence and at the end of the war, in August 1945, just for amusement, these women of St Ives in Cornwall dressed up in the uniforms which had been denied them during the war – that of the Home Guard – and won first prize in a VJ Carnival. Throughout the war, women in uniform had proved that they were an immensely valuable national resource of intelligence, good humour, bravery, endurance and compassion.

(By kind courtesy of St Ives Trust Archive Study Centre)

twenty-two

BP — SOE

'The British Secret Service has a great tradition. Germany possesses nothing comparable to it … The cunning and perfidy of the British Secret Service is known to the world, but it will avail them little unless Germans themselves are ready to betray Germany.'

Adolph Hitler

The Second World War was a war of secrets: nation attempted to deceive nation in a multitude of ways – spies, agents and double agents, surveillance and counter-surveillance, sabotage, espionage and counter-espionage – and stitched garments were to play quite unusual roles. In 1939, Germany possessed, it seemed, an impregnable secret means of communication using an encryption and decryption device named 'Enigma'. Looking like a portable typewriter with light bulbs on top and using 17,576 alphabets, it could give a possible 15 million alternatives for each message; in addition, its settings could be changed daily.[1] However, Polish Intelligence had begun to unlock the secrets of 'Enigma' in the 1930s, using the 'Bomba', a mechanical de-coding machine which could rapidly sift through the virtually infinite possibilities of combinations. Upon the imminent invasion of Poland by the Nazis, the work was hurriedly passed to the French and British Intelligence. When France fell to German occupation, Britain continued alone.

The task was taken up by the Government Code and Cypher School at Bletchley Park, Hertfordshire[2] and Bletchley Park itself became one of Britain's greatest secrets of the war. By 1945 nearly 10,000 people[3] were working within its security-fenced fifty-six acres, yet even the inhabitants of the nearby village of Bletchley were not aware of what was going on.

Strangely, stitch was to play a role in the progress of this vitally important work for relaxed clothing became part of the informal atmosphere which was allowed at Bletchley in order to encourage creative thinking. Newcomers were shocked by the mixture of civilians and military personnel and by the absence of the rigid 1940s social dress-codes by which the classes were easily identified.[4] So many and various were the uniforms of those who were called to work there, that even the obligatory practise of saluting had to be abandoned.[5] For security, visiting senior officers of the forces were requested to wear civilian clothing, although the Royal Navy refused to comply.[6]

Everyone who worked at Bletchley Park was required to sign the Official Secrets Act, and the majority of people were not even told the purpose of their work – including Lieutenant Colonel Fillingham, who was in administrative charge of the camp's Army personnel – a number of whom were civilians who had been given an Army rank and uniform upon arrival.[7]

While for the officers in charge of the camp, we were a funny lot of soldiers who were doing some peculiar job or other. The sight of some soldiers – as they shambled about, uniforms awry, caps at strange angles and badges and boots uncleaned – must have galled the CO, Colonel Fillingham, deeply. From time to time, goaded beyond endurance, he would explode with rage... [He] did what he could to keep us up to some sort of military scratch and to repel the egalitarianism and informality of BP...[8]

What mattered more than a parade-ground appearance was intelligence, and at the core of Bletchley Park were some of the finest brains in Britain who had the seemingly impossible task of deciphering the mass of unfamiliar and complex material which was being being received from intercepted German 'Enigma' broadcasts.[9] Three quarters of the British national chess team were brought in, and winners of the *Times* crossword contests, or those who could solve a *Times* crossword without writing down a single clue.[10] Bletchley also co-opted Egyptologists, amongst others, with experts on porcelain, university dons, scientists, business executives, booksellers and mathematicians.[11] In their preliminary interviews, they might be asked to complete the *Daily Telegraph* crossword puzzle in twelve minutes.[12] This core group of outstandingly intelligent 'Boffins', as they were known, were affectionately respected by all, and there was a feeling of responsibility for their well-being, for as well as being conspicuous by their dress, they could be a little absent-minded.[13] Josh Cooper once left for home, hat in hand and briefcase held over his head[14] and Max Newman, carrying a dead hare, was found worriedly searching the platform of Bletchley station for his lost railway ticket, to find out whether he was on his way to Oxford or Cambridge.[15]

They wore a strange assortment of ancient overcoats, old macs tied with string, woolly hats made from tea cosies and sometimes pyjama trousers showing underneath everyday clothes.[16]

Angus Wilson: He used to mince into the room, swaggering, and wore what were outrageous clothes in those days – a bright yellow waistcoat, red bow tie and blue corduroy trousers.[17]

Alan Turing: He dressed in a way that put the average tramp to shame [wearing] his tie to hold his trousers up, and … a piece of rope to tie his voluminous raincoat around him as he cycled along. (John Bowring, nearby Corps of Signals)[18]

By 1940, Alan Turing, with W.G. Welchman,[19] had designed a British 'Bombe', and, to break the even more complex codes used by German High Command in their *Lorenz* machine, the 'Colossus' was designed and built in 1943. The first cipher to be broken was that of the *Luftwaffe*, in May 1940,[20] and then the *Heer*, but it was not until U-boat 110 was captured on 9 May 1941,[21] and Bletchley received its 'Enigma' machine plus related documents,[22] that the vital *Marine* and *Kriegsmarine* keys were broken, allowing German naval communications to be monitored almost daily. There was now advance warning of bombing raids and the appalling losses of British shipping in the Atlantic could be dramatically reduced. Also through the indexing and cross-referencing of deciphered information, a closely detailed knowledge was built up of all that was happening in Germany, including details of the uniforms and regiments of men who had escaped from prison camps – thus proving that they were still alive – which was wonderful news to their wives and relatives in the Bletchley personnel.[23]

To retain this advantage, complete secrecy was essential, and the 'Ultra'-coded information was only passed on to forces' commanders and the ARP if its source was not revealed. However, in the early spring of 1942, the German Navy replaced the three rotors of its 'Enigma' with four, and Bletchley could no longer break the codes. Again, the U-boat 'wolf packs' decimated British shipping, which continued until October 1942 when three members of the Royal Navy courageously entered the sinking U-559 to retrieve its vital 'Enigma' documents. Two of the men were drowned, but their sacrifice was of tremendous significance to Britain, for, by December 1942, Bletchley was once again in command of the German *Kriegsmarine* communications[24] and such was the subsequent devastation to enemy U-boats that by mid-1943 they were withdrawn from the Atlantic and the Battle of the Atlantic was over.

Churchill insisted that the latest information from Bletchley be relayed to him directly, from his 'geese who lay the golden eggs and never cackle' of which one-third of were civilians and three-quarters were women,[25] including WRNS, WAAF and ATS. In 1942, 3,000 WRNS took over the eight-hour around-the-clock 'spells' of the men who were operating[26] the Bletchley 'Bombes',[27] and despite the informality of Bletchley Park, they were expected to maintain their uniforms to the usual high standard,[28] somehow managing to remove the black grease of the machines' drums from their white shirts so as to appear once again in immaculate uniform for their next eight-hour shift.[29]

However trying, this problem was trivial compared to those encountered by the Intelligence agents of another top-secret British organisation, the 'Special Operations Executive' (SOE), who lived as apparently innocent individuals in enemy-occupied countries across Europe, Africa, the Middle East and the Far East.[30] For them, wearing the correct garments meant the difference between life and death.

Churchill's plan in 1940 was that SOE should 'set Europe ablaze'[31] with networks of resistance, escape lines to aid RAF aircrew who had been shot down over Europe, and supply vitally needed Intelligence.[32] However, this was soon extended to undermining the morale of the enemy, raising the morale of the occupied population, and sabotage … even assassination, of which the British military establishment did not approve, and SOE was given the name of 'The Ministry of Ungentlemanly Tactics'. One of the most disapproved of these tactics was the recruiting of women[33] – some 3,000[34] out of the 13,000-strong organisation,[35] for SOE agents operating radios in German-occupied France had a life expectancy of no longer than six weeks.[36] Agents who felt that they would break under torture could request a poison pill to be sewn into their cuff.[37]

SOE women were fully combatant, being trained to kill, sabotage such vital enemy communication links as railways and bridges, and use clandestine radios to send and receive messages in Morse. To protect them under the Geneva Conventions, all were given commissions in the WAAF or FANYS;[38] however, if captured, they would not be wearing their uniforms and could therefore expect to be executed as spies. Fifteen of the fifty female agents sent to France were caught, interrogated and sent to concentration camps including Violette Szabo, who was taken prisoner in France shortly after D-Day and executed;[39] only three survived.[40]

Each agent took on an assumed identity and it was vital to be dressed for the part. Fortunately the stitchers working for the SOE, who had signed the Official Secrets Act, were masters in disguise, maybe padding jackets to give the wearer a hump, or using clothing which had been worn by European refugees, including accessories such as suitcases, hats, gloves and ties[41] and being particularly careful to follow the different stitching practises for each country, such as sewing on buttons with parallel stitches on the clothes of an agent departing for France.[42] A workroom would turn out around 200 shirts in a week based on the careful observation of a collection of clothes from each country showing collar and cuff shapes, positions of buttonholes, shapes of plackets, construction of seams and manufacturing processes.[43] They made suitable underwear for prostitutes gathering information in Parisian brothels and worked closely to the instructions of agents who knew exactly what should be worn.[44] One invaluable tailor was a German who had escaped from the Nazis and knew every detail of men's suits from Germany, Spain, Italy and Czechoslovakia. Not only were his suits for the SOE in Germany completely authentic in construction but he made sure that they looked well worn, often wearing a suit for a week, day and night:

> …we used to gently rub a very thin film of Vaseline over the creases, so that when you hung your jacket up you got a dirt mark where the creases had been. You used rotten stone again to dust on them to take the newness out of them and on the lapels like you'd use a bit of very fine sandpaper to take the gloss off them. (Darlow Smithson)[45]

Most of the personnel at Bletchley Park had overlooked – or completely forgotten about – the appearance of their clothing in the relaxed atmosphere where the important task was to unlock and use the secrets of 'Enigma'; yet the clothing of Britain's SOE agents could not have been more closely scrutinized – and if not perfectly designed and stitched would have led to their death.

twenty-three

'For You the War is Over'

Capture

The shock of being captured was tremendous. A mind and body geared to constant danger, exhausted, or in the thick of the deafening noise of battle, killing or being killed, was thrown into complete confusion when suddenly denied action. Already overloaded senses had now to respond to the shock of being completely under the control of the enemy and, as such, useless to the Allied war machine. If a German soldier knew no other English, he learnt to say 'For you the war is over'. Stitch helped to alleviate the situation, or even provide a means of escape.

It was preferable to be captured in uniform, for in civilian clothing one had no protection under the Geneva Conventions and Gestapo treatment of 'spies' or enemy agents was severe – interrogation and torture, then execution or incarceration in the inhuman conditions of a labour or concentration camp.

Hunger, Thirst, Frostbite, Disease, Boredom

Conditions in prisoner-of-war camps varied considerably, however for many their months and years would be haunted by hunger, thirst, cold or humid heat, illness and boredom or the extreme physical exhaustion of overwork. The Red Cross were allowed to provide a weekly food parcel for each prisoner, although these were not always received. The JWO also sent clothes and items which would provide mental stimulation, plus parcels from next-of-kin, who were given, from 1942 onwards, an initial allowance of forty coupons plus a further twenty coupons every three months for purchases.[1] These parcels meant the difference between starvation and survival, sanity and psychological collapse. Even more important were the precious letters from home, also organised by the Red Cross.

Uniform

One of the stipulations of the Geneva Conventions was that the Detaining Power must provide clothing and footwear for its prisoners,[2] however so many prisoners were taken by both sides in the Second World War that it was not possible to provide even such a basic necessity. Taking a pride in appearance was a boost to morale whilst giving an impression of independence from one's captors and many officers employed a batman or orderly to care for their clothing.[3] A shared determination not to let standards fall also created the bonds of comradeship which were essential to survival.

Prisoners of war collecting Red Cross parcels. (Courtesy of British Red Cross Museum and Archives IN433)

When a man did not have his own uniform, he was given various items from the uniforms of other armies which had fallen to Germany as a form of humiliation. This resulted in some strange combinations, which men were able to exploit, either wearing their outfits with ostentatious enjoyment, or cultivating a deliberate, contemptuous slovenliness, as was so effective when practised by the prisoners of Colditz.[4] However, by 1943, when Germany was convinced that Britain must be on the brink of defeat, camp guards were disturbed to find that their British prisoners were smartly uniformed and healthy, readily giving away the chocolate and cigarettes from their Red Cross parcels, instead of the beaten, tattered men of previous years.[5]

Seams

The blocks of three-tier bunks in POW camps allowed typhus-carrying lice to fall on sleepers during the night, which then hid in the seams of clothing; they could sometimes be killed by running a lighted paper over the seams.[6] Sometimes, in badly infested camps, partly for their own protection, to kill both eggs and insects, guards gave permission for clothes to be hung outside overnight to freeze; or prisoners were stripped, and their clothes hung on racks to be wheeled into ovens.

Escape and Evasion

Around 35,000 British men and women escaped to freedom from prison camps during the Second World War: it was their duty.

MI9 issued top-secret escape maps printed onto 21in squares of silk,[7] rayon or mulberry paper, which could be sewn into the recesses of uniforms, worn as neck-scarves, stuffed into hollow boot heels, or hidden in cigarette packets. Large-scale maps printed on rice-paper could also be sewn into air crews' uniforms. MI9 also issued 2.3 million tiny compasses to hide behind cap badges or in collar studs and epaulettes; or to sew onto uniforms in the guise of 'tunic buttons' or 'fly buttons'.[8]

Stitch was essential for successful escape and evasion, for it depended largely upon having the right clothing so as to remain unnoticed. The inventive genius of MI9, Christopher Clayton-Hutton, designed 'a new RAF mess dress' which could easily be turned into a *Luftwaffe* uniform, and made sure that a pamphlet describing this 'new uniform' 'accidentally' fell into enemy hands, thus ensuring that it was accepted without suspicion. He recalled:

> With the aid of the Wool Association, we saw to it that the correct cloth was employed. Then, attractive wire facing had to be included, so we simply used suitable lengths of wire to bind up our parcels. The prisoners, we knew, had learnt to fashion their own Iron Crosses, but we thought it would help if we sent them packets of handkerchiefs tied up with strips of black and white material, from which the right ribbons could be made.[9] (© Ian Dear, 1997)

However, only the most perfect clothing was essential for escape through Italy:

> The Italians are fascinated by the minutinae of dress and the behaviour of their fellow men… suits made from dyed blankets, the desert boots cut down to look like shoes and the carefully bleached Army shirts were hardly ever sufficiently genuine-looking.[10]

Stitch also played another vital role in the digging of escape tunnels Tom, Dick and Harry at Stalag Luft III. The sand from the tunnels was yellow and as the soil of the compound was grey, it had to be subtly scattered and the solution was to sprinkle it out of bags stitched from German-issue towels[11] or the long underpants supplied by the Red Cross 'Bless their maternal hearts. They were the only things we had plenty of'.[12] Filled with the excavated yellow sand, these were hidden inside trouser-legs, attached to a cord running round the neck: '… the bottom of each sack secured by a pin on a length of string extending inside the pocket' which, when released, allowed the sand to trickle out. 'The sheer amount of sand to be dispersed was enormous. …the maximum amount of sand disposed of in one day was four and a half tons.'[13]

While the tunnels were being dug, the camp's tailor, Tommy Guest, and his team of 'anyone who could sew'[13] were secretly hand-stitching nearly fifty outfits to disguide the excapees once they were outside the wire,[15] which was made easier by the similarity in colour between the *Luftwaffe* and RAF uniforms.[16] Men stitched secretly about the camp using fabric which had been smuggled in or taken from old de-constructed uniforms and the linings of greatcoats, using Guest's collection of patterns made from German newspapers for the cutting out. The old, heavy serge Polish uniforms which had been sent by the Red Cross provided more fabric after it had been shaved of nap and dyed with beetroot juice, diluted boot-polish or even the dye taken from book covers. The prisoners worked quickly – a man who wanted a German porter's uniform was fitted at 1 p.m. and the uniform, with cap, was finished at 5 p.m.[17] At the last minute, each man sewed his 'special kit' into the hidden pockets.[18] The clothing was so convincing that on the night of the escape, 24 March 1944, would-be escapers, nerves stretched to breaking-point, almost passed out with shock, believing that their fellow-prisoners were Germans.[19] Sadly, fifty of the seventy-six officers who escaped were later caught and shot. After the camp's memorial service, each remaining prisoner sewed a black cloth diamond onto his sleeve.[20]

Individuals and smaller groups also took their chance to escape, maybe when outsiders came into the camp: Pat Leeson escaped with the tophat and blackened face of the camp's German chimney sweep and a group of prisoners walked out dressed as a visiting party of Swiss camp inspectors.[21]

However, months of painstaking secret preparation could be lost in just a few devastating minutes in one of the frequent and sudden camp searches, as was the fate of Richard Pape's laboriously assembled escape kit including a knapsack, jacket and blanket-lined mittens made from the curtains of the camp *Kommandant's* waiting room, and a white over-suit for camouflage in the surrounding snow made from a sheet pulled from beneath a newly deceased prisoner's body in the camp hospital.[22] Persistent escapers were sent to the *Sonderlag* at Colditz, near Leipzig,[23] where they continued to endeavour to escape.

'Lines'

Once through, over or under the wire, an escapee depended for his clothing, food, maps, transport and identity papers upon the tremendous courage of partisans and the 'lines' of secret Resistance which stretched across occupied Europe. Those who sheltered or helped them faced terrible consequences if caught. MI9's PAT-line, which aided up to twenty-five men each week,[24] referred to the evaders and escapers as 'parcels', and messages were passed such as 'I am sending the shirt and trousers in two parcels, which should arrive by goods train at the Gare du Nord on November 8 at 8.45'.[25] (© Ian Dear, 1997) Sadly, after around 600 people had reached freedom, the network was betrayed.

The Final Months

Late in 1944, as the Russian Red Army closed in on the German Reich from the east, sick and starving prisoners were forced to leave their camps and march hundreds of miles along frozen roads to camps deeper within Germany. Stitching then became a desperate and last-minute means of survival as clothes and shoes for the march were hastily repaired, patched and darned. Shirts, with sleeves tied to form shoulder-straps and bottom opening stitched across, were turned into rucksacks,[26] but the conditions were appalling and clothing which was already worn soon fell apart, as did the rags being used to bind the prisoners' frozen feet. One soldier who took off his trousers for the first time in three weeks discovered that his underpants had disintegrated. The starving men who survived, covered in sores and abscesses, were often saved only by the determination of the Red Cross to find their shuffling frozen columns and distribute food parcels.[27] To add to their woes, Allied planes sometimes mistook their lines for columns of German infantry and clothing became a last defence for one group when men had the idea of spreading their greatcoats on the ground to spell out 'RAF'.[28] These terrible marches were essential, however, for over the following months some 30,000 British POWs who were still held within northern European prison camps, disappeared, presumably into the labour camps of Siberia.

Liberation

When the liberation of Germany's prisoner-of-war camps finally came, the prisoners were asked to 'stay put' until relief organisation was arranged and the cold, starving men raided their camps' stores for food, clothing and alcohol. Discarding their tattered and inadequate clothes, some put on whatever they could find, including the uniforms of the enemy – which greatly confused the soldiers sent to release them.[29]

However, many men decided to leave as fast as possible and 'liberated' whatever German vehicles they could find to begin their journey home,[30] looting wherever, and whatever, they could – including sewing machines, clothing and household linen, all to be loaded onto the bombers and transport planes sent to fly them back to Britain.

When the ex-prisoners finally arrived back in Britain, the nation was shocked by their appearance, not realising the terrible conditions under which they had been living. Louse-ridden clothing had to be stripped off and burnt and bodies de-loused, although some men asked to keep what clothes they had as evidence of their time of extreme hardship. Once cleaned thoroughly, dressed in new uniforms, their medals and badges carefully sewn into place, they were at last able to do what they had dreamt of for so long – go home.[31]

Burma

As the war dragged on in Burma, prisoners of the Japanese were enduring the same infestations of biting insects and hunger, but with a humid heat which rotted uniforms within weeks.[32] Against the orders of their officers, who could not be forced to work, and were quartered in relatively luxurious accommodation, the exhausted lower ranks who were being used as slave labour abandoned the British uniforms in which they sweated and risked the septic sores which developed from the rashes caused by sweating[33] and adopted instead the Japanese-style 'fundoshi', a small loincloth which tied at the waist, made from a rectangle of cloth cut from a pair of trousers or a shirt, or whatever they could surreptitiously pilfer.[34]

Civilians in Singapore

In 1942, upon the British surrender of Singapore, its civilians were forced into severely over-crowded internment camps and, believing that internment would last just a few days, many of the women hastily equipped themselves with their work-baskets containing threads, needles, scissors and patterns as a way to pass the time. As their incarceration stretched into years, this hand-stitching and embroidery became a means of survival both bodily and psychologically.

Elizabeth Ennis was married just four days before she and her husband were taken into their three-year imprisonment, and she quickly organised a Girl Guide Company of twenty girls, in Changi Prison, their 'uniform' being a white dress, which every girl possessed, and their first task was to stitch their emblems using as a pattern the trefoil which Mrs Ennis had with her. After begging and bartering for a piece of old navy skirt and some embroidery threads, they were each given threads, circles of fabric and cardboard and a safety-pin with which to make their trefoils, and more emblems followed, chosen and designed by the girls from Malayan wild flowers. Then, discovering the date of Mrs Ennis' birthday, the company secretly stitched a 'Grandmothers' Garden' quilt composed of seventy-two hexagon-rosettes in scraps of donated fabric, and each embroidered her name onto a piece.[35] (See colour illustration 15.)

This 'Girl Guide Quilt' inspired three more quilts of stretcher or single-bed size, which were organised by Ethel Mulvany of the camp's Canadian Red Cross using the unbleached calico of Red Cross flour, rice and sugar bags to make sixty-six squares[36] 8in in size,[37] the intention being that stitch might be used to send messages to husbands, friends and relatives in the separate men's camp with which they were allowed no communication. The first quilt, embroidered with Japanese-style motifs, was diplomatically presented to the Japanese Red Cross and, as had been hoped, this opened the way for more quilts to be given to the British and Australian Red Cross. Each woman stitched 'something of herself' into her square[38] to convey that she was still alive, or sew a specific message such as the mother rabbit with her baby wearing a blue ribbon to tell of the birth of a son.[39] Once each quilt was joined, the squares were outlined in Turkey red stitching before the white fabric border was added.

A message was embroidered onto the white cotton backing sheet of each of the quilts. The 'Japanese Quilt' bore the words 'Presented by the women of Changi Internment Camp 1942 to the wounded Nipponese soldiers with our sympathy for their suffering. It is our wish that on cessation of hostilities that this quilt be presented to the Japanese Red Cross Society. It is

Cell 8 × 12 feet accomodation for three men or two women.

The Flag of Tyranny

Detail of 'Sheet' embroidered by Hilda Lacey while held prisoner in internment camps, Singapore. (Courtesy of the Imperial War Museum, London EPH 4566) (See colour illustration 16.)

advisable to dry clean this quilt.' and the other two quilts were similarly dedicated to 'British soldiers' and the 'British Red Cross'; 'Australian soldiers' and the 'Australian Red Cross'. (See colour illustrations 14, 17 and 18.)

Despite malaria, dysentery and an almost starvation diet, the women of Changi Prison kept on resolutely stitching such items as clothing, tablecloths, patchwork jackets and quilts. Mrs Constance Ethel Dickenson used her scant supply of embroidery materials and paints to create a picture of a 'dream' thatched cottage surrounded by a beautiful, flowering garden, which in fact closely resembled the house which she and her husband were to buy upon their return to England.[40]

Hilda G. Lacey, of the Malayan Nursing Service, was also an internee of Changi, the Katong and Sime Road Camps. Her work is a memorial to those who did not survive, for, using stem-stitch, she embroidered the signatures of every internee onto a linen sheet, with images of prison life.[41] (See colour illustration 16.)

Another prisoner of the Japanese, interned in Stanley Prison, Hong Kong, was Day Joyce of the Hong Kong Auxiliary Medical Corps who kept two diaries: one written – *Ordinary People: the Sheet*, and one stitched – her 'Sheet', which included 'about 1,100 names, signs and figures'. She wrote: 'Itself, it is gay and colourful, though not very beautiful, and it is much stained.' Such records were forbidden and punishment would have been severe if the 'Sheet' or diary had been found. At times illness, disease and exhaustion prevented any sewing, and sometimes it was an achievement to add just two stitches, but Day's 'Sheet' ends joyfully in August 1945, after 1,342 days of imprisonment, her needle left rusting in the fabric.[42] (See colour illustrations 19 and 20.)

POW UK

As the Allies battled their way across mainland Europe, the deconstruction of stitch became a quick and useful means of controlling the German prisoners who were being taken in increasingly large numbers: belts were cut so that one hand was needed to hold up the trousers, tunics slashed, fly buttons cut off, and boot laces cut.[43] Stitch was also an aid to the organisation of the Italian and 402,000 German prisoners of war who were held in Britain from 1944, for after interrogation, patches were sewn onto German uniforms to signify the wearers' strength of allegiance to the Nazi Party: grey – no particular opinions; white – scant interest in politics; and black – a strongly opinionated Nazi. 'Black' POWs were held in camps located in the wilds of Scotland,[44] but many became an invaluable resource of farm labourers and building workers who were often befriended by British families, welcomed into the community and appreciated for their skills, such as farming or in the case of many Italians, singing; their nationality being identified by a green, yellow or red patch underneath which a hole had been cut in the jacket to prevent removal.[45]

Only one German prisoner, Franz von Werra, a pilot of the *Luftwaffe*,[46] managed to escape, after being moved to Canada: for even in faultless civilian clothing, escapees would make such mistakes as clicking the heels and bowing to a bus conductor in thanks for their bus ticket.[47]

Britain's prisoners of war, who were awaiting repatriation, were even an enormous help in the immediate post-war reconstruction, filling in anti-tank ditches, removing barbed-wire and mines from beaches, and tackling the enormous task of transforming ground-up air-raid shelters and rubble into sorely needed houses.

twenty-four

Wartime Embroidery

During our struggle with Germany we need to help ourselves in every possible way to
maintain a balanced and calm spirit. To many women (and indeed men, too) sewing and
especially embroidery, makes the type of appeal we now need. There must be in our work
a quality which will claim the attention of our minds and at the same time give us scope to
satisfy an impulse within us which urges us to make something of beauty.' (Margaret Purves)[1]

The Second World War was a time of the tearing apart of relationships, buildings, bodies, and
the fabric of society. However, there was an opposite influence at work in the massive use of
stitch, for stitch is a process of joining. In a multitude of ways it protected, comforted, kept up
morale, camouflaged, sheltered, and joined strangers in strong bonds of comradeship. Stitch, in
the form of embroidery, settled the nerves and healed the mind.

An massive amount of embroidery was needed in the Second World War for the organisation
of troops, Civil Defence, medical staff and voluntary workers of all ages. Millions of embroidered badges, brevets, stripes, insignia, and shoulder titles had to be issued to signify rank,
function and the particular group within a service or voluntary organisation and an enormous
variety of symbols and lettering were used in a wide range of colours, gold and silver-gilt.
Produced in factories such as Firmin & Sons and Hand & Lock, and the homes of out-workers,
these small pieces of stitch were worn with pride on the cap or beret, jacket front, shoulder or
sleeve, and formed the links with others which often led to acts of gallantry, courage and hero-
ism. (See colour illustration 22.) At home, they were worn as 'Sweetheart Badges', so valued
that they were bought as jewellery, maybe from Aspreys, who transformed the embroidered
colours into diamonds, rubies and sapphires.[2] The most famous badges of the war were possibly
the 'wings' of fighter-pilots, and in 1942 a fashion began for embroidering them onto pale blue
silk pyjamas.[3] (See top illustration page 96.)

In the Army, the embroidered formation signs which identified each unit had to be cleverly
designed to make their significance obscure so as not to betray information to the enemy
and men chose the symbols themselves: for example, the fig leaf of the BEF 3rd Army Corps
was chosen in reference to its commander, Lieutenant-General Sir Ronald Adam.[4] Sometimes
hand-stitched by the owner himself, they were proud symbols of the formation and the strength
of its spirit;[5] small but potent visual signs of the group bonds, comradeship and mutual support
which brought many men through days and nights of strain to their limits of exhaustion and
endurance. Embroidered badges were also anchors in a surreal and intensely threatening world
and a serviceman's embroidered badge, his beret or identity disc, were also his essential guar-
antee of relative safety when attempting escape or evasion in enemy territory whilst wearing
clothing other than his uniform, for they proved that he was a member of His Majesty's Forces
and not a spy, who would not be protected from execution under the terms of the Geneva
Conventions.[6]

Right Embroidered
RAF 'Wings' were
worn with pride on
pale blue pyjamas.
(Courtesy of Hulton
Archive 26598229 (RM).
Photograph by Felix
Man)

Far right Sir Andrew
Cunningham, Admiral
of the Fleet. The
uniform of this rank was
embroidered around
the sleeves with four
medium and one wide
lace rings with a curl
on the uppermost. Gold
lace also comprised
the shoulder straps,
and on the cap, a

silver embroidered crown above an open laurel wreath and crossed batons, the cap peak being richly
embroidered with golden oak leaves. (Courtesy of the Imperial War Museum, London A 15702)

In the Royal Navy, seamen were issued with 'Tallies' or cap ribbons bearing only the letters 'HMS', which would betray no information to the enemy if they should be captured and
WRNS proudly received a taffeta ribbon also embroidered with the letters HMS.[7] However,
the cap peaks of leading seamen were embroidered with blue worsted laurel leaves and the
uniforms of the upper ranks were progressively more embellished with richly embroidered
gold or silver-gilt laurel wreaths to the cap, gold lace rings and stripes and loops on the sleeves.

For home-embroiderers, the Royal School of Needlework designed a series of 132 badges
based on those of the British and Canadian Forces in England, including the Canadian Maple
Leaf, which were approved by the War Office and marketed by William Briggs & Co. Ltd,
Manchester in their book published in 1940: '*Badges of H.M. Services*', kits or sold as individual transfers.[8] (See colour illustration 25.) The popularity of such embroidery is evidenced by
reprints of the book being made available in 1943 and even after the war in 1946.

…two badges I worked when I was at school during the war. They were both worked for
competitions in connection with the National Savings Scheme. The Royal Air Force badge
was worked in 1943 and the Duke of Cornwall's Light Infantry badge the following year.
(Maureen Spencely) (See colour illustrations 23 and 24.)

In the 1930s, embroidery had usually been inspired by a desire to enhance the home or clothing, however when the war began embroiderers who were used to always having a piece of
work 'on the go' soon found that they had very little time to spare after long hours of war
work, Make Do and Mend, and the difficulties of day-to-day living. Their stores of transfers
(linear designs in thick ink on tissue-paper, which could be transferred to fabric with a hot
iron), and Anchor embroidery 'silks' would now have to be used with care if they were to last
'for the duration'. In her article, 'Embroidery in Times of Stress', for the Embroiderers' Guild
Journal *Embroidery*, Phyliss M. Platt wisely advised:

It is only natural that the first reaction of the needlewoman in war time is to concentrate on the useful. But, if we are to continue cheerful and efficient, we cannot go on indefinitely without some regular relaxation and refreshment of mind. Even in the busiest, and especially anxious times, it is important to keep in contact with the activities we value most in normal times, and exercise faculties and interests beyond those called into use by stark necessity. … even if only a small piece of work can be attempted it can be exquisite of its kind, its value being in the thought and knowledge put into its idea and planning and the interest and peace which has been found in its working.[9]

Of course, the most determined home-embroiderers somehow managed to carry on. Colour illustration 27 shows a chair-back which was made some time between 1940 and 1944 from parachute 'silk' and the stitcher's pre-war collection of transfers.

Started nursing training [1943] and still embroidering when I had the time (12-hour days, 12½-hour nights and one day off a week). (Hazel Sims)

In 1945, as my mum was going past a market stall she saw a firescreen kit, but no threads. The fabric was blue cotton for the sea; on it was a transfer of the British Isles, key war sites with embroidered features e.g. a barrage balloon flying in the sky over Stanton and Stavely iron works, people, the coal mines, whales in the sea, and the royal coat-of-arms in one corner. Mum said it only cost her coppers to buy. Threads were in short supply, but she had a few at home of her own which enabled her to complete it. … She used to stitch when she got home from work. The shelter was too dark, dirty and smokey to stitch in, all the old men smoked heavily, and [she had] two children to take care of. (Susan Monks)

…my mother often used transfers – they were still fairly easily obtained where we were, even if there wasn't a lot of choice – if she couldn't get yellow transfers for the blackout material she would tack the transfers onto the material and embroider through the paper which was torn off on completion. (Anita Seamons)

I still have two tea-time tablecloths – one embroidered with bunches of violets (one of my mother's favourite flowers) the other with pink and blue butterflies. The colours were dictated by what embroidery threads were available in the sewing basket. These tablecloths were made from sugar, or flour, bags, made of linen and begged from a grocer. They were carefully unpicked and bleached to remove the printing – on one of them the wording is still faintly discernible. To save on material they weren't hemmed but the edges bound with bias binding … (Anita Seamons)

I have a tablecloth which was made by my mother during the war. It was made from flour sacks which have been faggotted together and then the floral design hand embroidered. I believe the sacks came from an uncle who worked on the waterways – barges. (Chris Watkins)

Blackout material was used for cushions – these were brightly embroidered with floral motifs and the inevitable crinoline ladies! (Anita Seamons)

…we had what I think were floor cloths with a close heavy weave. We used mending wool … to weave in coloured stripes, going under one thread and over several. The effect was like Florentine work and when finished would be stitched to a piece of fabric to make a cushion cover … (Sheila Westall)

We made cushion covers out of floor cloths – they were heavy weave and we pattern darned in the chevron pattern using darning wool – this was not on ration and came in cut skeins or plaits so they were in various shades of brown, grey and navy. I have a chair back made at one of these sewing bees (held in an air-raid shelter during the winter evenings), made out of a flour sack – the printing never washed out. I don't know where the thread came from to decorate the chair backs but presume that it was given to us by relations who had old stock… (Susan Reynolds)

By 1941, production had long ceased in embroidery materials as metal thread, beads and sequins were deemed 'inessential' by the Government. Regulations were brought in to restrict their use. Supplies varied throughout the country, but when Woolworths, department stores and the 'Mecca' of embroiderers – The Needlewoman on Regent Street, London – soon ran out of stock, embroiderers had to look around for alternatives, and explore designs and techniques which would be appropriate to the wartime situation. Phyllis M. Platt recommended that work should be designed which was 'easy to take up at odd moments, and perhaps in odd places', maybe Winchester canvas work, for 'It will not suffer unduly from being carried about.'[10] *Embroidery* also recommended consideration of Norwegian embroidery, which gave 'bold, quick effects',[11] and quoted 'Miss Ann Macbeth', whose work had become 'gay bunches made for wall panels': 'I feel, in these days, that one wants bright colours before anything. I go for clean, bright colours, and find the knitting yarns stand the light best.'[12]

Innovative embroiderers discovered that they actually thrived on the shortages and improvisation soon became a matter of course, including the use of parachute fabrics, recycled clothes, dish cloths, floor cloths, sacking, woven interfacing (washed and boiled) parachute silk cords which were easily stranded and dyed, knitting wool, string, raffia, unravelled fabric, fabric strips, binder twine (orange and blue), piping cord, bias-binding, tape, crochet cotton, sewing cotton, two or three strands of mixed colours: 'In fact anything that could be unravelled, washed and dyed.' (Hazel Sims)

This tablecloth, designed to express the embroiderer's dreams of a servicemen's longed-for return, was bought ready-stamped with flower motifs and edged with victory 'lace' bearing the words 'Welcome Home'. The embroiderer worked the flowers in white and added the signatures of her husband's naval colleagues, as a 'permanent memory of their service time together'. (By kind courtesy of Rosemary Dishington)

I have always done embroidery and in wartime I used linen maps, after they had been washed to remove the markings. Another source of material was the Irish Linen that was used to cover aircraft. After it was put onto the bombers it was painted with 'dope' and then became rigid. The girls who did the doping knew I sewed and used to give my father offcuts. (Angela Cole)

My main memory of that time was the shortages of materials. We could always rip up worn bed-linen for ground fabric but had great difficulty in finding any threads. My mother remained in London and would send me embroidery cottons when she could. I remember sewing with a particularly unpleasant shade of pink for many months because when mother found a supply she purchased it all – but they only had pink! I still dislike pink. (Doreen Green)

Triangular bandages were precious. We hemmed and embroidered them, and two joined made lovely table cloths. (Barbara Parsons)

Mother worked mainly in chain stitch during the war and so used mainly stranded embroidery thread wherever and whenever she could. Owing to the shortage of embroidery thread, she developed the design as she went along and as material became available. (Roberta Page)

Ann Macbeth also encouraged stitchers to create their own designs rather than depending upon transfers[13] and Agnes M. Miall, in *Pearson's Complete Needlecraft*, addressed the trepidation which many embroiderers felt:

Invaluable as ready-made transfers are, no home embroideress should feel lost without them. … Don't think of home-designed patterns as complicated things which must first be drawn out laboriously on drawing paper and then be transferred to the material with a black carbon. Most women doing simple embroidery for their own and their children's clothes, or to beautify their homes, don't want to be bothered with anything so reminiscent of an art school!

Encouraging embroiderers to develop their own 'built-up' patterns by letting their stitches keep suggesting the next step, just using the barest guidance of ruled lines or circles traced around coins or tea-cups, she also recommended using this simple method to create a border around designs using transfers. 'You will find it great fun to evolve your own built-up patterns by trying experiments on a bit of stuff with one stitch and another till you get something that pleases you. … And it is thrilling working them out in one or more pretty colours.'[14]

The work of embroiderers who had created their own personal responses to the wartime situation was to be particularly treasured:

I was a young mother, living with my baby son, with my mother … and I made the sampler as a present for my father, who was at sea in command of … a naval Repair ship. We kept chickens, ducks, and grew masses of fruit and vegetables, and I bought a pony and jingle, in which, with the baby in a moses basket at the back, I would drive to Tavistock to shop and meet trains etc. The other two figures are my teenage brother, who was in the Home Guard, and my sister, a Visual Signaller in the WRNS My husband, under the palm tree, was in the R.E. (Royal Engineers) in Burma. He came back safely, thank God, in 1945. (Virginia Leonard-Williams) (See colour illustration 29.)

Embroidery was also used by the Scottish grandmother of six-year-old Janet Mary Ness who lived in 'Hell-Fire Corner' Kent, with enemy bombers and fighter planes roaring overhead, as a means of conveying comfort, love and a sense of security to the little girl. 'Jan' must have been delighted to receive her 'Covering Blanket', a feast of lovingly stitched embroidered and appliquéd images which resound with re-assurance, humour and a bracing Scottish common-sense. (See colour illustration 26.)

The Embroiderers' Guild had been formed in 1932 to support the nation's embroiderers and it managed to continue its much-appreciated work throughout the war, although the Guild's postal library of 'boxes' containing reference books and embroidery samples had, for safekeeping, to be removed from their London headquarters, and in 1941 it was necessary to move into the smallest of their three offices on Grosvenor Street, London – which was subsequently bombed in February 1943, with the loss of 'all our stored furniture (books and stationery) and some, but not the best, embroideries'. It seemed to the Guild's staff that '…with the advent of war … the Guild had received its death blow. … With big things, important institutions crumbling round us, how could a craft so fine and delicate as embroidery hope to survive?'[15] But 'some obstinate spark of life persisted, and the work went on…' despite disruption to the Guild's journal, *Embroidery*, which, due to paper shortages, could not be published again in regular quarterly issues until 1948. An article entitled 'Embroidered Crafts as War Work – Members' Work in War-Time' agonised: 'It is hard to see today, how, except indirectly, needlecraft can help the national effort', however the Embroiderers' Guild *was*, in fact, to be of great use in 'the national effort', for members replaced destroyed church textiles, taught embroidery in hospitals, put on exhibitions of their work in aid of the Red Cross, kept the skills of embroidery alive in schools and colleges and sent out embroidery kits to wounded servicemen and prisoners of war.[16]

Members were joined by professional embroiderers such as Beryl Dean to aid occupational therapists and Sheila Fraser was to write, in *Embroidery*, December 1945:

> In orthopaedic hospitals needlework can be used for hand disabilities … The treadle machine has proved an excellent medium in helping mobility of knee and ankle. While the patient is absorbed in making something, the required exercises are performed voluntarily. The making of clothes often keeps a mother (who is otherwise separated from her family), in touch with growing children, and by so doing helps to counterbalance any growing depression or neurotic tendencies. The electric machine is a boon to convalescent patients. Garments for immediate wear hold universal appeal. The main urge is to make something useful for a member of their family, or for themselves. The making of a quilted bed jacket is always a source of joy. Men are particularly keen on canvas embroidery….[17]

Embroidery kits were in such great demand for occupational therapy that the Red Cross was asked to take over distribution, including 2,000 kits to prisoners of war and the wounded in the Middle East.[18]

> My mother and I embroidered a tablecloth each. They were worked from Penelope kits obtained by my father from Staff at the Naval hospital in Plymouth. I made for my mother a firescreen out of another Penelope kit. I worked it in tent stitch. (Delcia Miles) (See colour illustration 28.)

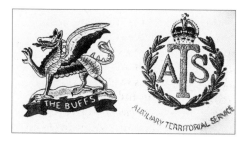

These badges were worked by 'wounded soldiers': Left: 'A dragon is worked in shades of gold and green; his tongue is red. A band of rich blue shows up the lettering.' Right: 'The red berries glow charmingly in a green wreath. Dull gold lettering.' (Reproduced by courtesy of the Embroiderers' Guild)

My father was in hospital in Germany during the war and I have the embroidery of the Intelligence Corps badge which he worked. (Jane Rodgers)

Towards the end of the war, with the advent of V.2 rockets, Ack-ack and Searchlight sites became obsolete. It was then I was transferred to the Education Corps and had to organise activities to alleviate boredom. We were glad to buy the Penelope wool embroidery kits at a special rate for our girls. (Anon.)

In 1943, Embroiderers' Guild members began to supply the kits of 'commenced' embroidery to British and Dominion prisoners of war, including fabric, design, threads, scissors, thimbles and needles. These were so much appreciated that in the autumn of 1944 the BBC broadcast an appeal for donations on behalf of Guild members who were forming needlework groups so as to enable them to supply even more kits, particularly for men suffering from TB, for before the assembly of kits could begin, the funds had to be raised, materials and threads obtained. Demand was continuous, and the twelve members of the Woldingham Occupational Needlework Group kept up the work for five years, their weekly meetings coming to be called their 'Tuesday Tonic', for they were 'thrilled' to read letters sent from grateful servicemen, such as: 'I am rationing myself to 10 rows of tapestry work per day so that the work shall last a long time'; or 'My needlework is the one high spot in my day that I look forward to, and I dare not do too much of it at one time because I shall finish it too soon.' The group eventually sent off 1,800 pieces of embroidery.[19]

Civilian men also worked their own embroidery, maybe to pass the hours and keep nerves steady while on solitary duty in a church tower, plotting the positions of falling bombs before phoning the information through to the ARP Post:

Father embroidered a firescreen kit, Jacobean style, canvas work from a chart. He was badly injured in WWI, only one arm and not much use left in his left arm – it was his version of physiotherapy to encourage his left arm. (Jean Panter)

The provision of embroidery for occupational therapy was still needed in the immediate post-war years in collaboration with Brabazon to aid in the recovery of the physically and mentally wounded, prison inmates and also the poverty-stricken. In December 1945, Cecil Briant informed the readers of *Embroidery* that:

We're told that our hard won 'peace' will be in some ways worse than war. Let us see to it that these Service men and women, who have given their health and vigour, that we may live, have a serenity built up by pleasant occupations and comradeship, and help them as we did in the prisoners' cage, to gain that freedom of thought and spirit, which leads to the grandeur of God's Universe.[20]

An unfailing inspiration to all of Britain's embroiderers who resolutely continued to produce beauty by stitch through the years of the war was Her Majesty Queen Mary, a Patroness of the Embroiderers' Guild, and one of her wartime pieces was a magnificent 'Three Leaf Screen' of fifteen panels depicting a graceful luxuriance of flowers and foliage. (See colour illustration 30.)

The Royal School of Needlework also played its part in the nation's wartime embroidery by holding charity sales of their own work and that of the royal family in aid of the JWO and forces' charities. Staff and members helped with occupational therapy, and those on active service overseas passed on their skills by holding embroidery classes. In addition to their *Badges of HM Services*, the RSN also produced a series of eleven correspondence lessons in home sewing:

Needlework in War-time, which included: 'embroidery wools, silks and cottons, designs, and offers of individual help to 'all those who encounter difficulties'. Stitchers could book lessons all over the country in the eleven subjects: Lingerie Making (elementary *or* advanced), Cutting and Making of Children's Clothing, Canvas Work, Quilting and Patchwork Quilts, Church Work, White Work (drawn and pulled threads), Embroideries in Silks, Cottons or Wools on Materials Other Than Canvas, Suggestions for Teaching Beginners or Convalescents, Renovating (mending, darning and patching), Remodelling, and Dressmaking. The introduction to each volume was written by the Principal, Lady Smith-Dorrien, who was later to become a Dame of the British Empire:[21]

> As a secondary object 'Needlework in War-time' aims at helping those whose thoughts are constantly with their men on active service, whose vivid imagination pictures tragedy whenever their minds are not fully occupied... I have the entire medical profession with me, I believe, when I say that working out an intricate design is the best possible remedy for overstrained nerves – for it is literally fascinating and all worries are forgotten for the time being.

In her introduction to Volume 8 *On Teaching Convalescents*, she described how embroiderers could 'try to take the minds of our patients off their own troubles – at any rate, temporarily', for:

> Doctors seem all agreed on one point, which is, that peace of mind is almost essential to successful treatment in cases were inertia and long suffering cannot be avoided. The man sitting up in bed, or tied to his wheelchair, must be given an interesting occupation to prevent him from brooding on his calamity.

She advised that once men had accepted that stitching could be of benefit, it had then to be discovered which form of embroidery would most suit each individual, for:

> No two men are satisfied with the same work – some need the most intricate design and complicated shading before they can become absorbed in their task, others ask for a mechanical occupation for their hands to keep them busy and happy. Then there are still others who enjoy working out geometrical patterns on canvas, which entails endless counting of stitches and needs great accuracy only.[22]

For students of embroidery art colleges and trade schools continued the instruction of artist-embroiderers throughout the war in hand- and machine-stitching, albeit with students of an unusual age range – from thirteen to seventeen years and older people unfit for war service. Existing students who had been conscripted part-way through their course had to wait until the victory of 1945 before they could resume their studies. Tutors such as Iris Hills and Elizabeth Grace Thompson somehow managed to maintain high standards despite the lack of materials, and the interruption when classes had to move swiftly into air-raid shelters where light was poor and conditions cramped and work had to be suited to the situation, recommending that students should aim for 'bold, quick effects'.[23]

Embroidery students also contributed to the war effort: in Dundee, Scotland, where Angela Radshaw taught 'enormous classes', her students repaired banners, uniform decorations, and garments for the Free French Navy, Norwegian, Dutch and Polish soldiers, sailors and airmen; and in London, undeterred by the dust and disruption of the Blitz, Constance Howard organised students at the Kingston School of Art to produce large padded and embroidered maps for the RAF on:

> ... very tough, waterproof fabric that gave us sore hands from the effort of pushing the needles through the close weave... Trees were defined by French knots placed solidly together, and stitches worked over one another for hills, stem stitch to represent fields and roads. The accuracy being greater for the texture.[24]

ON TEACHING CONVALESCENTS

By LADY SMITH-DORRIEN, D.B.E.

THESE notes and suggestions have been compiled with a view to helping those who intend to bring the solace of needlework into the lives of men handicapped by ill health or crippled.

The need of starting a handicraft centre in connection with each Hospital or Convalescent Home showed itself before the end of 1914, and as was to be expected, voluntary workers at once stepped into the breach. Many of these organisations were admirable, others had to start on their task with a very limited knowledge of their subject. It is to be of assistance to the latter type of voluntary teacher that I put at their disposal the sum total of my own experience and that of several others who worked in hospitals during the last War.

Our primary object was, of course, to try and take the minds of our patients off their own troubles—at any rate, temporarily.

Doctors seem all agreed on one point, which is, that peace of mind is almost essential to successful treatment in cases where inertia and long suffering cannot be avoided. The man sitting up in bed, or tied to his wheel chair, must be given an interesting occupation to prevent him from brooding on his calamity.

It is very important that those undertaking to teach even beginners should be themselves practical needlewomen with quick perceptions, limitless patience and the power of imparting enthusiasm without which little can be accomplished. Your first task must be to prove to your patient that needlework is not derogatory to his manhood—make him understand that thousands of able-bodied men all over England who work hard all day with their brains have, during the last ten years or so, realised that stitching away in the evenings is the very best way of resting their over-tired nerves, and many of them have become very expert workers, doing the finest petit point and arranging their own colouring. No two men are satisfied with the same work—some need the most intricate design and complicated shading before they can become absorbed in their task, others ask for a mechanical occupation for their hands to keep them busy and happy. Then there are still others who enjoy working out geometrical patterns on canvas, which entails endless counting of stitches and needs great accuracy only.

Luckily, there are so many different forms of stitchery that a suitable piece of work can easily be found for nearly every type of mind. I can do little more in this lesson than give you suggestions and advice on how to start off interesting your patients. Once this is accomplished and they

Page Three

Introduction to Volume 8 of *Needlework in War-time* by the Royal School of needlework. (Reproduced by courtesy of The Royal School of Needlework)

Professional embroiderers who had not been conscripted were also personally challenged by the wartime conditions, for they still needed to exhibit, receive commissions and sell their work. In Scotland, generous owners of the great Scottish houses offered employment in the repair of tapestries and embroideries, and one hundred embroiderers, including Dorothy Allsopp, Rebecca Crompton, Kathleen Harris and Rosamund Willis, contributed work to an exhibition at the Art Gallery in Sunderland, County Durham, entitled 'Modern British Embroiderers'. *Embroidery* reported that it was 'like a refreshing oasis in these desert days of war... It breathes beauty and tranquillity in an unquiet world.'[25]

Passing on her skills as a professional embroiderer, Lilian Dring gave inspiration to the nation's teachers of embroidery in her series 'Thriftcraft', published by *Art and Craft Education*, 1939–40. She wrote:

Imagination goes a long way in this craft. Begin to **look** at materials and see what they suggest to you. You will find endless possibilities. Tweeds looking like brickwork, fields, mountains. Search for silks and cottons that suggest animals, fish, water, skies. Old clothes must, of course, be used with discretion. Very worn parts cut away, or tactfully covered with other materials. Please, **never** sew on a button just as a piece of decoration, or 'because it wants something there'. Always have a reason for everything. Stitches should be kept as simple as possible. I use few but the ordinary sewing stitches – hemming, over-sewing, herring-bone, etc. Couching is useful and very easy.[26]

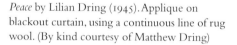

Peace by Lilian Dring (1945). Applique on blackout curtain, using a continuous line of rug wool. (By kind courtesy of Matthew Dring)

Then, in 1941, 'hurling her materials together with an urgency provoked by her subject [she] made a statement about World War II that has no parallel in the annals of 20th century embroidery.'[27] 'Parable I' (36¾in x 25½in) was designed to be hung at a bombed-out window, the couching, appliqué and hand embroidery being worked on a ground of tailors' canvas. (See colour illustration 21.) It was exhibited by the Arts and Crafts Exhibition Society in 1941 and by the Embroiderers' Guild in 1945 at the Royal Watercolour Society, where its pioneering, free expression 'caused considerable comment'.

By 1948, war work and shortages had brought to an end the immense popularity of embroidery in Britain, tradition. Embroiderers no longer wanted to spend hours stitching exquisite copies of older pieces or work on the mass-produced designs of transfers. *Pearson's Complete Needlecraft* of 1949 stated:

> In modern times we have greatly developed simple and quick forms of embroidery and those who take a great deal of time are seldom made. Also, styles change almost every year and we have little use for things which won't wear out! So the old rule about using only the best materials should be applied with discretion.[28]

The war had forced upon embroiderers a vision of free and adventurous work in colour, technique and design, which was captured by Constance Howard in her establishment of a Department of Embroidery at Goldsmiths College, London. Victory had won a new and exciting era for the embroiderers of Britain.

twenty-five

Weddings and Babies

Arranging a wedding ceremony during the Second World War was such an obstacle course that more weddings had to be cancelled than actually went ahead. This was a beaurocratic process calculated to ensure that only the most committed couples were married.[1] The creation of wedding clothes and later, baby clothes, were tasks on which stitchers often had to exercise their skills.

Once a couple had decided to marry, if they were under twenty-one, they had first to seek the permission of their parents. The groom then asked the permission of his commanding officer and the bride had to obtain a letter from her employer confirming her good character. A medical examination was next, and forms had to be filled in before obtaining a 'permission to marry' form, buying a licence, meeting a chaplain to set the date, and hoping that all would go through before the licence expired.

But all this did not stop people getting engaged and marrying during the Second World War. There was a feeling that one had to take one's chance at happiness in the moment for who knew what tomorrow would bring. Relationships with servicemen had to be sustained by hand-written letters, between their short, often unexpected, and infrequent leaves and women knew that their love might come to a sudden end with his death: it was happening to couples all the time.

Society expected marriage in the 1940s, and a 'white' church wedding was accepted as the 'proper' start to married life, for the British wife was 'an icon of decency and stability'.[2] As for wedding clothes – the groom had no problem, he could wear his service uniform or dress uniform; but brides had to exercise great ingenuity in the face of rationing and shortages as wedding dresses were virtually unobtainable, except for the very wealthy. However, relatives, friends and neighbours were glad to help, for in the destruction of war, weddings had become a glad statement that love, happiness, hope and normality were still as strong as ever.[3]

It was particularly difficult for servicewomen who had no clothing coupon allowance and, realising their plight, Eleanor Roosevelt, wife of the American President, was moved to send a collection of used wedding dresses to be hired complete with veils and head-dresses[4] and the novelist Barbara Cartland arranged the loan of a number of society wedding dresses for members of the WAAF.[5] The Land Army was also sent a collection of ten wedding dresses from America.[6]

By 1943, after two years of clothes rationing, and making a virtue of a necessity, it was considered much more patriotic to be married in a 'best' suit or day dress which could be worn again, made special for the occasion with a hat[7] or small veil,[8] and magazines offered ideas for hats which could be quickly stitched.

I was married during the war so being in the forces I had no clothing coupons. I borrowed a friend's dress to get married in. (Kathleen Lever)

Stitching for Victory

The wedding of Ernest John Osborne to Susie Mollard at the High Street Chapel, Penzance, on 8 February 1940. (By kind courtesy of Mike Osborne and the St Ives Archive Trust)

Many brides had to be content with getting married in their uniform; however, the most determined stitchers made their dresses out of whatever was available, including 'under-the-counter' pre-war bridal satin, butter muslin or curtain lace (worn over a white nightgown)[9], or even bleached and dyed blackout fabric. Oyster-coloured parachute 'silk' was beautiful if one could get it, but it was difficult to make a wedding dress out of the many bias-cut triangles which radiated out from the centre. (See colour illustrations 32, 33 and 34.) Narrow skirts saved on material and the most popular designs had a heart-shaped or square neckline with tight-fitting sleeves gathered into a 'puff' at the shoulders.[10]

> Wedding dresses were very scarce. I made mine – it was a short dress, pale blue wool, princess style, with lots of tiny buttons down the back. (Evelyn Taylor)

Brides of the 1940s were also expected to provide themselves with a newly made trousseau, or a nightdress, at least, and sometimes precious coupons were put towards this, rather than a wedding dress which would be worn just once:

> When my younger sister was married in 1945, all the family contributed coupons for her trousseau, and I made her a rather grand-looking embroidered nightdress out of peach-coloured furnishing satin! I don't know how it stood up to washing. (Virginia Leonard-Williams)
>
> (In 1950-51) a white silk parachute made undies for my trousseau; two pairs of cami-knickers and a petticoat embroidered in blue. The top of the petticoat was trimmed with a rouleau stitched in place with faggot stitch. The cami-knickers had some shell edging. (Sheila Fowles)

This wedding dress was made by
the bride out of a length of Liberty's
export-reject Broderie Anglaise which
'needed some stitching where there were
faults!' and was lined with mapping fabric
from the American Air Base on Gresham
Common. The starched, blue material
had first to be boiled and rinsed until
the fine, white linen emerged. 'With the
wedding dress's short train cut off and the
sleeves and yoke removed it made me a
great evening dress for my married life
in West Africa, as the dress was washable.'
(By kind courtesy of Denise Cochrane)

Wedding clothes also had to be made for bridesmaids and page boys: 'My cousin Sylvia and I were
bridesmaids for another cousin and my mother made both our short dresses in …organdie in a lilac
colour with a funny sort of flat ribbon trimmed thing for our heads.' (By kind courtesy of Anita
Seamons)

'My brother, on the left, was in maroon velvet (he wasn't a pageboy). My cousin's trousers were blue velvet and his blouse was blue crêpe-de-chine, the same fabric as my dress. All these clothes … were made by a dressmaker two villages away (about ten miles) working in her front room. My mother used to cycle with us for "fittings". After the wedding my dress was shortened and I wore it for "best" until I couldn't be squeezed into it anymore! I didn't wear the cap again, though.' (By kind courtesy of Sheila Westall)

Having overcome all the problems of beaurocracy, clothing and food, weddings could still suffer at the last minute from the wartime situation. It was quite common for servicemen to have leave cancelled just before their wedding, or be unexpectedly given just a few hours to get married and then ordered to report back to their unit immediately. Sometimes the church was bombed, and couples had to quickly make arrangements at another.

Then, once the wedding was finally achieved, if the dress was not to be lent to other brides, the precious material was re-made into a day dress or evening gown, underwear, nightwear, or even baby clothes:

At the start of the war, my mother still had a cook, but she soon left to work in a factory. When she got married, I made her a really beautiful wedding dress, out of very shiny cream-coloured furnishing brocade. Furnishing fabrics were still unrationed _if_ you could get them. It was a great success, but less so when she cut it short for every day! (Virginia Leonard-Williams)

But now the problems *really* started, for couples might be working on different shifts and rarely be at home at the same time, they might not see one another again for months, years – or maybe never:

> … a gunner came in asking if he could have the morning off later in the week to get married. He was given a seventy-two-hour pass, came back, and was killed on his next Op, so he had a three-day honeymoon and a three-day married life. Such things were everyday, common-place. It happened all the time.[11]

Pregnancy presented yet another series of problems. From 1941, once a doctor's or midwife's cer-tificate had been obtained, there was a clothing allowance of fifty coupons for expected babies which could alternatively be spent on fabric.[12] This was later increased to sixty coupons which still hardly covered basic needs, for just a pack of terry towelling nappies took twenty-four cou-pons.[13] However, butter-muslin for nappy linings was coupon-free. Bombed-out babies could be provided with more clothing, but by 1944 they were bigger and healthier and too big for the 1940 baby clothes.[14] Expectant mothers often had to adapt their existing wardrobe, laboriously hand-stitching the garments if they had no sewing machine. The Ministry of Information *Make Do and Mend leaflet No. 1* 'Adapting Your Ordinary Clothes for Maternity Wear advised the addi-tion of an 'attractive matching or contrasting gathered or pleated panel' to the front of dresses.
    The same leaflet also included 'Getting ready for baby':

> Don't go in for frills and trimmings and elaborate designs when making Baby's layette. You must aim to make the clothes from as little material as possible, yet in such a way that they are loose and Baby can wear them longer than he would have worn his first clothes in peace-time.

The wartime edition of *Elizabeth Craig's Needlecraft* was for more ambitious stitching mothers-to-be:

> Modern Layettes Baby's First Outfit' 'LONG SLIPS. – Make these of fine cotton lawn, nain-sook or cambric for wearing under cotton, lawn, nainsook, or cambric day gowns, with a sleeveless yoke and skirt of the same length as the skirt of the day gowns. If the slip is to be worn under a silk day gown, make it of nun's veiling, Jap silk, or crêpe-de-chine. If it is to be worn instead of a long flannel, known as a 'barracoat', make it of flannel or any other fine, soft woollen material. Allow 1½ yards of material for each long slip. Trim with Valenciennes lace edging. If you like, a frill can be added to the slip. Join the frill to the slip with insertion to match the edging. The usual length for slips is 24 inches, but sometimes they are made 27 inches long. (© 1947 Elizabeth Craig)

The book also pointed out that fabric could be saved by breaking with the tradition of dressing a baby in long clothes for its first three months:

> Before starting to prepare a layette you must decide for how long you wish baby to wear long clothes, then make a list of the long clothes necessary. … Many modern mothers will have nothing to do with long clothes for babies. They prefer to put babies straightaway into short clothes.[15] (© 1947 Elizabeth Craig)

> I was married in 1941 and my son was born in 1943. By that time things were getting scarce. … The previous year, I started getting together terry nappies, making long gowns etc. You kept your baby in long gowns until he was old enough to be 'shortened' then he was put into

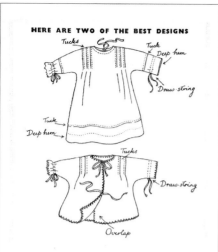

HERE ARE TWO OF THE BEST DESIGNS

The local Welfare Centre or your Health Visitor will be ready to advise you

COTS.—A laundry basket, or even a deep drawer suitably lined and padded, can be adapted to make a very useful cot for the first months. No permit is required for a Utility cot.

BEDCLOTHES.—If you live in the country there is probably no need to buy a mattress. A corn chandler or farmer may be able to sell you some clean chaff. Bake it in a moderate oven for one hour, then fill a pillow-case with it. A small piece of old blanket or rug should be placed under chaff mattresses to provide warmth in winter.

If a pillow is thought necessary a small flat pillow-case can also be filled with chaff.

Left Simple baby clothes and tips on baby's bedding. (Make Do and Mend leaflet No.1. By courtesy of The National Archives)

Below left Traditional baby clothing – long slips.

Below Elizabeth Craig's 'Rompers For All Occasions':'Some modern mothers put their children into rompers before they are able to crawl. Others dress their babies in rompers from the age of five or six months until they are three or four years old… Make rompers of gingham, holland, linen and other washable materials for everyday wear, and of tussore for special wear.'

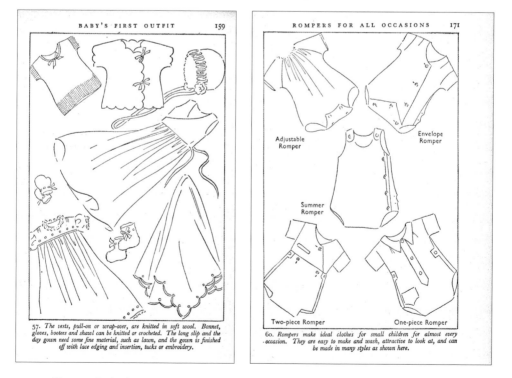

BABY'S FIRST OUTFIT 159

57. *The vests, pull-on or wrap-over, are knitted in soft wool. Bonnet, gloves, bootees and shawl can be knitted or crocheted. The long slip and the day gown need some fine material, such as lawn, and the gown is finished off with lace edging and insertion, tucks or embroidery.*

ROMPERS FOR ALL OCCASIONS 171

Adjustable Romper

Envelope Romper

Summer Romper

Two-piece Romper

One-piece Romper

60. *Rompers make ideal clothes for small children for almost every occasion. They are easy to make and wash, attractive to look at, and can be made in many styles as shown here.*

(© 1947 Elizabeth Craig. Reprinted by kind permission of HarperCollins Publishers Ltd) rompers. I made romper suits for the baby from shirt tails and sleeves. I remember cutting up my husband's cream cricket flannels and producing a skirt for myself and a pair of little trousers (with a bib front) for my son. (Evelyn Taylor)

Babies might be born to the sound of screaming bombs[16] in hospitals filled with injured servicemen, or lacking in even their most basic needs:

They'd no clothes for the babies, no napkins or anything like that. So half the time they had old pieces of khaki round them, sometimes for a whole day. Half the babies got sore bottoms, and our Keith was in a dreadful state when I brought him out.[17] (Ethel Robinson)

Although some arrived in the relative luxury of large country houses which had been converted into maternity homes.[18]

The 'best part' of old sheets or blankets often had to be turned into cot bedding. 'Getting ready for baby – Bedclothes' advised:

If you live in the country there is probably no need to buy a mattress. A corn chandler or farmer may be able to sell you some clean chaff. Bake it in a moderate oven for one hour, then fill a pillow-case with it. A small piece of old blanket or rug should be placed under chaff mattresses to provide warmth in winter. If a pillow is thought necessary a small flat pillow-case can also be filled with chaff.[19]

I recall standing on tiptoes to peer over a crib next to my mother's bed to see my new brother; all I knew was that he came in the night. His crib was swathed in lemon material with rose springs on it, a year or so later this lemon material was made into summer frocks for my sister and I. (Delcia Miles)

I had my son in 1944. … His night clothes were made out of anything soft and warm. A little bit of embroidery added made them look a little less like old shirts etc. … When he reached the toddler stage and was out of nappies I would buy a five-shilling roll of white lint, which made five pairs of underpants, quite soft and warm. I used the legs and any other reasonable pieces of his dad's trousers to make him daywear trousers. I managed to get two grey Army blankets (I have forgotten how – just as well, I think). I had them dyed a very dark red. One made our son a grand three-piece outfit – leggings, coat and hat. (Wyn Trevitt)

… .the earliest memory I have, I was wearing a coat and beret, this later was turned into a coat and peaked cap for my baby brother. (Delcia Miles)

I was married in 1940, at the age of twenty, and had my first son in March 1942 … I made all his clothes – his first baby clothes out of new (and rationed) material, but after that, out of anything I could lay my hands on – old blankets, old clothes, unravelled woollies. (Virginia Leonard-Williams)

Fortunately I could sew and to combat the cold, when junior kicked off his bed-clothes I made 'shoe-bags' in fine woollen cloth and popped him into them (from the waist down) and he could kick all he wanted to without getting too cold. (Diana Trotter)

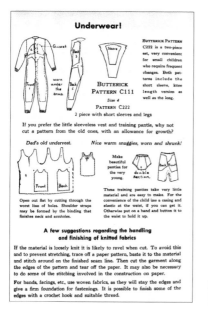

How to make 'training panties' out of Dad's old underwear.
(*Girls Own Paper* courtesy of Lutterworth Press)

Then, at the end of the war, 43,454 British brides of Canadians or American GIs with their 20,997 babies and children had to wait patiently to be reunited until ships were available to take them across the Atlantic in 'Operation Daddy'.[20]

But despite all the obstacles and tragedies, weddings and babies, and the stitches which went into their clothing, had taken on a special significance during the Second World War: in them was hope for the future and servicemen, especially those incarcerated as prisoners of war overseas, found the strength to endure even the harshest conditions knowing that they had a girlfriend, fiancée, wife or child at home.

The love for a wife or sweetheart which they silently possessed was the food that fed their hearts, the fuel for their enthusiasm and optimism in the unswerving purpose to live. It was the love in a prisoner's heart which, more than anything else, prevented him from swallowing the bitter pill of hopelessness and defeat.[21]

It was a victory of love.

twenty-six

VE – VJ

Victory in Europe was declared in a radio broadcast by Prime Minister Winston Churchill
on Tuesday 8 May 1945.

> At the end of the War I remember the church bells ringing. I had never heard such a wonderful noise and they went on and on. Everyone was happy and smiling and parties were going on all over the town. It was so exciting. The lights were shining everywhere. I only remembered going out after dark by torch-light and the 'black-out' was an every day occurrence for me so lights were also exciting and the singing and the laughter. There was a fancy-dress competition at our street-party and Mum dressed me up as 'Little Bo Peep' complete with crook. I won second prize which was a doll dressed in knitted clothes. (Stroma Hammond)

The surrender of Japan was declared over the radio by Prime Minister Clement Attlee at
12 p.m. on 14 August 1945.
The Second World War was finally over.

As the announcement came so late in the evening, people were woken by their neighbours and went out into the streets in their dressing gowns. Again, the royal family appeared to wildly celebrating crowds; there were church bells ringing, parties in streets draped with flags and bunting, children parading in fancy dress, bonfires and fireworks.

Overseas, demobilisation began for many ragged, undernourished, newly released prisoners of war in Singapore with a bare-foot walk of nearly 800km to a Japanese Army base where they were 'freely and amiably' given kitbags to fill with, amongst other things, blankets and clothing in which to begin the long journey back to Britain and home.[1]

From 18 June 1945 and on into 1946, 4,243,000 servicemen[2] were in the process of returning home. Each man was given a cash gratuity, a demob outfit valued at not more than £12, plus ninety clothing coupons.[3] But Japan's unexpected surrender had resulted in a massive need for suits and even when 20 per cent of the nation's military textile workers, including 7,000 from blanket factories, were released to meet the demand, there was still not enough labour, time or materials. Demob suits had to be made hastily, from as little material as possible.[4]

The suits, which were usually light in colour in order to save dyes, and easily identifiable by the buttonholes on each lapel, were of 1930s design – a welcome resumption of the familiar pre-war style[5] – and it was accompanied by a shirt with two detachable collars, a tie, cufflinks, shoes and two pairs of socks, a hat,[6] two collar studs and a raincoat and the complete outfit was that of a typical 'middle-class family man dressed for church'.[7] There were the choices of single or double-breasted styles, in dark blue, brown or pin-stripe.[8]

Children of the 1940s were used wearing fancy dress for parties and competitions and it was natural for mothers to stitch something for this most special celebration. Third and fourth from the left on this photograph are 'The Make Do and Mend' sisters. (By kind courtesy of Glory A. Chenery)

Stepping out as civilians again, wearing new demob suits. (By kind courtesy of *The News*, Portsmouth, 3309)

'To celebrate the end of the war, red, white and blue ribbon was available and she [mother] made lots of rosettes by gathering up a length of ribbon onto a flat circle and stitching a safety pin on the back. Everyone wore them. My father shaped some scrap metal into V shapes, and my mother covered these with felt and decorated them. Some of the V for Victory brooches and the felt buttonholes and necklaces were sold from her shop, others were sold to family and friends. We proudly wore our V for Victory brooches.' (By kind courtesy of Wendy Corner)

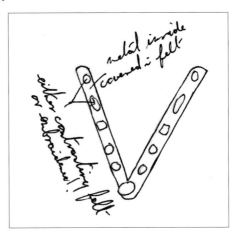

And it was like another uniform! Everybody walked around with the same. Thousands of men all dressed the same, just the same…[9] (Eddie Mathieson, ex-Commando)

Returning servicemen were advised to shake hands with their wives and then go upstairs to inspect their pre-war clothing[10] – but there was often a shock in store when they opened their wardrobes to discover that shirts, suits, coats and cricketing flannels were missing, for their wives had, in desperation, used the fabric to stitch clothes for themselves and the children. However, many of these same wives had used up their own coupons to buy new clothes for the children to wear as they greeted their father, hoping to give the impression that all was well despite the shabbiness of their home. Stitchers were fortunate if their men-folk had brought home fabrics and threads, maybe in glorious colours from Burma; or a 'liberated' sewing machine from Germany – although it was difficult to obtain replacement needles.

British troops had, for six years, lifted their spirits by singing: 'When I get my civvy clothes on, Oh how happy I shall be!' (to the tune of the hymn 'What a friend we have in Jesus'), but now that the 'civvy' clothes had actually arrived, the reality of reversal back to civilian life was often a deeply uncomfortable and challenging experience. Britain, which had dressed its men to fight, was now dressing them as civilians and workers again, and once more expected them to find the inner resources with which to cope.

'Constant wearing of official costume can so transform someone that it becomes difficult or impossible for him or her to react normally',[11] and some of the newly demobbed men found that they did not fit in civilian life after serving in uniform for up to six years. In uniform they had become used to living rough in the company of their close comrades, seeing – or carrying out – violent, abhorrent acts and obeying orders without question, and they knew that no civilian, not even those closest to them, could ever be able to truly understand the nightmare memories of the appalling horrors of the war.

> Most men created a barrier between the two sets of clothing – those things which had happened when wearing military uniform would not apply to civilian life, would not be spoken of or referred to, so as to preserve their identity as peacetime father, husband, brother, uncle. Yet the expected behaviour of the years in uniform could not, in truth, be just switched off.[12]

The demob suit was now identifying a man with his job, career or vocation and family. Relationships would have to be forged anew and family members would have to get to know each other again since everyone had experienced the war in different ways and everyone had changed since they were separated. Children had grown and many had been living in other households in another part of the country; wives were used to living independently or had maybe found a new partner; and the returned servicemen were considerably changed by close-knit masculine comradeship, giving or obeying orders, the experience of foreign countries, physical or psychological injury. Divorces in Britain soared to 47,041 by 1947.[13]

As for the 437,000 demobbed British servicewomen,[14] they were not issued with an outfit, but were instead given a cash gratuity and ninety clothing coupons to spend on clothes of their own choice. The Women's Land Army was aggrieved to find that, as it was not a military organisation, 'Land Girls' were not entitled to any demobilisation clothing allowance or post-war benefits.[15] The only reluctant concession was that they could share in a £150,000[16] Benevolent Fund donation and keep their shoes and greatcoat.[17] Their jerseys would be sold through the Army Surplus Stores, even though patched and darned – often inexpertly – stained and maybe smelling irretrievably of the farmyard and its animals.[18]

The return to wearing feminine clothes could be an enormous challenge after years of constantly wearing a masculine-style uniform. 'For many of them uniform had become almost second nature; they felt exposed and vulnerable when this carapace was removed…'.[19] It was also difficult to deal with the sudden freedom of choice, especially as coupons and money had to be spent extremely wisely in the continuing shortages of clothing and high shop prices and the situation was particularly difficult for those women who had never chosen clothes for themselves, having joined the forces as young girls whose wardrobes were dictated by their parents.

Women's magazines offered advice and department stores put on tempting displays of outfits which could be bought with the demob coupon allowance.

In the West End, John Lewis employed advisers to show demobbed women the new lines in clothes … and Selfridges held a services' dress parade every Friday at 3pm during September and October 1945 … showing sample wardrobes, each totalling between £8 and £10, consisting of either a coat, dress and overall or a suit, blouse and mackintosh. Some shops with women billeted nearby staged special mannequin parades at their units (see illustration page 146) and 'many firms were prepared to dye and alter uniforms so that they could be used as civilian suits'.[20] However, tailors were so besieged by requests for alterations of pre-war clothing that waiting times could be up to six to nine months.[21] To be able to sew was a valuable skill.

Once the celebrations were over and demob was well under way, the next challenge was a result of victory – the re-building of a battered, almost bankrupt Britain. Now it was 'Back to Work'.

twenty-seven

Luxury and Austerity

By 1945, Britain had been at war for a greater length of time than any of the Allies.[1] The massive amounts of money which had been borrowed from America had to be repaid; the millions of refugees and displaced people within the British administrated zone of north-west Germany needed aid;[2] and there were the financial commitments of the Commonwealth and Dominions. At the same, the newly elected Labour Government needed to spend money in Britain itself to establish a new 'Fair Shares For All' Welfare State as had been outlined in the best-selling Beveridge Report of 1942, to end the 'five giant evils' of 'want, disease, ignorance, squalor and idleness'.[3] The solution was obvious – Britain needed to somehow dramatically increase income from exports and at the same time drastically cut expenditure on imports – which demanded yet more years of sacrifice, frugality and austerity.

Now, even those essential wartime possessions, the sewing machine and radio, had to become luxury items: '… If Dad has his new wireless he must do without tobacco, newspapers, and the wood for his chair – all imports. Mother can have her sewing machine, but nothing to sew – all our cotton and most of our wool are imported….' (Ministry of Information). Yet people were tired and needed rest after six years of war effort; their possessions were shabby and they had been looking forward to returning to lives which had been interrupted in 1939. Austerity was such a gloomy prospect that between 1946 and 1948, some 150,000 Britons emigrated to Canada, Australia and New Zealand.[4] But even in these years of continuing hardship, stitch would overcome the after-effects of war and provide solutions to Britain's financial situation.

Rationing had to be so severe that 'Flying Squads' of retired policemen were employed to keep an eye on the distribution of resources[5] and Government 'agents' even observed plates of food to make sure that no one was eating more than the 5s worth that they were allowed.[6] In 1948, a London dressmaker was arrested for embroidering flowers on underwear (which had been banned under the 'Civilian Clothing Order' of 1942)[7] and governmental control was becoming increasingly like the Gestapo state which Winston Churchill had been so condemned for predicting. Thefts from military stores proliferated, including four Beaufighter and two Mosquito bombers.[8] A wave of burglaries swept the country[9] and rebellion simmered. Then, after bread was rationed in June 1946, the British Housewives' League presented the House of Commons and the Ministry of Food with petitions of some 600,000 signatures, demanding more food, clothes and household goods with which to properly care for their families.[10] Misery increased still further during the freezing winter of 1947 with the acute shortages of coal and electricity.

Utility regulations concerning women's clothing were removed in the spring of 1946,[11] but prices were high and choice severely restricted, which was particularly a problem for women in employment whose employers insisted that they resume a pre-war standard of smartness – or lose their jobs.[12] The situation was only made worse by magazine illustrations of desirable 'export-only' clothing which could not be bought in Britain,[13] and the Council for Industrial

Poster stitched by Lilian Dring for the ERP promotion competition. (By kind courtesy of Matthew Dring)

Design's exhibition, 'Britain Can Make It', held at the Victoria & Albert Museum, London, in 1946, caused huge resentment by its displays of 'For Export Only' goods including exquisite clothing from the Incorporated Society of London Fashion Designers and rapidly became known as 'Britain Can't Have It'.[14]

To earn urgently needed revenue by the promotion of British fashion, Frederick Starke founded the 'Model House Group' in 1947, which was soon re-named the 'Fashion House Group of London'. In 1948, its fourteen members won contracts in Europe, the British colonies and America for a range of ready-to-wear clothing.[15] Additionally, Molyneux organised a London Fashion Week held immediately before the French collections were shown in Paris, to attract buyers to the collections of The Incorporated Society of London Fashion Designers. Unfortunately, their efforts were hampered by governmental beaurocracy and 'red tape',[16] the severe post-war shortage of materials and labour, for British textile factories were still waiting for their workers to be demobbed.[17] Molyneux returned to Paris in 1946 and British couture soon returned mainly to dependency on its pre-war aristocratic clientele. However, the society 'Season' was resumed in 1947, and there was a surge of clients, particularly from Hardy Amies,[18] for events such as Ascot races, Henley Regatta, and the 'coming out' of some 20,000 debutantes[19] who required wardrobes of new clothes and gowns for their presentation at Court which had been delayed by the war.

In 1947, Britain received a four-year loan from America,[20] and the Government organised a competition for posters to advertise this 'European Recovery Programme' ('ERP' or 'Marshall Aid'). An entry by the textile artist Lilian Dring represented Europe and the newly formed 'Iron-Curtain' countries in checks and ginghams against a deep-blue-painted canvas background, with an overlay of black net edged with red machine-stitching to define the new Russian territories. Countries receiving Aid were linked by threads in the colours of their national flags to the letter 'R' in E R P. The lower section evoked the aftermath of war with dull brown scrim and fabric taken from old grey flannel trousers.

The gloom of austerity in Britain was lifted in the spring of 1947, by the presentation in paris of the first collection of the French couturier Christian Dior which took the world by storm with its unexpected, uninhibited extravagance and luxurious, corseted and padded feminity. The fashion press called it the 'New Look'.

Dior's designs were shocking to the eye after six years of drab, frugal, masculine uniformity. Enormous skirts swept down from nipped-in waists to within 8 or 14in of the ground in clouds of beautiful colour, using at least 25 yards of expensive fabric and maybe 300 hours of labour to construct,[21] involving complicated Victorian dressmaking techniques and Dior's own similarly time-consuming new methods.[22] At a time of such shortages, the collection was received with very strong, sometimes violent public and governmental disapproval in Britain, America and even Paris itself. Yet, it was the 'Look' of women's dreams:

> Soft neat shoulders, a wasp waist, a bosom padded for extra curve, and hips that swelled over shells of cambric or taffeta worked into the lining … She was delicious and she made all other women green with envy.[23]

Women were thoroughly weary of frocks made from just 3½ yards of fabric and tired of the military Schiaparelli-style clothing which had been so necessary during the war. Heads turned and people stopped to stare at the 'New Look' being worn in the street and any initial reluctance to wear such an extremely different style was soon swept away by the joy of the outrageous feminity. Stitch was providing a restoration of beauty and a sense of new beginnings. The Deréta shop in London's West End sold its complete stock of 700 un-rationed grey flannel 'New Look' suits in just a fortnight[24] and even the royal Princesses managed to wear the 'New Look' by appearing in coats by Molyneux which had insertions of velvet bands to lengthen and widen the skirts.[25] By 1950, Princess Margaret felt free to enjoy her twenty-first birthday in the unashamed luxury of an exquisite ballgown by Dior himself. In fact, such was the effect of Dior's romantic designs that even an ordinary woman clothed in 'New Look' could find herself standing straighter and taller, feeling like a queen.[26]

A 'New Look' Dior evening gown. (Courtesy of Hulton Archive 3364180 (RM) Photograph by Keystone)

'New Look' dress patterns were available, however they required at least 20 yards of fabric costing over two coupons a yard when the allowance for adults had been reduced to an unprecedentedly meagre thirty-two. Even so, stitchers made dresses for themselves in any fabrics which were available in sufficiently large quantities, such as blackout fabric, parachute silk or khaki. *Weldon's Ladies' Journal* offered a cut-out-and-ready-to-sew model, or one could make a 'New Look' skirt by unpicking the hem and side seams of a gathered dirndl skirt and turning it sideways[27] and there were other ways of obtaining enough fabric for a 'New Look' outfit, of course, if one did not object to the black market:

> I got some 'Black Market' materials – my first New Look skirt and some lovely woven medium weight woollen material from which I made a two piece, skirt and jacket. I made bound buttonholes and cut them on the wrong side! It was a Vogue special pattern. (Doreen Newson)

When retailers and clothing manufacturers found that they could not sell their existing stocks, the Government was forced to revise its regulations and allow the production of a Utility 'New Look' range, even though the designs more closely resembled crinolines.[28] The stitches of couture had overcome the after-effects of the war!

In 1947, the controversy of 'New Look' was joined by that of Princess Elizabeth's wedding to Lieutenant Philip Mountbatten RN – should it echo the nation's need for austerity or should it be a truly royal occasion? Public opinion was divided: a survey discovered that 50 per cent of those questioned saw a royal wedding-gown as a waste of money[29] but the Princesses Elizabeth and Margaret Rose were leaders in fashion and young girls were eager to see the wedding dress and going-away outfit,[30] as was the world's press, and extensive precautions had to be taken to keep the design of the gown a secret.[31] The Queen once more called upon Norman Hartnell to

'… the dress I altered when the new look came in. Pieces let in skirt and waist, piping at neck and added pieces to sleeve. After so many regulations to dress during the war, I guess we were pleased when longer dresses came in.' (By kind courtesy of Kathleen Lever)

strike a balance between the nation's frugality and the provision of a spectacle in keeping with the marriage of the heir to the throne, and, of course, design a gown which would please the bride. He submitted twelve designs, from which was chosen a gown befitting the splendour of the occasion, inspired by Botticelli's painting *Primavera*, symbolic of new beginnings both for the couple and the nation.[32] Requested by the Queen to use satin from Lullingstone Castle in Kent, Hartnell found that it was suitable for the gown's train but too heavy for the dress itself; but when a lighter, more supple satin was ordered from Winterthur of Dunfermline, Scotland, the Press questioned whether the silk worms were 'enemy Italian', only to be re-assured that they were, in fact, from Nationalist China.[33] With only three months to the wedding from the acceptance of the design, his embroiderers worked with silver thread, crystals, diamonds and the 10,000 tiny seed pearls which Hartnell had brought from America. The delicate gauzy 15ft train which fell from the Princess's shoulders, woven in Braintree, Essex[34] was appliquéd with five-petalled star-shaped satin blossoms, the White Rose of York and embroidered ears of wheat embellished with shimmering crystals and pearls.[35] Star-shaped blossoms also garlanded the gown itself with rich sprays of roses and smilax worked in pearls and diamonds.[36] (See colour illustration 35.)

On their cold, grey wedding day of 20 November 1947, the couple were, in fact, greeted with crowds lining the route some fifty people deep and there was a definite feeling in the nation of happiness and new beginnings.[37] The going-away outfit was, after all, not New Look but the 'matronly' style which young women of the late '40s strove to achieve.[38]

For the vast majority of women, the only thing to do was to keep on making-do and stitching garments at home from the few materials which were available, including the silk escape maps printed for issue to RAF personnel, which were now being sold off.[39] Patterns could be bought from companies such as McCall, Butterick, Simplicity and Vogue, who brought out a fresh collection bi-annually.[40] In July 1947, a Research Services Ltd survey of the domestic sewing habits of 4,000 wives and working women revealed that:

> Three-quarters of all sewers had something in hand … most of them were doing darning and mending, particularly the housewives. Twenty-seven percent were doing more creative work – making women's clothes for themselves or their families; or babies' and children's clothes for their own or other people's families; or, to a smaller extent, things for the house – curtains, pillow cases and cushion covers. … The average weekly time given to sewing in the early Spring is about three hours – the equivalent of half an hour each day, or one whole evening a week. … Sewers expect to cut down their sewing time in the summer (June-September), but for seasonal reasons only; there is a general desire to do as much or more during the twelve months as a whole. … The impulse to sew comes primarily from the need to do repairs – household repairs, and keeping personal things in order. 'Saving' is also very important, but nearly half the sewers said they enjoyed sewing. Fashion appeal is low.[41]

The survey also discovered that the women who had stitched to keep family and home respectable throughout the war still placed a great deal of importance on stitching in education: 'The broad picture is very clear; there is a strong desire among mothers to see their daughters better equipped than they are themselves, and to regard sewing as an essential part of school curricula'.

There was a shortage of many things for several years after the war and the rationing of clothes and textiles continued. Army surplus goods such as pillow cases, cotton snow suits and nylon parachutes were sold off cheaply at the close of the war and were eagerly sought after by people who were good at sewing, like my mother. (Heather Fogg)

[I made] woollen shorts for both boys out of their grandfather's plus-fours. They were a bit on the large side and worn with … thick jackets they looked like a pair of orphans – but that was after the war of course. (Doreen Newson)

The continuing shortages of sewing materials were also an acute problem for embroiderers. In 1947, St Osyth Mahala Eustace Wood embarked upon a twelve-page concertina-folded book of samplers and declared upon the first page:

We have had six years of war and two of uneasy peace. Of silks and threads and linens are there none. Nor yet sheets, or pillow-cases or towels. We have few clothes and most things that can be bought are shoddy. I am weary of darning and patching and mending. So I shall use what skeins and remnants I have left over from better days and plan my samplers to fit them. With care, there will be enough for a few pages and samplers can be great fun. But the colour schemes may look odder and odder as my small store dwindles. (See colour illustration 36.)

In December 1946, ever encouraging and supportive, the Embroiderers' Guild printed an article in *Embroidery* by Captain Geoffrey Edwards entitled 'Let Us Now Praise – Austerity' which told readers: 'Good for Austerity – the Goddess who has arrived and who seems to be with us for some time. She is going to compel us to make our own designs, trace them, finish them.'[42] He continued:

Now, dear reader, will you come with me to see how you are going to have great fun in making a potential work of art out of nothing – making bricks with very little straw! First examine your assets (we will call this P.P. for short, ie. Pitiful Pile) … To those who don't know their Museums, there is a treat in store …'; choose 'crude bold patterns that you get in wood-cut or brass rubbings' and draw the design on 'decent drawing paper'; make an outline in Indian ink, trace, transfer to 'dead-white' lining fabric and 'scrub colours in firmly' using water-colour or water-proof ink. Then, remembering that 'Every stitch as long as it crosses another casts a shadow – therefore that stitch is equal to two, put in 'as few stitches as possible'. 'So Rule 1, make every stitch cross another, viz. Blanket etc. Rule II, make up any sort of stitch as long as it is a <u>surface</u> stitch. … Rule IV … Goodbye satin stitch … resisting the temptation for outlining, use any sort of CONTRAST in tone or colour. If there is very little [background] showing, leave well alone, but if a lot, then perhaps the 'dead white' (now coloured) will appear a bit mean – so a few loose stitches (trellis or buttonhole) will soon get rid of the mean look … You have now experienced austerity and accomplished *something* and if others will do the same on their own lines and pool their ideas, then good will come. There are surely many ways of making bricks without straw, but if the methods are written down, it will avoid much wastage of everyone's precious P.P.[43]

In 1947–48, to promote the nation's recovery, the Fine Arts department of the British Council organised an exhibition of Britain's finest embroidery to tour the world for three years from

CARTOON

Reproduced by permission of G. Edwards

ORIGINAL TRACING AND REVERSE OF PANEL

Illustration from 'Let Us Now Praise Austerity' by Captain Geoffrey Edwards. (*Embroidery*, 1947. Courtesy of the Embroiderers' Guild)

London to Ankara, Istanbul, Cyprus, Egypt and Smyrna until 1950. Pieces ranged from world-renowned medieval Opus Anglicanum ecclesiastical vestments to contemporary work, some taken from the Royal Scottish Museum, the Royal School of Needlework and private owners. When approached for contributions of member's work, the Embroiderers' Guild lent eleven pieces and were pleased that their young embroiderers, who had only known the shortages of war, would be able to see the standard of excellence which could be achieved with a wide choice of high-quality materials.[44]

At the same time, in 1947, the British Government also called upon the nation's home-stitchers to provide work which could be sold in the United States through their 'Home Industries Ltd' scheme. Samples of work had to be submitted to the Board of Trade through the WVS,[45] and if deemed to be 'of the highest standard' all materials would be provided for the completed piece – which was essential in the continuing scarcity of fabric and thread. The problem of continuing shortages was addressed in *Embroidery* in December 1947:

> Under the impending threat of still greater austerity, the search for materials suitable for embroidery is likely to make ever more demands upon the time and tenacity of the enthusiastic worker. Fortunately, the surplus government stocks of mattresses, etc., which are in all the shops from time to time, provide good material for those willing to give time and care to the soaking and laundering sometimes required to make them soft and pleasant to work upon.

Other recommended fabric sources were: 'parachutes, architects' tracing canvas, old cambric shirts, sugar bags … even sacking in which overseas parcels have been packed',[46] but it was not until 1948 that embroiderers could again – after nine long years – buy the Anchor 'silks' which were the mainstay of 1940s home embroidery. In 1949 the choice widened still further with the launch of Anchor's 'Soft Embroidery' range.

This photograph of a twenty-one year old was taken by a street photographer in London – she is wearing her first shop-bought coat, a 'New Look'. (Her father is worriedly searching his pockets for the receipt for a watch which he has just bought for her twenty-first birthday.) (By kind courtesy of Enid Mason)

Utility restrictions on clothing were ended in 1948[47] and, in addition, the adult coupon allowance was also raised to thirty-six for a six-month period;[48] then, at the end of the year the number of coupons required for clothing purchases was reduced – men's suits were marked down from twenty-six to twenty coupons and women's suits from eighteen down to twelve – which was fortuitous as the winter of 1948 was the most bitter winter on record. Snow blizzards obliterated the sun for weeks on end and 'only one road remained open to connect London and the north, via Birmingham'.[49] Britain shivered yet again as power supplies were cut for up to five hours each day for twelve days in February, one of the coldest months. Factories had to lay off thousands of workers,[52] shops and offices were lit by candles and oil lamps, and people risked a massive fine of £100 or three months in prison for disobeying the Government's use of fuel regulations such as 'no electricity to be used in relation to superfluous activities' – which included listening to the radio – even during its severely shortened transmission times.[50] Ex-military duffel coats which had been worn on the Russian Convoys came in particularly useful.

Despite the gloom, the weather and its financial difficulties, Britain managed to host the 1948 Olympics, which came to be known as the 'Austerity Olympics'. Female athletes had to stitch their own clothing, or have it stitched for them; German prisoners of war constructed the 'Olympic Way'; Boy Scouts re-painted Wembley stadium and ex-military convalescent homes were used to accommodate the visiting athletes.[51]

The icy weather lasted through until March of 1949, and by then, not surprisingly, nearly half the nation – 42 per cent – wanted to emigrate.[52] However, the worst was over, and life was to gradually become a little easier. In the spring of 1949, as part of the Labour Government's 'bonfires' of controls, the end of clothes rationing finally arrived;[53] however, even though there was a marvellous freedom from coupons, choice was limited and prices too high for many to afford the items which they sorely needed.[54]

Even if one could afford new clothes, the transition from wartime 'make-do' wardrobe to smart new shop-bought clothing could be embarrassing at times:

My sister too trained as a teacher and her P.E. garb was a pair of long brown bloomers called Erics. Goodness knows why. The shops were beginning to stock clothes again so she and I went shopping together to spend my precious earnings. Imagine her embarrassment in stripping off in front of the assistant. What was I wearing but a pair of the hideous Erics. The suit was my pride and joy particularly for walks with boy friends. It was muted red tweed and suited me very well. (Denise Cochrane)

By 1950, the WVS were still administrating the Board of Trade's 'Home Industries Ltd' scheme, however the most valuable piece of embroidery to earn export revenue had been stitched by Her Majesty Queen Mary: an impressive carpet originally intended as a furnishing for Buckingham Palace. The Royal School of Needlework had created the design, to be worked on cotton canvas, after taking inspiration from eighteenth-century designs in the collections of the Victoria & Albert Museum, and Queen Mary had chosen the colours. (See colour illustration 37.) The press was invited to see the almost-finished piece and the news magazine *Time* reported that it consisted of twelve panels depicting birds and flowers on a beige background, surrounded by a floral border, informing readers that the carpet would be displayed in London for a fortnight and then shipped to the United States and Canada for further exhibition, with the intention that it would be sold to the highest bidder and the proceeds donated to the British Treasury with the stipulation that it should eventually be presented to a public institution.

Such a large and beautiful work was a tremendous achievement and after crossing the Atlantic on board the RMS *Queen Mary* in March 1950, it was exhibited in a twelve-week tour of America and Canada; and under the auspices of the 'Committee for Queen Mary's Contribution to the Dollar Drive'[58] of the 'Imperial Order of Daughters of the Empire (Canada)' (IODE), $100,000 was raised for its purchase on behalf of the Canadian people. In 1951, it was presented to Princess Elizabeth on her State Visit to Canada, who in turn presented it to the National Gallery of Canada, Ottawa. The expert workmanship of the carpet also resulted in increased sales of British needlework in the United States of America.[59]

Weary of year upon year of Labour's intrusive austerity, Britain voted in a Conservative Government in 1951, headed by Winston Churchill, but rationing still did not end until 1954, 'long after the rest of western Europe'.[60]

twenty-eight

Men's Fashion and the War

'I know all the women will look smart, but we men may look shabby. If we do
we must not be ashamed. In war the term 'battle-stained' is an honourable one.'
(Broadcast by Oliver Lyttleton, President of the Board of Trade,
upon the introduction of clothes rationing, 1 June 1941.)

For centuries, British royalty had set the style and dress-codes for men's fashion in Britain and in 1939, a man's clothing instantly identified his place in society and therefore the way he should be treated. Clothing instantly proclaimed one a gentleman – or not. A man's clothing was a form of social shell into which he fitted.

At one end of the scale, the very poorest, the unemployed, lived in tatters and could hardly manage to keep warm and dry. At the other end of the scale of wealth, gentlemen of the aristocracy possessed extensive wardrobes of garments and accessories made from the highest-quality materials by expert tailors and craftsmen, which were appropriate for every activity in their day throughout the year and the society Season; these were maintained by trained staff. Sons of all classes were expected to dress in the same style as their fathers; however, following the example of Edward VIII, formerly Edward Prince of Wales, young men of the aristocracy shocked their fathers by adopting the more casual style of *chic fatigue*.

But all this was to change upon the outbreak of the Second World War in September 1939.

Smiling Through – Thin Trousers 'Don't stand against the light, Henry. Those trousers have worn a bit thin.' (Courtesy of Solo Syndication)

Immediately men became, first and foremost, the defenders of Britain and freedom. The whole spectrum of men's clothing was replaced by uniforms and the class divisions were now expressed by rank and the quality of uniform design and fabric. However, all men now received respect; their uniform declared that the wearer was prepared to serve, or even die, for his country.

These thousand upon thousand of military uniforms swallowed up the insufficient supplies of imported raw materials which had survived the depradations of the enemy during long sea passages, and it was no longer possible to issue servicemen with the usual full dress, undress and mess uniform.[1] Male civilians had to make what clothes they possessed last as long as possible and gentlemen had to forgo the practice of changing their clothing in the evening, maybe just altering their appearance by wearing a different hat. Wealthier men were at an advantage,

Old Sunday suits with
waistcoats were worn for
gardening, with hats or
caps. (By kind courtesy of
The News, Portsmouth, 78)

having ample hard-wearing wardrobes including the tough wool-tweed suits worn for shoot-
ing and fishing, but as the years of war passed, even they would find it difficult to keep up a
respectable appearance. Formal attire was replaced by more casual knitted pullovers and open-
neck shirts worn with flannel or corduroy trousers,[2] however it was always necessary to wear a
hat or cap.

   In 1942, the Government's Utility Scheme banned men's double-breasted jackets and coats;[3]
limited jacket lapel size; required that jackets or coats have only three pockets, or two in a
waistcoat;[4] specified the number of buttons and button-holes; required that the width of trouser legs should be 19in maximum; and created a storm of objections over the ban on trouser
turn-ups[5] – to which Hugh Dalton, President of the Board of Trade, replied: 'There can be no
equality of sacrifice in this war. Some must lose lives and limbs; others only the turnups on
their trousers.' Objections were also made to the ban on braces and pocket flaps which would
otherwise hide fraying and bagginess. Hugh Dalton also asked male civilians to give up wearing
socks, collars and ties in order to save the nation's materials and did not, himself, buy a new suit
during the five years and nine months of war.[6]

   In August 1945, the shabby and tattered men of Britain finally had a turn of fortune when
the United States decided to sell off its surplus Army, Navy and Air Force military clothing and
the duffle coats were particularly highly prized.[7] The US Airforce bomber-jacket became a
cult item and American blue jeans were to become tremendously popular from 1947, both for
males and females.[8] Khaki could be seen everywhere as 4 million items, including jeeps, filled
Britain's streets.[9] Some of these hard-wearing and useful American additions to men's wardrobes were to influence the clothing industry for decades to come: for instance, the cotton
T-shirt, with arms cut at right angles to the body like a letter 'T' which had been used as an
undershirt by the US Navy from 1942.[10] It's possible that the Chino trousers included in the
British sale were actually completing a circle, having originated in Britain and exported to
China in the 1930s; the Chinese then exported them to the Philippines where they were
named 'Chinos' and were popular with the American servicemen stationed there from 1936
to 1946.[11]

   The synthetic fabrics which had been produced in Britain during the war for military use
could be used for civilian clothing once the war was over and it was interesting to discover

Instruction in how to prepare a seed-bed, Kew Gardens. Note the absence of pocket flaps. (Courtesy of the Imperial War Museum, London. HU 63787)

the new nylon shirts did not need ironing, although, on the morning of a cool day they were uncomfortably cold to put on and did not 'breathe' on a hot day. Suits could be also made in the lightweight Terylene, Orlon and Dralon, or woollen merino and cross-breed mixtures[12] and a lighter, less stiff method of lining was devised – the 'English' lining, or 'skeleton' lining.[13]

However, Britain's men still had to cope with the serious clothing shortages and in meeting their needs the black market prospered. Young men who had been demobbed from the services, and were looking for a way of making a living, found that there were opportunities in the world of crime, but, far from making themselves inconspicuous, they prided themselves on their highly distinctive appearance. These 'spivs', or black marketeers, traded in goods which had 'fallen off the back of a lorry'[14] and a typical 'Flash Harry' or 'Jack the Lad'[15] sported a 'pencil moustache', hair parted in the middle, a narrow-waisted coat designed to emphasise the padded shoulders,[16] a thickly knotted tie, tight shirt collar, and trilby hat.[17] The first issue of the humorous *Spiv's Gazette* in March 1948 declared that 'All members must wear the official spiv uniform and shoulders to be not less than 46in wide'.[18] Suffering under a dreary tangle of strict Government and oppressive rules and regulations, the British public either applauded the 'spiv' for his independence – or 'threatened to shoot him'.[19]

Young British men also took great pleasure in wearing the latest version of the 'Zoot suit' which had caused such public condemnation and even street violence in America in the early years of the war for the look was of an impeccable, determined civilian extravagance at a time of severe shortages, with over-sized wide-shouldered jackets worn over roomy trousers.[20] Public outrage was also aroused when a similar style was later adopted by the young men of Paris – the provocative 'Zazous', whose large-check suits demanded yet more material to allow for matching the pattern at the seams.[21] However, by the time the 'Zoot suit' arrived in London in 1946,[22] it was warmly welcomed by tailors and clothing manufacturers, particularly as it generated a fresh interest in the jacket as a fashionable garment; for young men were tired of the short, fitted, 1930s-design 'bum freezer'. As the latest women's fashion was named the 'New Look,' the 'Zoot suit' was called the 'Bold Look'.[23]

There was also the option for young men of leaving their shirt tail hanging out,[24] which in turn led to the relaxed open-necked, three-quarter-length Chat Way shirt incorporating two hip-level pockets, which was, in its turn, the inspiration for the casual 'shirt-jacket'.[25]

British 'Zoot suit'. (Courtesy of the Victoria & Albert Museum)

The most exciting garments for men in the post-war years were from America – the brightly coloured 'Hawaiian' loose-fitting, short-sleeved shirts and ties which could be purchased from shops such as Cecil Gee in Charing Cross Road, London. Colour-starved ex-servicemen queued determinedly for their own luxuriant images of sun, sea, sand and prosperity – vivid sunsets and flowers, pin-up girls, skyscrapers, rodeos and American limousines.[26]

However, not all men were swept along with the wartime tidal wave of American influence: the officers of the Guards, who had carefully cared for their uniforms throughout the long and demanding crossing of Europe after D-Day, now made their own unique statement of British quality. Tailors were asked to make their quintessentially British neo-Edwardian suits with narrow trousers and brocade waistcoats displayed beneath narrow-shouldered, long, single-breasted jackets, the collars trimmed with velvet Accompanied by Chesterfield overcoats, rolled black umbrellas or silver-headed canes, gloves and Derby hats, the style did not catch on, for the strong prevailing mood in Britain was a forceful rejection of pre-war aristocratic domination. Yet the Guards had given birth to a new 'uniform', the business suit of office upper-management – the aristocrats of the business world. The style also inspired another extreme – the subversive 'street fashion' of the 'Teddy Boy' who might live in poverty, but spent what money he had in challenging the wealthy aristocracy with his own perfectly cut neo-Edwardian, velvet-trimmed suit, mirror-polished shoes, and immaculate haircut.[27]

By 1951, men's fashion had undergone radical changes: tailors who had joined the forces returned to find that the ready-to-wear industry was rapidly supplying High Street shops with affordable, good-quality men's wear; American leisure and sportswear was on its way and a new age-group was about to be defined – the teenager – which would be the basis of a whole new fashion industry. Savile Row had successfully weathered the war with overseas orders and tailor-made uniforms and now there were waiting lists for British suits to be taken back to America by servicemen who were returning home;[28] but Britain's tailoring industry would never regain its celebrated pre-war status, although the under-stated, perfectly crafted elegance would always be respected.

The men of Britain had fought for freedom, in the armed forces or as civilians. By 1951, it was becoming possible to enjoy the benefits of peace – properly dressed!

twenty-nine

Peace and Freedom

An overriding air of conformism, monarchism, and patriotism prevailed.[1]

It was a time to re-build. It was a time for change. Under the new Welfare State no one would starve, wear rags, or be denied an education or medical aid for lack of money. It was time for the the workers of Britain to have a voice, and they became a powerful force. Trades Union members now sat at boardroom tables with company bosses[2] and Britain was wracked by a series of strikes as the working man made his point of view known. It seemed to many that office jobs, particularly those in the service sector, were 'parasitic' for *real* men did the *real* work upon which Britain depended.[3] Men who sweated during the day at heavy, dirty physical work enjoyed great respect within their own communities and were proud to wear the working man's cloth cap,[4] especially the coal miners upon whom the prosperity of Britain had depended.

Stitch had defined the classes by military uniform during the war and it would now continue to do so – in the workplace – for despite the Government's increasing provision of 'Fair Shares for All', class resentments still simmered. To men dressed in overalls, the collar and tie of the office worker was to be resented as a statement of the 'easy' life enjoyed by the upper classes yet at the same time they wanted more for their sons than they themselves had found through a life-time's employment in heavy industry, believing that only a fool would take the sort of job which demanded wearing overalls.[5]

It was true; office work produced high incomes and the office worker could also be easily identified by his clothing. At the top of the company hierarchy could be seen: 'an elite predominantly blessed with the accents of the officers' mess: men bowler-hatted or homburged, wearing suits of military cut either bespoke or at least bought from such approved outfitters as Aquascutum or Simpsons of Piccadilly; gentlemen indeed, confident of manner, instantly recognisable by stance and gesture.' Beneath them were the aspiring 'upwardly mobile' and 'the snobbery of the socially unsure' – men with regional accents who 'bought their ready-made suits from Meakers, Dunn or Horne Brothers; wore at weekends blazers with breast-pockets adorned with the crests of such uncrack regiments as the Royal Army Service Corps; drove staidly respectable motor cars … and were blessed with "lady wives" who were proud of their well-furnished "lounges".'[6]

These were men who wanted their business success and high incomes to be demonstrated by wives who stayed at home,[7] and also to show the control which men had re-asserted over the workplace, sweeping away the fulfilling world of independence, freedom which had been opened up to women during the war.[8] Women now discovered that they were usually relegated to repetitive and unstimulating jobs and the best that they could hope for was a 'light' job which allowed the opportunity to chat to friends; or 'clean' work, for as with men, dirty work-clothes classed a person as being in some way inferior.[9] However, many women were glad to be able to return to the satisfying creativity of home-making once again, and this was carefully encouraged by media propaganda:[10] the number of women in paid employment in Britain reverted to that of the pre-war years.[11]

Television broadcasting had resumed on 7 June 1946 with the continuation of the Mickey Mouse cartoon which had been interrupted in 1939,[12] and the news announcers wore dinner jackets[13] and by the spring of 1949, some 100,000 housewives had an entirely novel problem to deal with: how to accommodate a newly purchased television set in the living-room – for, to be viewed properly, it needed a darkened room.[14] *House and Garden* suggested that stitch be used to divide the room by curtains, or Venetian blinds, creating both viewers' and non-viewers' spaces for 'the viewers need less light (especially around the set), while others may be distracted by the performance.'[15] However, stitchers could continue to work happily in adequate light as the majority of people still gathered around the hearth to 'listen in' to the radio.[16]

In 1946, the National Federation of Women's Institutes set about making a record of 'Women's Work in Wartime'. It was to be a momentous task, comprising some 2 million stitches, measuring over 9ft high and 15ft 3in wide and weighing 47lb. Single-mesh hemp canvas and 35lb of mothproof wool had to be sourced and stitchers trained to work the twenty-one images surrounded by richly designed borders. The quotation along the lower edge, intended to amuse, was taken from *Henry VIII* Act 1, Scene 1:

> '........the madams too,
> Not us'd to toil, did almost sweat to bear
> The pride upon them, ...'

This ambitious piece was based upon water-colour sketches by the artist-embroiderer Sybil Blunt, which were transposed onto squared paper to be given to representatives from each

'Women's Work in Wartime' stitched by 400 members of the WI. (Courtesy of the Imperial War Museum, London MH 4443)

county who met at two one-day workshops in Winchester to meet Miss Blunt, familiarise themselves with the design and master the stitches ready to pass on the information and skills at their respective branches. Members who wished to take part were asked to stitch a sample and in 1947 around 400 were chosen to start work on the fifteen separate panels, supervised by Mrs G.L. Parnell of Rogate WI, West Sussex. The tapestry, which appears to have been stitched by just one expert hand, was completed in Winchester and later exhibited at the Victoria & Albert Museum in an exhibition of WI crafts.[17] (See colour illustration 39 for the image of one of the many vital tasks which were performed by the WI during the Second World War – that of fruit preservation, which did much to make the most of Britain's scanty food resources.)

Britain could finally begin to relax: the working day was being shortened, wages were higher and there were now paid holidays.[18] After the long, hard years of war, pleasure and enjoyment was needed, and on each Bank Holiday enormous queues stretched out from major railway stations as holiday-makers patiently waited in their Sunday-best clothes for seats on the many trains and relief-trains which had to be laid on to transport them to seaside resorts all over Britain – if space could be found on the sand when they got there.

Trousers might be rolled up for a paddle, or a knotted handkerchief used for covering the head if the sun shone, but only a few people wore clothing actually designed for sunbathing or swimming.

Casual clothing was still an ocean away in America and by 1949 British fashion was dictated by Dior's two main silhouettes – pencil-slim skirt with back-pleat or vent, or curve-enhancing dresses with fitted bodices, wide collars, tiny waists and full, swishing skirt over layers of petti-coats with low-cut off-the-shoulder necklines, or halter-necks. A ready-to-wear bestseller was a taffeta dress with matching coat, however women continued to wear head-scarves and many shops still only stocked only drab 'Utility' clothing.[19] But consumer expectations were rising, if unambitiously – maybe just a second slip – one to wear and one in the wash.[20]

Embroidery was also gradually emerging from the constraints of the war: an exhibition pictures and samplers at Heals in London in 1946 was the first to feature decorative pieces for the home. However, Heals included a somewhat controversial picture by Constance Howard, *Bird in a Cage* – her first to be exhibited – which challenged the widely held concept that the achievement of perfect technique and finish in embroidery were of prime importance, rather than freedom and innovation in design.[21] But this sense of post-war immediacy and informal-ity was being encouraged by the newly resumed Needlework Development Scheme with its collection of mainly cut-paper and chalk designs by Mary Kesel to be circulated in schools

Post-war holiday clothes. (Hunstanton.)
(By kind courtesy of Anita Seamons)

The 'Country Pavilion', Festival of Britain. See 'Country Wife' background left. (By kind courtesy of the National Federation of Women's Institutes)

A day out on Ramsgate Sands., newly cleared of barbed wire, concrete blocks and mines. (Courtesy of the Kent Messenger Group)

Constance Howard working on *The Country Wife*. (By kind courtesy of the National Federation of Women's Institutes)

and colleges for individual interpretation in stitch whilst retaining the linear framework.[22] In October 1950, *Vogue* remarked on the 'renaissance of embroidery'. In 1950, the Embroiderers' Guild journal *Embroidery* was put on sale to the general public for the first time.[23]

Britain was ready for a turning point; a declaration that the war and its after-effects were finally overcome; and by 3 May 1951, twenty-seven acres of the bombed-out South Bank in London had been transformed into 'an environment of "fun, fantasy and colour"'[24] to commemorate the Great Exhibition of 1851 and create a showcase for British design and technology. Battersea Park was turned into the Festival Pleasure Gardens and 8.5 million visitors enjoyed the exciting, futuristic, playful, eccentric, '… all very British' experience.[25]

Exhibits such as those of the Needlework Development Scheme were displayed in the 'Dome of Discovery' and themed pavilions included the 'Country Pavilion' in which was displayed a 10ft x 16ft hanging depicting the accomplishments of the WI – *The Country Wife*, designed by Constance Howard and stitched by her students from Goldsmiths College.[26]

The activities represented included embroidery, dress-making, baking, weaving and flower arranging and the rounded and padded ⅝th life-size figures attached to the heavy felt backing were accompanied by items expertly crafted by WI members, such as a pair of gloves, a basket, knitting and richly embroidered fishes – which 'disappeared' a number of times and had to be replaced.[27] (See colour illustration 38.)

Communities across the nation also put on their own local festivals and the exhibition *Women of the Century*, at York House in Twickenham, included another large textile piece measuring 10ft x 10ft: a patchwork hanging entitled *The Patchwork of the Century* composed of one hundred squares representing the years 1851 to 1951. It had been a community project, involving some eighty women from local organisations who had worked for two months under the organisation of the textile artist Lilian Dring, and although many had no prior experience of embroidery, they were encouraged to produce their own designs. Four of the squares were worked by Lilian herself, including '1851' and '1951', which showed the new Royal Festival Hall.[28] Materials were provided by the stitchers themselves from items which they already possessed, such as blackout fabric, tablecloths and Air Force uniforms.[29]

After Britain's massive and sustained effort, stitch could once more become a pleasurable enjoyment of design, texture and colour. It was time to enjoy the fruits of the victory. But the habits of 'Make Do and Mend' were to last a lifetime!

End Notes

Chapter 1 'Ten Thousand Children'

1. Turner, Barry, *And the Policeman Smiled*, Bloomsbury Publishing Ltd, p.31
2. Harris, Mark Jonathan and Deborah Oppenheimer, *Into the Arms of Strangers*, Bloomsbury Publishing Ltd, p.87
3. Liesl Munden in conversation with the author
4. Harris and Oppenheimer, p.88
5. Leverton, Bertha and Shmuel Lowensohn, *I came alone*, The Book Guild Ltd, p.15
6. Ibid. p.95
7. Ibid. p.117
8. Ibid. p.95
9. Ibid. p.291
10. Ibid. p.347
11. Harris and Oppenheimer, p.114
12. Turner, p.58
13. Harris and Oppenheimer, p.145
14. Ibid. p.84
15. Imperial War Museum Photographic Archive EPH 3872
16. Harris and Oppenheimer, p.171
17. Turner, p.151
18. Leverton and Lowensohn, p.109
19. Ibid. p.99
20. From the autobiography of Ester Friedman. Reprinted by kind permission of Ester Friedman
21. Leverton and Lowensohn, p.101

Chapter 2 'The Royal Family'

1. 'Robb' and Anne Edwards, *The Queen's Clothes*, Beaverbrook Newspapers Ltd, (Book Club Associates edition 1977) p.16
2. Forbes, Grania, *Elizabeth the Queen Mother A Twentieth Century Life*, Pavilion Books Ltd, p.160
3. Vickers, Hugo, *Elizabeth the Queen Mother*, Hutchinson, p.178
4. Vickers (quoting the diary of Joseph P. Kennedy, April 1939). Reprinted by permission of the Random House Group Ltd
5. Ibid. p.178
6. Ibid. p.178
7. Forbes, p.159
8. www.gov.uk/output/page4342.asp
9. Vickers, p.186
10. Forbes, p.94
11. Vickers, p.205
12. Ibid. p.249
13. Gardiner, Juliet, *Wartime Britain 1939-1945*, Headline Book Publishing, p.345
14. Vickers, p.218
15. Forbes, p.90
16. Ibid. p.91
17. Vickers (quoting Mary A. Winter), p.218. Reprinted by permission of the Random House Group Ltd

Chapter 3 'Mr Churchill'

1. *Churchill's Bodyguard* by Tom Hickman. Original material © 1938-55 Walter Thompson. Additional text © 2005 Tom Hickman. Reproduced by permission of Headline Publishing Group Ltd, p.118
2. Lurie, Alison, *The Language of Clothes*, Heinemann, p.5. Reprinted by permission of the Random House Group Ltd
3. Hickman, p.95
4. Ibid. p.106
5. Mr Rowland Lowe – Mackenzie, Turnbull & Asser in conversation with the author
6. Best, Geoffrey, *Churchill A Study in Greatness*, Hambledon, p.166
7. Hickman, p.287
8. Mendes, Valerie and Amy de la Haye, *20th Century Fashion*, Thames & Hudson, p.104
9. Hickman, p.287
10. Best, p.165
11. *Churchill's Bodyguard* by Tom Hickman. Original material © 1938-55 Walter Thompson. Additional text © 2005 Tom Hickman. Reproduced by permission of Headline Publishing Group Ltd, p.90
12. Clayton, Tim and Phil Craig, *Finest Hour*, Hodder & Stoughton, p.147
13. Hickman, p.114
14. Clayton and Craig, p.282
15. *Churchill's Bodyguard* by Tom Hickman. Original material © 1938-55 Walter Thompson. Additional text © 2005 Tom Hickman. Reproduced by permission of Headline Publishing Group Ltd, p.122
16. Ibid. p.123
17. Best, p.190
18. Whittell, Giles, *Spitfire Women of World War II*, Harper Press, p.15
19. Bastable, Jonathan (Ed.), *Yesterday's Britain*, Terry Charman '1939-1945' (quoting Winston Churchill) Reader's Digest, p.153

Captions
1. Hickman, p.122
2. Best. p.243

Chapter 4 'Home'

1. Gardiner, Juliet, *Wartime Britain 1939-1945*, Headline Book Publishing, p.393
2. Ibid. p.395
3. Ibid. p.398
4. *Housewife* December 1939, Roger Smithell's 'Is Your House a Gloom-hole?' © IPC+Syndication, p.31
5. Ibid. p.96
6. Platt, Phyllis, *Embroidery*, Embroiderers' Guild, 1940
7. Gardiner, p.568
8. Board of Trade *Make Do and Mend* (1943) 'To Make Clothes Last Longer' 'Towels', p.11
9. Waller, Maureen, *London 1945*, John Murray Publishers, pp.134-35
10. *Make Do and Mend Keeping Family and Home Afloat On War Rations* 'Make Do and Mend' Leaflet No.3 'Your Household Linen Has Got To LAST!' 'Sheets and Pillowcases' reprinted by Michael O'Mara Books Ltd, pp.32-33
11. Felton, Monica, *Civilian Supplies in Wartime Britain*, Ministry of Information, London, 1944, p.44
12. Vickers, p.271
13. Thomas, Donald, *An Underworld at War*, John Murray Publishers, p.201
14. Ibid. p.371
15. Ibid. p.365
16. Ibid. p.371
17. Board of Trade, *Make Do and Mend Leaflet No.11* 'Simple HOUSEHOLD REPAIRS and How To Handle Them' 'A Carpet to Patch?'
18. *Home Chat* 26 October 1946 © IPC+ Syndication
19. Kynaston, David, *Austerity Britain 1945-51*, (quoting Mass Observation) Bloomsbury Publishing Plc, p.50
20. Judt, p.81
21. Kynaston, p.102

Captions
1. *Art and Craft Education* 1939-1940 © Scholastic Ltd

Chapter 5 'Blackout and the ARP'

1. Gardiner, Juliet, *The Children's War*, Portrait in association with the Imperial War Museum, p.99
2. Crocker, Emily, *The Home Front in Photographs*, Sutton Publishing Ltd, p.60
3. Gardiner, Juliet, *Wartime Britain 1939-1945*, Headline Book Publishing, p.384
4. Anderson, Janice, *Working Life in Britain 1900–1950*, Time Warner Books, p.104
5. Gardiner, *Wartime Britain 1939-1945*, p.54
6. Board of Trade *Make Do and Mend Leaflet No.11* 'Simple HOUSEHOLD REPAIRS and How to Handle Them' 'Blackout Curtains Ageing?'
7. *Housewife* December 1939 © IPC+ Syndication, pp.29-30
8. Jarrat, Melynda, *War Brides*, Tempus Publishing Ltd, p.122
9. Bastable, Terry Charman '1939-1945' p.123
10. Gardiner, *Wartime Britain 1939-1945*, p.61
11. Ibid. p.60
12. Bastable, Terry Charman '1939-1945' p.123
13. Gardiner, *Wartime Britain 1939-1945*, p.60
14. Ibid. p.53
15. Ibid. p.56
16. Ibid. p.435

Captions
1. *Art and Craft Education* October 1939, © Scholastic Ltd

Chapter 6 'Gas Masks and Bombs'

1. *British Red Cross Quarterly Review* January 1943 p.54
2. Wright, Michael (Ed.), *The World At Arms The Reader's Digest Illustrated History of World War II*, The Reader's Digest Association Ltd, p.52-57
3. Gardiner, *Wartime Britain 1939-1945*, p.383
4. Ibid. p.382
5. Ibid. p.370
6. www.fashion.era.com/1940s/1946
7. Bates, H.E., *Flying Bombs Over England*, Froglets Publications Ltd, p.11

8. Ibid. p.26
9. Gardiner, *Wartime Britain 1939-1945*, p.641
10. Bates, p.26
11. Ibid. p.52
12. Ibid. p.113
13. Ibid. p.136
14. Ibid. p.134
15. Gardiner, *Wartime Britain 1939-1945*, p.653
16. Bates, p.136
17. Parlour, A. & S., *Phantom at War*, Cerberus Publishing Ltd, p.192
18. Gardiner, *Wartime Britain 1939-1945*, p.65
19. Ibid. p.66
20. Croall, *Don't you know there's a war on? The People's Voice 1939-1945* (quoting Pat Palmer), p.193
21. The National Archives (TNA): Public Record Office (PRO) WO 188/395
22. Betty Davey in conversation with the author
23. TNA:PRO PCOM 9/172
24. O'Neill, Gilda, *Our Street East End Life in the Second World War*, Viking, p.24
25. Gardiner, *Wartime Britain 1939-1945*, p.66
26. Mulvagh, Jane, *Vogue History of 20th Century Fashion*, Viking, p.127
27. Mcdowell, Colin, *Forties Fashion and the New Look*, Bloomsbury Publishing Plc, p.114
28. Cawthorne, Nigel, *The New Look The Dior Revolution*, Wellfleet Press, p.70
29. Horth, Lillie B. and Arthur, *101 Things To Do In Wartime*, B.T. Batsford 2007 (first published 1940), pp.108-109. Reprinted by permission of B.T. Batsford and Anova Books.
30. Gardiner, p.658 and Waller p.69

Chapter 7 'Sandbags and Blankets'

1. TNA:PRO HO/186 444
2. Thomas, S. Evelyn, *A Concise, Fully Illustrated and Practical Guide for the Householder and Air-Raid Warden* (Seventh Edition)
3. TNA:PRO HO 186/212
4. TNA:PRO HO 186/212

5. TNA:PRO PCOM 9/172
6. TNA:PRO HO 186/212
7. TNA:PRO SUPP 3/45
8. TNA:PRO HO 186/212
9. TNA:PRO HO 186/444
10. TNA:PRO HO 186/212
11. TNA:PRO HO 186/444
12. TNA:PRO HO 186/140
13. TNA:PRO HO 186/444
14. TNA:PRO HO 186/212
15. TNA:PRO HO 186/444
16. TNA:PRO HO 186/444
17. TNA:PRO HO 186/736
18. TNA:PRO HO 186/444
19. TNA:PRO HO 186/736
20. TNA:PRO HO 186/444
21. TNA:PRO IR 34/192
22. TNA:PRO HO 186/140
23. TNA:PRO HO 184/549
24. TNA:PRO HO 186/140
25. TNA:PRO HO 186/736
26. Fowler, Will, *D-Day The First 24 Hours*, Spellmount, p.95
27. Waller, p.135 and Gardiner, p.392
28. Gardiner, *Wartime Britain 1939-1945*, p.392
29. Thomas, p.201
30. Hargreaves, E.L., *Civil Industry and Trade*, Her Majesty's Stationery Office and Longmans, Green & Co., p.382
31. Ibid. p.469
32. Gardiner, *Wartime Britain 1939-1945*, p.383
33. O'Neill, p.100
34. Ibid. p.35
35. Sladen, Christopher, *The Conscription of Fashion*, Scholar Press, p.14
36. From *One Fourteenth of an Elephant* by Ian Denys Peek published by Bantam Books. Reprinted by permission of the Random House Group. p.94
37. Ibid. p.114
38. Ibid. The Random House Group. p.311
39. Brickhill, Paul, *The Great Escape*, Cassell Military Paperbacks, p.165
40. Tory, Peter, *Giles at War*, Headline Book Publishing, p.119
41. Fowler, p.184
42. Longden, Sean, *To the Victor the Spoils*, Arris Books, p.136

Chapter 8 'Blimps'

1. Peter Garwood, Barrage Balloon Re-union Club (BBRC) www.bbrclub. org
2. Bacon, Leonard, www.17balloons.co.uk, *The Story of a Book, Hull's Own Airforce Station*, private publication, 2002
3. Atkins, Jacqueline M. (Ed.), *Wearing Propaganda Textiles on the Home Front in Japan, Britain and the United States, 1931–1945*, 'Potatoes are Protective Too: Cultural icons of Britain at War', Antonia Lant, Yale University Press, p.115
4. www.bbrclub.org
5. www.17balloons.co.uk
6. Ibid.
7. Gardiner, *Wartime Britain 1939-1945*, p.509
8. www.bbrclub.org
9. Bacon, www.17balloons.co.uk
10. www.bbrclub.org
11. Ministry of Information, *What Britain Has Done 1939. 1945*, p.95
12. www.17balloons.co.uk
13. www.bbrclub.org
14. www.17balloons.co.uk
15. www.bbrclub.org
16. Ibid.
17. www.17balloons.co.uk
18. Hawkins, Ian, *Destroyer*, Conway Maritime Press, p.43-44
19. Whittell, p.50
20. www.17balloons.co.uk
21. Jarrat, Melynda, p.183
22. Thorburn, Gordon, *Bombers First and Last*, Robson Books, p.35
23. Gardiner, *Wartime Britain 1939-1945*, p.325
24. www.17balloons.co.uk
25. www.bbrclub.org
26. Ibid.
27. www.17balloons.co.uk
28. From the Diary of Frank Taylor Lockwood, Acocks Green History Society. Re-printed courtesy of Arthur Lockwood and Jean Barnsby, son and daughter of Frank Taylor Lockwood
29. www.bbrclub.org
30. Ibid.

31. Ibid.
32. www.17balloons.co.uk
33. Gardiner, *Wartime Britain 1939-1945*, p.509
34. www.17balloons.co.uk
35. Ibid.
36. Gardiner, *Wartime Britain 1939-1945*, p.509
37. www.17balloons.co.uk
38. Gardiner, *Wartime Britain 1939-1945*, p.510
39. www.17balloons.co.uk
40. Ibid.
41. Bates, p.47
42. Ibid. p.46
43. Ibid p.47
44. Ibid. p.120
45. Ibid. p.122
46. Atkins (Ed.), Lant p.115

18. Hargreaves, E.L., p.319
19. Mulvagh, p.174
20. www.worldwar2exraf.co.uk
21. Waller, p.390
22. Gardiner, *Wartime Britain 1939-1945*, pp.520-21
23. Atkins, p.218
24. Gardiner, *Wartime Britain 1939-1945*, p.521
25. Waller, p.389
26. Wood, Maggie, p.47
27. Ibid. p.61
28. Waller, p.390
29. Wood, Maggie, p.39
30. McDowell, p.68
31. Atkins (Ed.), 'London Squares: the Scarves of Wartime Britain', Paul Rennie, p.237
32. McDowell, p.64

Chapter 9 'Factory Work'

1. Lampe, David, *Invasion Plan*, Greenhill Books, p.113
2. Gardiner, *The Children's War*, p.161
3. Ministry of Information, *What Britain Has Done 1939-1945*, p.103
4. Gardiner, *Wartime Britain 1939-1945*, p.305
5. Ministry of Information, *What Britain Has Done 1939-1945*, pp.95-99
6. Ibid. p.13
7. Crocker, p.16
8. Ministry of Information, *What Britain Has Done 1939. 1945*, p.14
9. Gardiner, *Wartime Britain 1939-1945*, p.515
10. Ministry of Information, *What Britain Has Done 1939. 1945*, p.14
11. Gardiner, *The Children's War*, p.160
12. *Millions Like Us*, Gainsborough Pictures
13. Crocker, p.12
14. Mendes, p.116
15. Jarrat, Melynda, p.123
16. Wood, Maggie, *'We wore what we'd got' Women's Clothes in WWII*, Warwickshire Books, Warwickshire Country Council, Wheaton Publishers, p.39
17. Reynolds, Helen, *Couture or Trade: Pictorial Record of the London College of Fashion*, Phillimore & Co. Ltd, p.250

Chapter 10 'In and Out the Classroom'

1. Westall, Robert, *Children of the Blitz*, Macmillan Children's Books, p.99
2. Croall, Jonathan, *Don't You Know There's A War On? The People's Voice 1939-45*, Century Hutchinson Ltd, p.194
3. Parsons, Martin, *War Child Children Caught in Conflict*, Tempus Publishing, p.34
4. Nicholson, Heather V., *Prisoners of War*, Gordon Publishing, p.182
5. Gardiner, *The Children's War*, p.19
6. Parsons, p.101
7. Ibid. p.94
8. Gardiner, *Wartime Britain 1939-1945*, p.406
9. Nicholson, p.29
10. Croall, *Don't You Know There's A War On? The People's Voice 1939-45* (quoting Mary-Rose Murphy) p.99
11. Nicholson, p.12
12. Westall, p.12
13. Reynolds, p.249
14. Gardiner, *Wartime Britain 1939-1945*, p.52
15. Goodman, Susan, *Children of War*, John Murray, p.267
16. Thorburn, p.217

17. Croall, *Don't You Know There's A War On? The People's Voice 1939-45*, p.92
18. Reynolds, p.257
19. Connell, Linda (Ed.), *Textile Treasures of the WI*, The National Needlework Archive, p.90
20. Ministry of Information, *Make Do and Mend*, p.35
21. Workman, Charlie, *From Hardships to Steamships*, United Writers' Publications Ltd. Reprinted by kind permission of Charlie Workman, p.113
22. Croall, *Don't You Know There's A War On? The People's Voice 1939-45*, p.5
23. Miall, Agnes M., *Pearson's Complete Needlecraft*, C. Arthur Pearson, p.173
24. *Housewife* March 1948 p.28-29 © IPC+ Syndication
25. Ibid. p.29
26. Reynolds, p.256
27. Gardiner, *The Children's War*, p.158
28. Ministry of Information, *Make Do and Mend*, p.39
29. Gardiner, *The Children's War*, p.164
30. Jarrat, Melynda, *War Brides*, Tempus Publishing Ltd, p.122
31. Parsons, p.82
32. Eaton, Faith, *Dolls For the Princesses*, Royal Collection Enterprises, p.68
33. Croall, *Don't You Know There's A War On? The People's Voice 1939-45*, p.180
34. Gardiner, *The Children's War*, p.137
35. Ibid. pp.140-41
36. Croall, *Don't You Know There's A War On? The People's Voice 1939-45* (quoting Cynthia Gillett) p.3
37. 'Robb' and Edwards, p.14
38. Goodman, p.212
39. Ibid. p.214

Chapter 11 'Royal Navy – Royal Naval Reserve – Merchant Navy'

1. Kaplan, Philip and Jack Currie, *Convoy Merchant Sailors at War 1939-1945*, Aurum Press, p.8
2. Hamilton, John, *War at Sea 1939-1945*, Blandford Press, p.38
3. Kaplan and Currie, p.65
4. Ibid. p.8
5. Ibid. p.115
6. Greer, Louise and Anthony Harold, *Flying Clothing*, Airlife Publishing Ltd, p.119
7. Chester, Len, *Bugle Boy*, Long Barn Books, p.111
8. Ibid. p.54
9. Jarrat, Dudley, *British Naval Dress*, J.M.Dent & Sons Ltd, p.133
10. Kaplan and Currie, p.19
11. US Naval Intelligence, *Uniforms and Insignia of the Navies of World War II*, Greenhill Books, p.10
12. Wells, Captain John, *The Royal Navy*, Alan Sutton Publishing, p.166
13. Kaplan and Currie, p.138
14. Workman, Charlie, *From Hardships to Steamships*, United Writers Publications Ltd, reprinted by kind permission of Charlie Workman, p.33
15. Kaplan and Currie, p.11
16. Gardiner, *Wartime Britain 1939-1945*, p.497
17. Kaplan and Currie, p.25
18. Mollo, Andrew, *Naval, Marine and Air Force Uniforms of World War 2*, Blandford Press Ltd, p.75
19. Wells, p.33
20. Kaplan and Currie, p.11
21. Ibid. p.105
22. Workman, p.194
23. Ibid. p.29
24. Ibid. p.78
25. Ibid. p.194
26. Hargreaves, p.323
27. Kaplan and Currie, p.138
28. Ibid. p.119
29. Hawkins, Ian, *Destroyer*, Conway Maritime Press, p.196
30. Ibid. p.290
31. Cawthorne, p.97
32. Deighton, Len, *Blood, Tears and Folly*, Jonathan Cape. Reprinted by permission of the Random House Group Ltd (quoted by Hawkins, p.256)
33. Kaplan and Currie, p.17
34. Deighton (quoted by Hawkins, p.113)

Chapter 12 'Royal Air Force'

1. Bowyer, Chaz, *History of the RAF*, Bison Books Corp., p.65
2. Bishop, Patrick, *Fighter Boys Saving Britain 1940*, HarperCollins, p.65
3. Mollo, Andrew, *The Armed Forces of World War II*, Little, Brown and Company, p.69
4. Kaplan and Currie, p.153
5. Mollo, *Naval, Marine and Air Force Uniforms of World War 2*, p.141
6. Nesbit, Roy Conyers, *An Illustrated History of the RAF*, Colour Library Books Ltd, p.109
7. Crocker, p.97
8. Mollo, *Naval, Marine and Air Force Uniforms of World War 2*, p.141
9. Ibid. p.224
10. Gardiner, *Wartime Britain 1939–1945*, p.327
11. Bishop, p.203
12. Ibid. p.271
13. Greer and Harold, p.86
14. Thorburn, p.7
15. Ibid. p.214
16. Bishop, p.61
17. Ibid. p.320
18. Mollo, *The Armed Forces of World War II*, p.69
19. Bishop, p.91
20. Gibson, Guy V.C. D.S.O. D.F.C., *Enemy Coast Ahead – Uncensored The Real Guy Gibson*, Crécy Publishing Ltd, p.63
21. Bishop, p.193
22. Ibid. p.194
23. Imperial War Museum, Duxford
24. Bishop, p.43
25. Robinson, Derek, *Invasion 1940*, Constable and Robinson Ltd, p.127
26. Chant, Christopher, *An Illustrated Data Guide to World War II Fighters*, Tiger Books, p.22
27. Bishop, p.44
28. Mollo, *The Armed Forces of World War II*, p.68
29. Greer and Harold, p.84
30. Ibid. p.83
31. Ibid. p.94
32. Ibid. p.83
33. Bishop, p.371
34. Greer and Harold, p.109
35. Ibid. p.84
36. Ibid. p.89
37. www.ezinearticles.com/?expert=MichaelRussell
38. Gardiner, *Wartime Britain 1939-1945*, p.311
39. Murphy, Chris, *Kent Messenger*, 12 March 2006, p.12
40. Gardiner, *Wartime Britain 1939-1945*, p.306
41. Bishop, p.203
42. Greer and Harold, p.84
43. Bishop, p.339
44. Ibid. p.116
45. Saunders, Andy, *Jane A Pin-Up at War*, Leo Cooper, an imprint of Pen and Sword Books Ltd, p.16
46. Ibid. p.50
47. Ibid. p.96
48. Bishop, p.309
49. Ibid. p.338
50. Pape, Richard, *Boldness Be My Friend*, Headline Review, p.13
51. Greer and Harold, p.89
52. Ibid. p.94
53. Imperial War Museum, Duxford
54. Thorburn, Gordon, *Bombers First and Last*, Robson Books, p.221
55. Barrymore Halfpenny, Bruce, *Bomber Aircrew in World War II*, Pen and Sword Aviation, p.116
56. Thorburn, p.95
57. Greer and Harold, p.107
58. Gilbert, Adrian, *POW Allied Prisoners in Europe 1939-1945*, John Murray, p.35
59. www.io.com/tog/Horsa
60. Bates, p.52
61. Ibid. pp.114-5
62. Ibid. p.118
63. Lowry, Bernard, *British Home Defences 1940-1945*, Osprey Publishing Ltd, p.51
64. Bates, p.94
65. Mollo, *Naval, Marine and Air Force Uniforms of World War 2*, p.224
66. Falconer, Jonathan, *The Dam Busters Story*, Sutton Publishing, p.232

Chapter 13 'Parachutes'

1. Newton, John, *9th Parachute Battalion Re-enacted*, www.9thpara.net
2. Lucas, John, *The Big Umbrella*, Elm Tree Books Ltd, p.107
3. Buckingham, William F., *Paras: the Birth of the British Airborne Forces from Churchill's Raiders to the 1st Parachue Brigade*, Tempus Publishing Ltd, pp.62–63
4. Newton
5. Parlour, p.220
6. www.pointvista.com/ww2GliderPilots/thehorsa
7. Falconer, Jonathan, *The Dam Busters Story*, Sutton Publishing Ltd, p.235
8. Fowler, p.101
9. Zwey, Charles A., *A Parachute Technician*, Pan American Navigation Service
10. Fowler, p.101
11. Lucas, p.98
12. Forty, George, *British Army Handbook 1939-1945*, Headline Book Publishing, p.115
13. Ibid. p.263
14. Lucas, p.98
15. Clayton and Craig, p.323
16. Lucas, p.110
17. Waller, p.25
18. Gardiner, Juliet, *The Animal's War*, Portrait, in association with the Imperial War Museum, p.32
19. Ibid. p.33
20. Ibid. p.111
21. Ibid. p.95
22. Ibid. p.33
23. Whillans, T.W., *Parachuting and Skydiving*, Faber & Faber, p.130
24. Wright, Ian B., *Bale Out! Beginning of the Modern Parachute*, GMS Enterprises, 31
25. Prodger, Mick J., *Luftwaffe vs RAF Flying Equipment of the Air War 1939-1945*, Schiffer Publishing Ltd, p.9
26. Barrymore Halfpenny, p.187
27. Prodger, p.11
28. Ibid. pp.10-11
29. Ibid. pp.15-16
30. Ibid. p.16
31. Ibid. p.17
32. Ibid. p.19
33. Clayton and Craig, p.160
34. Barrymore Halfpenny, p.126
35. Ibid. p.183
36. Lucas, p.103
37. Zwey
38. Whillans, p.144
39. Zwey
40. Lucas, p.103
41. Waller, p.103
42. Cawthorne, p.50
43. Waller, p.27

Chapter 14 'Army'

1. Longden, p.124
2. Ibid. p.5
3. Ibid. p.118
4. Ibid. p.20
5. Forty, p.4
6. Ibid. p.8
7. Ibid. p.4
8. Hargreaves, p.383
9. Forty, p.9
10. Ibid. p.4
11. Mollo, *The Armed Forces of World War II*, p.64
12. Ibid. p.63
13. Longden, p.145
14. Ibid. p.150
15. Hargreaves, p.323
16. Forty, p.176
17. Ibid. p.171
18. Longden, pp.154-55
19. Imperial War Museum
20. Hargreaves, p.323
21. Adie, Kate, *Corsets to Camouflage Women and War*, Hodder and Stoughton, p.187
22. Gardiner, *Wartime Britain 1939-1945*, p.210
23. Ibid. p.207
24. Mollo, *The Armed Forces of World War II*, p.125
25. Longden, p.152
26. Ibid. pp.148-49
27. Ibid. p.109
28. Ibid. pp.150-51
29. Ibid. p.159

30. Ibid. p.158
31. Ibid. p.151
32. Ibid. p.160
33. Ibid. p.160
34. Mollo, *The Armed Forces of World War II*, p.277
35. Ibid. p.287

Captions
1. Forty, p.181

Chapter 15 'Home Guard'

1. Gardiner, *Wartime Britain 1939-1945*, pp.221-2
2. Binns, Stewart, and Lucy Carter, Adrian Wood, Gill Blake, Katie Chadney, Anna Price, Kyla Thorogood, *Britain At War in Colour*, Carlon Books Ltd, p.43
3. Lowry, p.11
4. Binns, Stewart, Carter, Wood, Blake, Chadney, Price and Thorogood p.43
5. Gardiner, *Wartime Britain 1939-1945*, p.226
6. Ibid. p.226
7. Lampe, David, *The Last Ditch Britain's Secret Resistance and the Nazi Invasion Plan*, Greenhill Books, p.113
8. Ibid. p.5
9. *Millions Like Us*, Gainsborough Pictures
10. *Giles at War* by Peter Tory, © Express Newspapers Plc, reproduced by permission of Headline Publishing Group Ltd, p.21
11. Gardiner, *Wartime Britain 1939-1945*, p.242
12. Ibid. p.243
13. Lowry, p.13
14. Ibid. p.15
15. *Giles at War* by Peter Tory, © Express Newspapers Plc, reproduced by permission of Headline Publishing Group Ltd, p.17
16. Gardiner, *Wartime Britain 1939-1945*, p.339
17. Lampe, p.62
18. Ibid. p.72
19. Lowry, p.40
20. Lampe, p.68
21. Ibid. p.117
22. Ibid. p.75

23. Robinson, p.108
24. Cabell, Craig, *Dennis Wheatley Churchill's Storyteller*, Spellmount, p.175
25. Binns, p.70
26. Lowry, p.17
27. Robinson, p.105
28. Ibid. p.106
29. Crocker, p.65
30. Lampe, p.5
31. Gardiner, *Wartime Britain 1939-1945*, p.246
32. Lowry, p.41
33. Bates, p.50
34. Crocker, p.65

Chapter 16 'JWO'

1. Wood, Emily, *The Red Cross Story*, Dorling Kindersley Ltd, p.32
2. Gilbert, p.298
3. St John Ambulance in partnership with the British Red Cross, *Caring on the Home Front*, St John Ambulance and British Red Cross, p.14
4. Ibid. p.11
5. Ibid. p.10
6. Ibid. p.19
7. Ibid. p.9
8. Teeple, p.416
9. Gardiner, *Wartime Britain 1939-1945*, p.387
10. *Caring on the Home Front*, p.13
11. Whitmarsh, Andrew, *Portsmouth at War*, Tempus Publishing Ltd, p.61
12. *Caring on the Home Front*, p.26
13. British Red Cross, *Protecting the Emblems*
14. Teeple p.416
15. *Caring on the Home Front*, p.17
16. *British Red Cross Quarterly Review* April 1942
17. *Caring on the Home Front*, p.39
18. Wood, Emily, p.36
19. *Caring on the Home Front*, p.25
20. Whitmarsh, p.109
21. Gardiner, *Wartime Britain 1939-1945*, p.208
22. *Caring on the Home Front*, p.31
23. Ibid. p.13

24. *British Red Cross Quarterly Review* 1945
p.47
25. Wood, Emily, pp.50-51
26. Ibid. p.35
27. Reid, Major Pat, *Prisoner of War*,
Chancellor Press, p.118
28. Wood, Emily, p.35
29. Bishop, p.227
30. *Caring on the Home Front*, p.28
31. Wood, Emily, p.37
32. *Caring on the Home Front*, p.41
33. Wood, Emily, p.77
34. Ibid. p.76
35. Ibid. p.68
36. Ibid. pp.40-41

Captions
1. Teeple, John B., *Timelines World of History*,
Dorling Kindersley Publishing Ltd, p.416

Chapter 17 'Under Canvas'

1. Lucas, p.105
2. Croall, *Don't you know there's a war on? The
People's Voice 1939-45*, p.131
3. Gardiner, *The Children's War* (quoting
Brian Poole) p.66
4. Gardiner, *Wartime Britain 1939-1945*, p.625
5. Neave, Airey, *Saturday at MI9*, Pen and
Sword Books, p.258
6. Forty, p.34
7. Fisher, David, *The War Magician*,
Weidenfeld and Nicolson, p.99
8. Ibid. p.97
9. Gardiner, *Wartime Britain 1939-1945*, p.619
10. Fisher, p.18
11. Ibid. p.280
12. Ibid. p.287
13. Ibid. p.101
14. Wright, Michael M.A. (Ed.), *The World At
Arms The Reader's Digest Illustrated History
of World War II*, The Reader's Digest
Association Ltd, p.226
15. Fisher, p.295
16. Wright, Michael M.A. p.226
17. Fisher, p.317
18. From *One Fourteenth of an Elephant* by Ian
Denys Peek, published by Bantam Books.

Reprinted by permission of the Random
House Group, p.53
19. Ibid. p.160
20. Hawkins, p.183
21. Kaplan, p.189
22. Workman, pp.151-52

Chapter 18 'Coupons'

1. Hargreaves, p.380
2. Gardiner, *Wartime Britain 1939-1945*, p.567
3. Hargreaves, p.381
4. Ibid. p.387
5. Ibid. p.375
6. Ibid. p.425
7. Ibid. p.402
8. Ibid. p.385
9. Ibid. p.402
10. Ibid. p.404
11. Ibid. p.386
12. Ibid. p.411
13. Ibid. p.402
14. Ibid. p.386
15. Ibid. p.352
16. Ibid. p.365
17. Ibid. p.307
18. Ibid. p.309
19. Ibid. p.308
20. Ibid. p.309
21. Howell p.16
22. Sladen, p.20
23. Mulvagh, p.128
24. Hargreaves, p.311
25. Gardiner, *Wartime Britain 1939-1945*, p.569
26. Hargreaves, p.394
27. Ibid. p.316
28. Kynaston, p.296-97
29. Thomas, p.392
30. Mulvagh (quoting a poster in the exhibition 'The Use of the Clothing Coupon'),
p.127
31. Gardiner, *Wartime Britain 1939-1945*, p.568
and www.fashion.era.com/1940s/1946
32. Mulvagh, p.128
33. Gardiner, *Wartime Britain 1939-1945*,
pp.567-68
34. Waller, p.212

35. www.fashion.era.com/1940s/1946

36. Cawthorne, p.40

37. Hargreaves, p.316

38. Thomas, p.157

39. Hargreaves, p.317

40. Waller, p.210

41. Gardiner, *Wartime Britain 1939-1945*, p.568

42. Thomas, p.150

43. Croall, *Don't You Know There's A War On? The People's Voice 1939-45*, p.107

44. Ibid. p.166

45. Ibid. p.170

46. *An Underworld at War* by Donald Thomas, © Donald Thomas 2003, reproduced by permission of John Murray (Publishing) Ltd, p.170

47. TNA:PRO 1/292 18-10 July 1944

48. Hargreaves, p.413

49. Ibid. p.431

50. Thomas, pp.158-59

51. Judt, p.163

Chapter 19 'Women's Fashion and the War'

1. *Vogue*, 1939, Vogue © The Condé Nast Publications Ltd

2. Mulvagh, p.161

3. Gardiner, *Wartime Britain 1939-1945*, p.60

4. Kennet, Frances, *Fashion*, Granada Publishing Ltd, p.65

5. Cawthorne, p.39

6. Atkins (Ed.), *Keeping up Home Front Morale: 'Beauty and Duty' in Wartime Britain*, Pat Kirkham, p. 213

7. Mulvagh, p.161

8. Atkins (Ed.), Kirkham, p.206

9. Mulvagh, p.161

10. Soames, Mary, *Clementine Churchill*, Doubleday, pp.339-40

11. Atkins (Ed.), 'London Squares: the Scarves of Wartime Britain', Paul Rennie, p.232

12. MacDowell, p.106

13. Mulvagh, p.127

14. Cawthorne, p.41

15. McDowell, p.151

16. Ibid. p.147

17. Mendes, Valerie and Amy de la Haye, *20th Century Fashion*, Thames and Hudson, p.112

18. Sladen, p.38

19. Atkins (Ed.), Kirkham, p.226

20. Ibid. Kirkham, p.223

21. Ibid. Kirkham, p.212

22. Gardiner, *Wartime Britain 1939-1945*, p.575

23. Howell, p.164

24. Hargreaves, p.433

25. McDowell, p.92

26. Hargreaves, p.437

27. Howell, p.163

28. Ibid. p.164

29. Gardiner, *Wartime Britain 1939-1945*, p.575

30. Atkins (Ed.), Kirkham, p.223

31. Ibid. Kirkham, p.213

32. Sladen, p.51

33. Atkins (Ed.), Kirkham, p.212-13

34. Hargreaves, p.436

35. Ibid. p.437

36. Cawthorne, p.50

37. Atkins (Ed.), Kirkham, p.211

38. Hargreaves, p.437

39. Mendes, p.112

40. Felton, Monica, *Civilian Supplies in Wartime Britain*, Ministry of Information 1944, p.39

41. McDowell, p.109

42. Ibid. p.103

43. Hargreaves, p.439

44. Mulvagh, p.183

Chapter 20 'Mrs Sew-and-Sew'

1. *Wartime Britain 1939-1945* by Juliet Gardiner; Text © 2004, reproduced by permission of Headline Publishing Group Ltd, p.569

2. Felton, p.41

3. Ministry of Information *Make Do and Mend* 'The "Stitch In Time"' 'General Hints', p.13

4. Board of Trade *Make Do and Mend Leaflet No.13* 'Hints on Renovating and Recutting!'

5. Miall, pp.171-2
6. Ibid. 'Turn Out and Renovate' 'Two Old Dresses into a Coat-Frock', p.43
7. Ibid. 'The "Stitch In Time"' 'Decorative Patches', p.20
8. Ibid. 'The "Stitch In Time"' 'General Hints', p.14
9. Ibid. 'The '"Stitch In Time"' 'Holes', p.18
10. Ibid. p.173
11. Reynolds, p.251
12. Board of Trade *Make Do and Mend Leaflet No.12* 'Some Useful Hints for Repairing Men's and Boys' Clothes'
13. Reynolds, p.248
14. Wood, Maggie, p.28
15. Goodman, p.213
16. Wood, Maggie, p.66
17. Board of Trade, *Miracles of Make-Do a Revision of Re-make Wrinkles*, p.2

Chapter 21 'Women in Uniform'

1. Mack, Angela, *Dancing on the Waves*, Benchmark Press, p.13
2. Rennolds Millbank, Caroline, *Couture: The Great Fashion Designers*, Thames and Hudson, p.230
3. Hill, Marion, *Bletchley People – Churchill's Geese That Never Cackled*, Sutton, p.80
4. Croall, *Don't you know there's a war on? The People's Voice 1939-45*, p.63
5. Waller, p.385
6. Ministry of Information, *What Britain Has Done*, p.15
7. Lurie, p.86
8. Ministry of Information, *What Britain Has Done*, p.13
9. Ibid. p.14
10. Clayton and Craig, p.280
11. Wood, Maggie, p.42
12. Atkins (Ed.), Kirkham, p.216
13. Turner, p.213
14. Harris and Oppenheimer, p.80
15. Westall, p.121
16. *Corsets to Camouflage* by Kate Adie, Text © 2003, reproduced by permission of Hodder and Stoughton Ltd, p.179

17. Turner, p.215
18. Adie, p.173
19. Soames, p.323
20. O'Neill, p.138
21. Wood, Maggie, p.42
22. Gardiner, *Wartime Britain 1939-1945*, p.514
23. Wood, Maggie, p.42
24. Mack, p.14
25. Crocker, p.106
26. *Corsets to Camouflage* by Kate Adie, Text © 2003, reproduced by permission of Hodder and Stoughton Ltd, p.168
27. Forty, p.318
28. Adie, pp.167-68
29. Sladen, p.200
30. Thorburn, *Bombers First and Last*, p.265
31. *Vogue*, 1939, Vogue © The Condé Nast Publications Ltd
32. Atkins (Ed.), Kirkham (quoting from a Yardley advertisement 'No Surrender', July 1942), p.206
33. Barrymore Halfpenny, p.198
34. McDowell, p.47
35. Lant, p.109-110
36. Atkins (Ed.), Kirkham, p.222
37. Ibid. Lant, p.132
38. Gardiner, *Wartime Britain 1939-1945*, p.514
39. Mack, p.23
40. Lampe, p.133
41. Whittell p.21
42. Ibid. p.108
43. Ibid. p.10
44. Ibid. p.11
45. Ibid. p.13
46. Ibid. p.95
47. Ibid. pp. 194-195
48. Ibid. p.109
49. MacDowell, p.58
50. Cawthorne, p.66
51. Gardiner, *Wartime Britain 1939-1945*, p.17
52. Turner, Mary, *The Women's Century*, National Archives, p.93
53. Bates, p.68.
54. Ministry of Information, *What Britain Has Done*, p.14
55. Gardiner, *Wartime Britain 1939-1945*, p.527
56. Ibid. p.527
57. Ministry of Information, *What Britain*

Has Done, p.107

58. Ibid. p.110
59. Crocker p.23
60. Gardiner, *What Britain Has Done*, p.524
61. Imperial War Museum Sound Archives
    Danher 9/526/3/1
62. MacDowell, p.34
63. Abbott, Dorothea, *Librarian in the Land
    Army*, Greenhill Books, p.10
64. Ibid. p.30
65. Wood, Maggie, p.44
66. Abbott, p.33
67. Gardiner, *Wartime Britain 1939-1945*, p.526
68. *Corsets to Camouflage* by Kate Adie, Text
    © 2003, reproduced by permission of
    Hodder and Stoughton Ltd, pp.181–82
69. *Corsets to Camouflage* by Kate Adie, Text
    © 2003, reproduced by permission of
    Hodder and Stoughton Ltd, p.189

Chapter 22 'BP – SOE'

1. Hill Prologue
2. Ratcliff, R.A., *Delusions of Intelligence
   Enigma, Ultra and the End of Secure Ciphers*,
   Cambridge University Press, p.2
3. Hill Prologue
4. Ibid. p.28
5. Ibid. p.72
6. Ibid. p.77
7. Ibid. p.73
8. Ibid. p.74
9. Ratcliff, p.78
10. Hill p.62
11. Ratcliff, pp.77–78
12. Hill, p.14
13. Ibid. p.62
14. Ibid. p.65
15. Ibid. p.63
16. Ibid. p.62
17. Ibid. p.67
18. Ibid. p.68
19. Ratcliff, p.205
20. Best, p.204
21. Parlour, p.88
22. Hawkins, p.118
23. Hill, p.42

24. Hawkins, p.186
25. Hill Prologue
26. Ibid. p.77
27. Ibid. p.54
28. Ibid. p.78
29. Ibid. p.55
30. Binney, Marcus, *The Women Who Lived
    For Danger The Women Agents of SOE in the
    Second World War*, Hodder and Stoughton,
    p.1
31. Ibid. p.xiii
32. Miller, Russell, *Behind the Lines*, Secker
    and Warburg, p.30
33. Ibid. p.10
34. Binney, p.8
35. Miller, p.30
36. Ibid. p.xi
37. Ibid. p.46
38. Binney, p.8
39. Miller, p.131
40. Binney, p.1
41. Miller, p.130
42. Ibid. p.133
43. Ibid. p.130
44. Ibid. p.131
45. Ibid. p.128

Chapter 23 'For You the War is Over'

1. Hargreaves, p.324
2. Gilbert, p.15
3. Ibid. p.129
4. Ibid. p.105
5. Dear, Ian, *Escape and Evasion POW
   Breakouts in World War Two*, Cassell
   Military Paperbacks, p.16
6. Pape, p.124
7. Dear, p.29
8. Ibid. p.30
9. Ibid. Reprinted by permission of
   Campbell Thomson & McLaughlin Ltd
   on behalf of Ian Dear, p.32
10. Reid, p.184
11. Rees, Ken Wing Commander and Karen
    Arrandale, *Lie in the Dark and Listen*, Grub
    Street, p.148
12. Brickhill, p.41

13. Rees and Arrandale, p.149
14. Brickhill, p.38
15. Ibid. p.159
16. Ibid. p.69
17. Ibid. p.12
18. Ibid. p.166
19. Rees, p.176
20. Brickhill, p.228
21. Ibid. p.10
22. Pape, p.137
23. Neave, p.34
24. Dear, p.37
25. Ibid. Reprinted by permission of
    Campbell Thomson & McLaughlin Ltd
    on behalf of Ian Dear, p.38
26. Longden, p.306
27. Ibid. p.309
28. Ibid. p.312
29. Ibid. p.315
30. Ibid. p.313
31. Ibid. p.321
32. Peek p.40
33. Ibid. p.29
34. Ibid. p.40
35. Alan, Sheila, *Diary of a Girl in Changi
    1941-1945*, Kangaroo Press, pp.239-40
36. Ibid. p.243
37. Ibid. p.240
38. Ibid. p.241
39. Ibid. p.242
40. Dorset County Museum
41. Imperial War Museum EPH 4566
42. Imperial War Museum Department of
    Documents The Private Papers of Mrs D.
    Joyce P324
43. Longden, p.268
44. Dear, p.62
45. Reid, p.146
46. Dear, p.63
47. Ibid. p.65

Chapter 24 'Wartime Embroidery'

1. Purves, Margaret, *Embroidery* June 1940,
   Embroiderers' Guild
2. Atkins (Ed.), Kirkham, p.222
3. *Picture Post* 13 February 1942 'Bedtime
   Fashions'
4. Rosignoli, p.109
5. Ibid. p.107
6. Thorburn, p.95
7. Gardiner, *Wartime Britain 1939-1945*, p.514
8. Royal School of Needlework
9. Platt, Phyllis M., *Embroidery* June 1940
10. Ibid. Platt
11. *Embroidery* June 1941
12. Macbeth, Ann quoted in *Embroidery* June
    1941 p.58
13. *Embroidery* Volume 25 Number 1, p.11
14. Miall, pp.49-50
15. *Embroidery* December 1945 p.76
16. Ibid. 'Embroidered Crafts as War Work –
    Members' Work in War-Time' p.40
17. Fraser, Sheila, *Embroidery* December 1945
    'Occupational Therapy', p.69
18. From the research of Lynn Openshaw
    at the Occupational Therapy School,
    London
19. *Embroidery* Autumn 1944 p.82
20. *Embroidery* December 1945. Cecil Briant
    *A Message To All Who Helped With Work for
    Our Sick Prisoners-of-War*, p.67
21. Smith-Dorrien, *Lady Needlework in
    War-time*, Volume 8 Royal School of
    Needlework, Introduction
22. Ibid. pp.3-4
23. *Embroidery* June 1941
24. Beaney, Jan and Jean Littlejohn,
    Conversations with Constance, Double
    Trouble Enterprises
25. *Embroidery* June 1941
26. Dring, Lilian 'Thriftcraft 1939-40', *Art
    and Craft Education*, Scholar Press
27. Edwards, Joan, *Textile Graphics by Lilian
    Dring*, Bayford Books, p.12
28. Miall, p.9

Chapter 25 'Weddings and Babies'

1. Jarrat, p.23
2. Lant, p.155
3. Atkins (Ed.), Kirkham, p.217
4. Croall, *Don't you know there's a war on? The
   People's Voice 1939-45*, p.8

5. Bastable, p.156
6. Abbott, p.64
7. McDowell, p.120
8. Atkins (Ed.), Kirkham, p.217
9. McDowell, p.118
10. Ibid. p.120
11. Thorburn, p.185
12. Hargreaves, p.318
13. Gardiner, *The Children's War*, p.156
14. Bates, p.90
15. Craig, Elizabeth, *Needlecraft* 'Clothing the Children' HarperCollins Publishers Ltd, p.168
16. Croall, *Don't you know there's a war on? Voices From the Home Front 1939-45*, p.8
17. Ibid. p.4
18. Ibid. p.9
19. Board of Trade in Collaboration with the Ministry of Health *Make Do and Mend Leaflet No.1* 'Getting Ready for Baby'
20. Jarrat, p.25
21. *Boldness Be My Friend*, by Richard Pape © Richard Pape, 2007, reproduced by permission of Headline Publishing Group Ltd, p.161

Captions
1. Craig, Elizabeth, *Needlecraft,* 'Rompers For All Occasions' p.169

Chapter 26 'VE – VJ'
1. Peek, p.512
2. Waller, p.427-28
3. Hargreaves, p.324
4. Waller, p.430
5. Cawthorne, p.99
6. Ibid. p.98
7. Waller, p.429
8. Gardiner, *Wartime Britain 1939-1945*, p.683
9. *Wartime Britain 1939-1945* by Juliet Gardiner; Text © 2004, reproduced by permission of Headline Publishing Group Ltd, p.683
10. Waller, p.430
11. From *The Language of Clothes* by Alison Lurie, published by William Heinemann Ltd. Reprinted by permission of the Random House Group Ltd, p.5
12. Waller, p.432-43
13. Gardiner, *Wartime Britain 1939-1945*, p.98
14. Waller, p.27
15. Twinch, Carol, *Women on the Land*, The Lutterworth Press, p.126
16. Ibid. p.129
17. Ibid. p.131
18. Ibid. p.129
19. McDowell, p.166
20. Ibid. p.167
21. Ibid. p.166

Chapter 27 'Luxury Austerity E.R.P.'
1. Judt, p.161
2. Ibid. p.98
3. Kynaston, p.21
4. Judt, p.163
5. Thomas, p.358
6. Ibid. p.391
7. Cawthorne, p.50
8. Thomas, p.364
9. Kynaston, p.113
10. Ibid. p.117
11. Hargreaves, p.439
12. MacDowell, p.168
13. Howell, p.167
14. McDowell, p.152
15. Mulvagh, pp.184-85
16. McDowell, p.165
17. Ibid. p.167
18. Mendes, p.142
19. Glynn, Prudence and Madeleine Ginsburg, *In Fashion dress in the twentieth century*, George Allen & Unwin, p.87
20. Judt, p.90
21. de Rethy, Esmerelda and Jean-Louis Perreau, *Christian Dior The early years*, Thames & Hudson, p.91
22. Howell, p.167
23. Howell, p.167. Reproduced by permission of Penguin Books Ltd
24. Cawthorne, p.122
25. Ibid. p.125
26. Kynaston, p.187
27. Cawthorne, p.121

28. Ibid. p.140
29. *The Queen's Wedding* Channel 4, 29 November 2007
30. Roberts, Jane (compiled by) *Five Gold Rings A Royal Wedding Souvenir Album from Queen Victoria to Queen Elizabeth II*, © Royal Collection Enterprises Ltd, p.104
31. 'Robb' and Edwards, p.34
32. Roberts, p.104
33. 'Robb' and Edwards, p.38
34. Roberts, p.104
35. 'Robb' and Edwards, p.38
36. Ibid. p.34
37. *The Queen's Wedding*
38. McDowell, p.188
39. Gardiner, *The Children's War*, p.156
40. Mendes and de la Haye, p.140
41. Research Services Ltd. *Survey of Domestic Sewing Habits* July 1947. Reprinted by permission of Coats Craft UK
42. Edwards, Captain Geoffrey, *Embroidery* December 1946, p.6
43. Ibid. p.6
44. *Embroidery* December 1947 and 1949
45. *Embroidery* December 1947 p.34
46. Ibid. Phyllis M. Platt
47. Mulvagh, p.184
48. Kynaston, p.297
49. Thomas, p.355
50. Kynaston, p.194
51. www.bbc.co.uk/radio4/todayreports/misc/austerityolympics_20080507.shtml
52. Kynaston, p.249
53. Ibid. p.297-98
54. Ibid. p.532
55. www.openlibrary.org
56. Judt, p.163

Captions
1. Edwards, Captain Geoffrey, *Embroidery* December 1946 p.6

Chapter 28 'Men's Fashion and the War'

1. Constantino, Maria, *Men's Fashion in the Twentieth Century*, B.T. Batsford, p.64
2. Mendes and de la Haye, p.112
3. Atkins (Ed.), Kirkham, p.211
4. Gardiner, *Wartime Britain 1939-1945*, p.574
5. Waller, p.214
6. Cawthorne, p.41
7. Chenoune, Farid, *A History of Men's Fashion*, Flammarion, p.212
8. Zeigler, Philip, *Britain Then & Now*, Weidenfeld & Nicholson p.204
9. Chenoune, p.212
10. Hayward, Catherine and Bill Dunn, *Man About Town The Changing Image of the Modern Male*, Hamlyn, p.85
11. Constantino, p.76
12. Ibid. p.88
13. Ibid. p.87
14. Bastable, p.182
15. Thomas, p.356
16. Kynaston, p.111
17. Thomas, p.356
18. Kynaston, p.255
19. Thomas, p.356
20. Constantino, p.69-71
21. Ibid. p.71
22. Ibid. p.84
23. Ibid. p.85
24. Ibid. p.85
25. Ibid. p.87
26. Ibid. p.84
27. Ibid. p.89
28. Mendes and de la Haye, p.115

Chapter 29 'Peace and Freedom'

1. Morgan, Kenneth O., *The People's Peace*, Oxford University Press, p.83
2. Kynaston, p.452
3. Ibid. p.398
4. Ibid. p.399
5. Ibid. p.428
6. Ibid. p.446
7. Ibid. p.416
8. Ibid. p.417
9. Ibid. p.419
10. *How TV Changed Britain* June 2008, Channel 4
11. Crocker, p.191
12. Kynaston, p.116
13. Morgan, p.83

14. Kynaston, p.304-5
15. *House and Garden* March 1949
16. Kynaston, p.306
17. Connell, Linda (Ed.) *Textile Treasures of the WI*, The National Needlework Archive, p.111
18. Anderson, p.118
19. Morgan, pp.77-78
20. Wood, Maggie, p.56
21. Howard, Constance, *Embroidery in Great Britain 1940-1963*, B.T. Batsford Ltd, p.19
22. Ibid. p.22
23. Ibid. p.48
24. Mercer, Derrik (Editor-in-Chief) *Chronicle of the 20th Century*, Jacques Legrand, Chronicle, p.718
25. Bastable, p.206
26. Connell, p.112
27. Howard, p.49
29. Edwards, p.13
30. Howard, p.50

Bibliography

Abbott, Dorothea, *Librarian in the Land Army*, Greenhill Books, Stratford-upon-Avon, 1984

Abbott, Dorothea, *Plenty of Mud!*, Greenhill Books, Stratford-upon-Avon, 1994

Adie, Kate, *Corsets to Camouflage Women and War*, Hodder & Stoughton, London, 2003

Allan, Sheila, *Diary of a Girl in Changi 1941-1945*, Kangaroo Press, Pymble, New South Wales, 2004

Anderson, Janice, *Working Life in Britain 1900-1950*, Time Warner Books, London, 2005

Atkins, Jacqueline M., Ed., *Wearing Propaganda Textiles on the Home Front in Japan, Britain, and the United States, 1931-45*, Yale University Press, New Haven and London, 2006 'Propaganda on the Home Fronts: Clothing and Textiles as Message' Jacqueline M. Atkins 'Potatoes are Protective, Too: Cultural Icons of Britain at War Antonia Lant 'Keeping Up Home Front Morale: 'Beauty and Duty' in Wartime Britain Pat Kirkham 'London Squares: The Scarves of Wartime Britain' Paul Rennie

Barrymore Halfpenny, Bruce, *Bomber Aircrew in World War II*, Pen & Sword Aviation, South Yorks, 2004

Bastable, Jonathan Editor Terry Charman 1939-1945 Dr Paul Addison 1945-1949 *Yesterday's Britain* Reader's Digest, London, 1998

Bates, H.E., *Flying Bombs over England*, Froglets Publications Ltd supported by Kent Council Arts and Libraries, Kent, 1994

Beany, Jan and Jean Littlejohn *Conversations With Constance*, Double Trouble Enterprises, Maidenhead 2000

Bernstein, David J., *The Mystery of the Bayeux Tapestry*, George Weidenfeld and Nicolson Ltd, Great Britain, 1986

Best, Geoffrey, *Churchill A Study in Greatness* Hambledon and London, London, 2001

Binney, Marcus, *The Women Who Lived For Danger The Women Agents of SOE in the Second World War*, Hodder & Stoughton, 2002

Binns, Stewart, Lucy Carter, Adrian Wood, Gill Blake, Katie Chadney, Anna Price, Kyla Thorogood, *Britain At War In Colour*, Carlon Books Ltd, London, 2000

Bishop, Patrick *Fighter Boys Saving Britain 1940* HarperCollins, London, 2003

Bowyer, Chaz, *History of the RAF*, Bison Books Corp, Greenwich Connecticut, 1977

Published by The Hamlyn Publishing Group Ltd, London, 1983

Brickhill, Paul, *The Great Escape*, Cassell Military Paperbacks, London, 2000

Bryan III, J. and Charles J.V. Murphy, *The Windsor Story*, Book Club Associates, 1980

Bryant, Mark, *World War II in Cartoons*, Gallery Books, New York, 1989

Buckingham, William F., *Paras: The Birth of the British Airborne Forces from Churchill's Raiders to the 1st Parachute Brigade*, Tempus Publishing Ltd, Gloucestershire, 2005

Cabell, Craig, *Dennis Wheatley Churchill's Storyteller*, Spellmount, Staplehurst, Kent, 2006

Cawthorne, Nigel, *The New Look The Dior Revolution*, Wellfleet Press, New Jersey, 1996

Chant, Christopher, *An Illustrated Data Guide to World War II Fighters*, Tiger Books International PLC, Twickenham, 1997

Chenoune, Farid, *A History of Men's Fashion*, Flammarion, Paris, 1993

Chester, Len, *Bugle Boy*, Long Barn Books, Gloucestershire, 2007

Clayton, Tim and Phil Craig, *Finest Hour*, Hodder and Stoughton, London, 1999

Collins, *The British Carry On*, London, 1940

Connell, Linda (Ed.), *Textile Treasures of the WI*, The National Needlework Archive, Southampton, 2007

Constantino, Maria, *Men's Fashion in the Twentieth Century*, B.T. Batsford, London, 1997

Conyers Nesbitt, Roy *An Illustrated History of the RAF*, Colour Library Books Ltd, Godalming, 1995

Croall, Jonathan, *Don't You Know There's A War On? The People's Voice 1939-45*, Century Hutchinson Ltd, London, 1988

Craig, Elizabeth, *Elizabeth Craig's Needlecraft*, Collins, London, 1947

Croall, Jonathan, *Don't You Know There's A War On? Voices From the Home Front*, Sutton Publishing Ltd, Gloucestershire, 2005

Crocker, Emily, *The Home Front in Photographs*, Sutton Publishing Ltd, Gloucestershire, 2004

Dean, Basil, *The Theatre at War*, George G. Harrap & Co. Ltd, London, 1956

Dear, Ian, *Escape And Evasion POW Breakouts in World War Two*, Cassell Military Paperbacks, London, 2000

Deighton, Len, *Blood, Tears and Folly*, Jonathan Cape

De La Haye, Amy (Ed.), *The Cutting Edge 50 Years of British Fashion 1947-1997*, V&A Publications, 1996

de Marly, Diana, *Fashion for Men An Illustrated History*, B.T. Batsford, London, 1985

Doherty, Richard, *A Noble Crusade The History of the Eighth Army 1941-45*, Spellmount Staplehurst, Kent, 1999

Eaton, Faith, *Dolls for the Princesses*, Royal Collection Enterprises Ltd, London, 2002

Edwards, Joan, *Textile Graphics by Lilian Dring*, Bayford Books, Dorking, 1988

Ewing, Elizabeth, *Fur In Dress*, B.T. Batsford Ltd, London, 1981

Falconer, Jonathan, *Stirling in Combat*, Sutton Publishing Ltd, Stroud, 2006

Falconer, Jonathan, *The Dam Busters Story*, Sutton Publishing Ltd, Stroud, 2007

Fawkes, Richard, *Fighting For a Laugh*, Macdonald and Jane's Publishers Ltd, London, 1978

Felton, Monica, *Civilian Supplies in wartime Britain*, Ministry of Information, London, 1944 (Reprinted by Department of Printed Books, Imperial War Museum 1997)

Fisher, David, *The War Magician*, Weidenfeld & Nicolson, London, 2004

Forbes, Grania, *Elizabeth The Queen Mother A Twentieth Century Life*, Pavilion Books Ltd, London, 1999

Fowler, Will, *D-Day The First 24 Hours*, Spellmount, Staplehurst 2004 first published 2003

Forty, George, *British Army Handbook 1939-1945*, Sutton Publishing Ltd, Stroud, 2002

Gardiner, Juliet, *Wartime Britain 1939-1945*, Headline Book Publishing, 2004

Gardiner, Juliet, *The Children's War*, Portrait, London 2005 in association with the Imperial War Museum

Gardiner, Juliet, *The Animals' War*, Portrait in association with the Imperial War Museum, London, 2006

Gibson, Guy VC DSO DFC, *Enemy Coast Ahead – Uncensored The Real Guy Gibson*, Crecy Publishing Ltd, 2003 first published 1946

Gilbert, Adrian, *POW Allied Prisoners in Europe, 1939-1945*, John Murray, London, 2006

Glynn, Prudence with Madeleine Ginsburg, *In Fashion dress in the twentieth century*, George Allen & Unwin (Publishers) Ltd, 1978

Goodman, Susan, *Children Of War*, John Murray, London, 2005

Greer, Louise and Anthony Harold, *Flying Clothing*, Airlife Publishing Ltd, Shrewsbury, 1979

Haining, Peter, *Chianti Raiders*, Robson Books, London, 2005

Hamilton, John, *War at Sea 1939-1945*, Blandford Press, Poole, Dorset, 1986

Harclerode, Peter, *Go To It! The Illustrated History of the 6th Airborne Division*, Bloomsbury, London, 1990

Hargreaves, E.L., *Civil Industry and Trade*, Her Majesty's Stationery Office and Longmans, Green & Co., 1952

Harris, Mark Jonathan and Deborah Oppenheimer, *Into the Arms of Strangers*, Bloomsbury Publishing Plc, London, 2000

Hawkins, Ian (Ed.), *Destroyer*, Conway Maritime Press, London, 2003

Hayward, Catherine and Bill Dunn, *man about town The Changing Image of the Modern Male*, Hamlyn, London, 2001

Hickman, Tom, *Churchill's Bodyguard*, Headline Book Publishing, London, 2005

Hill, Marion, *Bletchley People – Churchill's Geese That Never Cackled*, Sutton Publishing Ltd, Stroud, 2004

Horth, Lillie B. and Arthur C., *101 Things To Do In Wartime 1940*, Batsford, London, 2007 (first published 1940)

Howard, Constance, *Embroidery in Great Britain 1940-1963*, B.T. Batsford Ltd, London, 1983

Howell, Georgina, *In Vogue*, Penguin Books Ltd, Harmandsworth, 1978

Hyndman, Oonagh, *Wartime Kent 1939-1940* (a selection of memories from the BBC Radio Kent series), Meresborough Books, 1990

Innes, Miranda, *Rags To Rainbows*, Collins & Brown, London, 1992

Ireland, Bernard, *Naval History of World War* I,I HarperCollins, London, 1998

Ireland, Bernard, *War At Sea 1914-45*, Cassell, London, 2002

Jarrat, Dudley, *British Naval Dress*, J.M. Dent & Sons Ltd, London, 1960

Jarrat, Melynda, *War Brides*, Tempus Publishing Ltd, Gloucestershire, 2007

Judt, Tony, *Postwar A History of Europe Since 1945*, Pimlico, London, 2007

Kaplan, Philip and Jack Currie, *Convoy Merchant Sailors at War 1939-1945*, Aurum Press, London, 1998

Kelly, Terence, *Hurricane Over the Jungle*, Pen & Sword Aviation, South Yorkshire, 2005

Kennedy, Sarah, *The Swimsuit*, Carlton Books Ltd, London, 2007

Kennet, Frances, *Fashion*, Granada Publishing Ltd, London, 1983

King, Peter, *Women Rule the Plot*, Gerald Duckworth & Co. Ltd, London, 1999

Knopp, Guido, *Hitler's Henchmen*, Sutton Publishing Ltd, Stroud, 2000

Kynaston, David, *Austerity Britain 1945-51*, Bloomsbury Publishing Plc, London, 2007

Lampe, David, *The Last Ditch Britain's Secret Resistance and the Nazi Invasion Plan*, Greenhill Books, London, 2007

Lant, Antonia, *Blackout Reinventing Women for Wartime British Cinema*, Princeton Univ. Press, 1991

Laver, James, *Modesty in Dress*, Heinemann, London, 1969

Lee, David, *Up Close and Personal The Reality of Close-quarter Fighting in World War II*, Greenhill Books, Lionel Leventhal Ltd, London, 2006

Lee, Loyd E. (Ed.), *World War II in Asia and the Pacific and the War's Aftermath with General Themes A Handbook of Literature and Research*, Greenwood Press Westport Connecticut 1998 'Art Music and World War II' Ben Arnold 'Popular Culture and World War II' Ruth Elwell

Leverton, Bertha and Shmuel Lowensohn, *I came alone*, The Book Guild Ltd, Sussex, 1990

Longden, Sean, *To the Victor the Spoils*, Arris Books, Gloucestershire, 2004

Lowry, Bernard, *British Home Defences 1940-45*, Osprey Publishing Ltd, Oxford 2004

Lukacs, John, *The Hitler of History*, Phoenix Press, London, 1997

Lucas, John, *The Big Umbrella*, Elm Tree Books Ltd, London, 1973

Lurie, Alison, *The Language of Clothes*, Heinemann, London, 1981

Lyman, Robert, *First Victory Britain's Forgotten Struggle in the Middle East, 1941*, Constable & Robinson Ltd, London 2006

Mack, Angela, *Dancing on the Waves*, Benchmark Press Andover 2000

McDowell, Colin, *Forties Fashion and the New Look*, Bloomsbury Publishing Plc, 1997

Make Do and Mend Keeping Family and Home Afloat On War Rations (compilation of official Second World War instruction leaflets), Michael O'Mara Books Ltd, 2007

Mendes, Valerie and Amy de la Haye, *20ᵗʰ Century Fashion*, Thames & Hudson Ltd, London, 1999

Mercer, Derrik (Editor-in-Chief), *Chronicle of the 20ᵗʰ Century*, Jacques Legrand, Chronicle, London, 1988

Miall, Agnes M., *Pearson's Complete Needlework*, C. Arthur Pearson Ltd, London, 1949

Middlemas, Keith, *The Life and Times of George VI*, George Weidenfeld and Nicolson Ltd and Book Club Associates, 1974

Miller, Russell, *Behind the Lines* Secker & Warburg London, 2002

Ministry of Information for the Board of Trade *Make Do and Mend* 1943 (re-published by the Imperial War Museum, London, 2007)

Mollo, Andrew, *Naval, Marine and Air Force Uniforms of World War 2*, Blandford Press Ltd, 1975

Mollo, Andrew, *The Armed Forces of World War II*, Little, Brown and Company, 2000

Morgan, Kenneth O., *The People's Peace*, Oxford University Press, Oxford, 1990

Mulvagh, Jane, *Vogue History of 20ᵗʰ Century Fashion*, Viking, London, 1988

Neave, Airey, *Saturday at MI9*, Pen & Sword Books Ltd, Barnsley, Yorkshire, 2004

Nesbit, Roy Conyers, *An Illustrated History of the RAF*, Colour Library Books Ltd, Godalming, 1995

New Collins Concise English Dictionary, William Collins Sons & Co. Ltd, 1982

Nicholson, Heather V., *Prisoners of War*, Gordon Publishing, London 2000

O'Neill, Gilda, *Our Street East End Life in the Second World War*, Viking, Penguin Group, London, 2003

Overy, Richard (Introduction), *What Britain Has Done 1939-1945* (first published by the Ministry of Information, 1945), Atlantic Books, London, 2007

Pape, Richard, *Boldness Be My Friend*, Headline Review, London, 2007

Parlour, A. & S., *Phantom At War*, Cerberus Publishing Ltd, Bristol, 2003

Parsons, Martin, *War Child Children Caught in Conflict*, Tempus Publishing, Stroud, 2008

Peek, Ian Denys, *One Fourteenth of an Elephant*, Transworld Publishers, London, 2004

Prodger, Mick J., *Luftwaffe vs RAF: Flying Equipment of the Air War 1939-45*, Schiffer Publishing Ltd, Atglen, Pennsylvania, 1998

Reid, Major Pat M.B.E. M.C. and Maurice Michael, *Prisoner of War*, Chancellor Press, 2000

Ratcliff, R.A., *Delusions of Intelligence Enigma, Ultra, and the End of Secure Ciphers*, Cambridge University Press, 2006

Reader's Digest, *The World At Arms The Reader's Digest Illustrated History of World War II*, The Reader's Digest Association Ltd, London, 1989

Rees, Ken Wing Commander and Karen Arrandale, *Lie In the Dark and Listen*, Grub Street,

London, 2004

Rennolds Milbank, Caroline, *Couture The Great Fashion Designers*, Thames and Hudson, London, 1985

Rethy, Esmeralda de and Jean-Louis Perreau, *Christian Dior The early years 1947-1957*, Thames & Hudson, London, 1999

Reynolds, Helen, *Couture or Trade: Pictorial Record of the London College of Fashion*, Phillimore & Co. Ltd, 1997

Robb, and Anne Edwards, *The Queen's Clothes*, Beaverbrook Newspapers Ltd, London, 1977 (published by Book Club Associates by arrangement with Elm Tree Books Ltd 1977)

Roberts, Jane (Compiled by), *Five Gold Rings A Royal Wedding Souvenir Album from Queen Victoria to Queen Elizabeth II*, Royal Collection Enterprises, London, 2007

Robinson, Derek, *Invasion, 1940*, Constable & Robinson Ltd, London 2005

Rosignoli, Guido, *World Army Badges & Insignia Since 1939*, Blandford Press, 1983

Rosignoli, Guido, *Air Force Badges and Insignia of WW2*, Arco Colour Series, Blandford Press, Poole, 1976

St John Ambulance and British Red Cross, *Caring on the Home Front*, St John Ambulance and British Red Cross, 2005

Saunders, Andy, *Jane A Pin-Up at War*, Leo Cooper, an imprint of Pen and Sword Books Ltd, South Yorkshire, 2004

Seeling, Charlotte, *Fashion The Century of the Designer 1900-1999*, Konemann, Cologne, 1999

Sheean, Vincent, *Between the Thunder and the Sun*, Macmillan, London, 1943

Sladen, Christopher, *The Conscription of Fashion*, Scholar Press, Aldershot, 1995

Soames, Mary, *Clementine Churchill*, Doubleday, London, revised edition 2002

Sparke, Penny, *An Introduction to Design and Culture in the Twentieth Century*, Routledge, London, 1989

Steele Commager, Henry, *The Story of the Second World War*, Brassey, Washington 1998. First published by Little, Brown and Company, 1945

The British Red Cross Quarterly Review, 1942-51

Teeple, John B., *Timelines World of History*, Dorling Kindersley Publishing Ltd, London, 2002

Thomas, Donald, *An Underworld At War*, John Murray (Publishers), London, 2003

Thomas, Graham A., *Firestorm Typhoons Over Caen, 1944*, Spellmount Ltd, 2006

Thomas, Samuel Evelyn (Compiler), *Laughs With The Forces*, J.W. Vernon & Co., St Albans, 1943

Thomas, S. Evelyn *A Concise, Fully Illustrated and Practical Guide for the Householder and Air-Raid Warden*, Donnington Press, St Albans [Seventh Edition, undated]

Thompson, Julian, *The Imperial War Museum Book of Victory in Europe The North-West European Campaign 1944-1945*, Sidgwick & Jackson Ltd, London, 1994

Thorburn, Gordon, *Bombers First and Last* Robson Books, London, 2006

Tobin, Shelley, Sarah Pepper, Margaret Willes, *Marriage a[ar] la Mode*, National Trust Enterprises Ltd, 2003

Tory, Peter, *Giles at War*, Headline Book Publishing, London 1994 (copyright Express Newspapers plc)

Turner, Barry, *…And the Policeman Smiled*, Bloomsbury Publishing Ltd, London, 1990

Turner, Mary, *The Women's Century*, The National Archives, London, 2003

Twinch, Carol, *Women on the Land*, The Lutterworth Press, Cambridge, 1990

US Naval Intelligence (Compiled by), *Uniforms & Insignia of the Navies of World War II*, Greenhill Books, Lionel Leventhal Ltd, London, 1991

Vickers, Hugo, *Elizabeth The Queen Mother*, Hutchinson, London, 2005

Waller, Jane and Michael Vaughan-Rees, *Women in Wartime The Role of Women's Magazines 1939-45*, Macdonalds Optima, London, 1987

Waller, Maureen, *London 1945*, John Murray (Publishers), London, 2004

Wells, Captain John, *The Royal Navy* Alan Sutton Publishing Ltd, Stroud, 1994

Westall, Robert, *Children of the Blitz*, Macmillan Children's Books, 1995

Whiting, Charles, *Hitler's Secret War*, Leo Cooper 2000 an imprint of Pen & Sword Books Ltd, Barnsley, Yorkshire

Whitmarsh, Andrew, *Portsmouth At War* Tempus Publishing Ltd, Stroud, 2007

Whittell, Giles, *Spitfire Women of World War II*, HarperPress, London, 2007

Willans, T.W., *Parachuting and Skydiving*, Faber & Faber, 1964

Wood, Emily, *The Red Cross Story*, Dorling Kindersley Ltd, London, 1995

Wood, Maggie, *'We wore what we'd got.' Women's Clothes in World War II*, Warwickshire Books, Warwickshire County Council, 1989

Woodley, Charles, *BOAC An Illustrated History*, Tempus Publishing Ltd, Gloucestershire, 2004

Workman, Charlie, *from Hardships to Steamships*, United Writers Publications Ltd, Penzance, 2004

Worsley, Harriet, *The Hulton Getty Picture Collection Decades of Fashion*, Konemann, London, 2000

Wright, Ian B., *Bale Out! Beginning of the Modern Parachute*, GMS Enterprises, Peterborough, 1991

Wright, Michael M.A. Editor, *The World At Arms The Reader's Digest Illustrated History of World War II*, The Reader's Digest Association Ltd, London, 1989

Zeigler, Philip, *Britain Then & Now*, Weidenfeld & Nicolson, London, 1999

Zwey, Charles A., *Parachute Technician*, Pan American Navigation Service, California, 1944

Websites

www.bbc.co.uk/radio4/todayreports/misc/austerityolympics_20080507.shtml

www.bbrclub.org (Barrage Balloon Reunion Club)

www.embroidery.embroiderersguild.com/2002-6/leonard.html Polly Leonard *Pavilion'd in Splendour Textiles in the Festival of Britain 1951*

www.ezinearticles.com/?expert=MichaelRussell

www.fashion.era.com/1940s/1946

www.fashion.era.com/queen_mother

www.forum.keypublishing.co.uk

www.historylearningsite.co.uk/horsa_glider

www.historyofwar.org/articles/operation_dynamo

www.hullcc.gov.uk/museumcollections

www.io.com/tog/horsa

www.9thpara.net

www.paradata.org.uk/content/horsa-glider-0

www.pointvista.com/ww2GliderPilots/the horsa

www.royal.guv.uk/output/page4342.asp

www.17balloons.co.uk/pages/page-00.html ('The Story of a Book' *Hull's Own Air Force Station*' Len Bacon private publication 2002)

www.gov.uk/output/page4342.asp

www.thewi.org.uk

www.vehicles.com/unitedkingdom/aircraft/glider/airspeed-horsa.asp

www.worldwar2exraf.co.uk

www.yorkshireairmuseum.co.uk

Television programmes

British Style Genius – 4 November 2008 BBC 2
How TV Changed Britain – June 2008 Channel 4
The Queen's Wedding – 29 November 2007 Channel 4
When Britain Went Bananas – 13 June 2006 on BBC2

Film

Millions Like Us, Gainsborough Pictures

Documents

The Diary of Frank Taylor Lockwood
The private papers of Mrs D. Joyce. Department of Documents at the Imperial War Museum.
    P324
National Archives HO 184/549, HO/186 212, HO 186/140, HO 186/444, HO 186/736,
    PCOM 9/712, PRO IR 34/192, PRO SUPP 3/45
Ministry of Information, *Make Do and Mend Leaflets 3, 11*
Ministry of Information, *Make Do and Mend*, 1943 (re-published by the Imperial War Museum
    2007)
The Consumer Branch, The Wartime Prices and Trade Board, *MIRACLES OF MAKE-DO A
    REVISION OF RE-MAKE WRINKLES*
Research Services Ltd, Survey of Domestic Sewing Habits July 1947

Magazines

Art and Craft Education October 1939-1940 Scholastic Ltd
British Red Cross Quarterly Review January 1943
Embroidery 1939-1945 Embroiderer's Guild
Home Chat 26 October 1946 ©IPC+ Syndication
House and Garden March 1949
Housewife December 1939 ©IPC+ Syndication
Time 6 February 1950

Newspapers

Kent Messenger 12 March 2006, Chris Murphy p.12
The Times 3 November 2007, 'Warplanes' Allan Mallinson

Leaflet

Protecting the Emblems, British Red Cross 2007

Other sources

John at gallahad@twmi.rr.com
The Imperial War Museum Sound Archives Danher 9/526/3/1

Index

Visit our website and discover thousands of other History Press books.
www.thehistorypress.co.uk